UNMASKING the ANTICHRIST

Ron Rhodes

HARVEST HOUSE PUBLISHERS

EUGENE, OREGON

Cover by Harvest House Publishers, Inc., Eugene, Oregon

UNMASKING THE ANTICHRIST
Copyright © 2012 by Ron Rhodes
Published by Harvest House Publishers
Eugene, Oregon 97402
www.harvesthousepublishers.com

Library of Congress Cataloging-in-Publication Data
    Rhodes, Ron.
    Unmasking the Antichrist / Ron Rhodes.
        p. cm.
    Includes bibliographical references (p. 237).
    ISBN 978-0-7369-2850-2 (pbk.)
    ISBN 978-0-7369-4203-4 (eBook)
    1. Antichrist. I. Title.
    BT985.R49 2012
    236'.9—dc23

                                                2011025151

Printed in the United States of America

            12 13 14 15 16 17 18 19 20 / LB-NI / 10 9 8 7 6 5 4 3 2 1

To all who joyfully anticipate
the imminent rapture of the church

Acknowledgments

I continue to appreciate my professors of Bible prophecy at Dallas Theological Seminary in the late 1970s and early 1980s, including John F. Walvoord, J. Dwight Pentecost, and Charles Ryrie. I also appreciate the entire staff at Harvest House Publishers, not only for their commitment to excellence in Christian publishing but also for their unbending commitment to biblical truth. Most of all, I am thankful to God for the wondrous gift of my family—Kerri, David, and Kylie. Our God is an awesome God!

CONTENTS

Introduction:

RISING INTEREST IN THE EMERGENCE OF THE ANTICHRIST

As soon as the word *antichrist* is mentioned, all kinds of questions come to mind. Could the antichrist be alive somewhere in the world today? Could he be a child, or perhaps a teenager, a college student, or even an adult waiting in the wings to emerge as a world leader?

Could one of today's well-known political leaders be the antichrist—perhaps even a leader in the United States? And if he is in the world today, is he indwelt by Satan even now, or does that take place in the future?

Will he be a Muslim? Will he be a Jew? Is he the mysterious person named Gog in the book of Ezekiel?

Do any prophecies need to be fulfilled before the antichrist emerges on the world scene? If so, which ones? Can we calculate with precision when the antichrist might emerge?

Will the antichrist have some kind of supernatural birth? Will he be half human and half demon?

Will he actually claim to be God on earth one day? Will he really suffer a fatal head wound and then be resurrected from the dead, inspiring awe and wonder around the world?

What is the mark of the beast we keep hearing about? Will the antichrist control the world economy in the near future, preventing those of us who have not received his mark on our bodies from buying or selling anything? And what if we refuse?

For whatever reason, interest in the emergence of the antichrist is on the rise. In fact, as I engaged in research to write this book, I discovered more than 1.25 million Google searches for *antichrist* or *the antichrist* during a single month. More books were published on the antichrist in the last year alone than in the past three decades combined.

Of course, interest in the antichrist has been significant for a long time. It seems to have been a topic of interest and even fascination in many centuries throughout church history. For example, in the late second century, Irenaeus, the bishop of Lyons in Gaul, wrote a volume titled *Against Heresies* (5.30.1) in which he discussed the antichrist and his mark. One of Irenaeus's disciples, Hippolytus, a presbyter of Rome, wrote a rather detailed volume titled *On Christ and Antichrist* in about AD 200. Tertullian, a Christian apologist who lived in approximately AD 160–220, wrote a volume titled *Against Marcion* (an early heretic) in which he discussed the antichrist.[1] Many other examples are available, but these are sufficient to illustrate that from the beginning of church history up to the present day, the antichrist has been a topic of interest.

AVOIDING EXTREME ATTITUDES

There are two extreme attitudes we should avoid when studying the doctrine of the antichrist.[2] One extreme is to ignore the doctrine altogether, as some Christians have done in the past. These Christians seem to think that this is an unhealthy topic that should be avoided. Such a view, however, fails to recognize that it is a focus of God's revelation in the Bible, and God desires that His people understand all that is contained in His Word (see Acts 20:27). More than 100 passages of Scripture address the person, words, and works of the antichrist.

The other extreme is to focus on this doctrine to the exclusion of other important doctrines contained in Scripture. The proper approach is to seek to understand the whole of Scripture on all doctrines. The Word of God protects and edifies believers, so to be ignorant of any portion of Scripture is spiritually self-defeating.

There is another reason we need a balanced understanding of this doctrine. Scripture exhorts us to be accurate observers of the times.

> The Pharisees and Sadducees came, and to test him [Jesus] they asked him to show them a sign from heaven. He answered them, "When it is evening, you say, 'It will be fair weather, for the sky is red.' And in the morning, 'It will be stormy today, for the sky is red and threatening.' You know how to interpret the appearance of the sky, but you cannot interpret the signs of the times" (Matthew 16:1-3).

What a rebuke! These were the religious elite of the time, men who were supposed to know the teachings of Scripture, and yet they were completely unable to properly discern the times. The Pharisees and Sadducees had been surrounded by signs pointing to Christ's true identity, and they had missed them all. They were blind to the reality that the Messiah was in their midst. Jesus' miracles were clear signs of His divine identity, just as dark clouds in the sky are a sign of impending rain. The Old Testament had predicted the Messiah would perform these miracles (see Isaiah 35:5-6, for example), and the Pharisees and Sadducees—experts in the Old Testament—should have recognized that Jesus fulfilled these messianic verses. But in their blindness, they could not interpret the signs of the times. Let's not follow the example of the Pharisees and Sadducees. Rather, let's learn from the prophetic Scriptures so we can determine whether the stage is being set for the eventual emergence of the antichrist.

Jesus also urged, "From the fig tree learn its lesson: as soon as its branch becomes tender and puts out its leaves, you know that summer is near. So also, when you see all these things, you know that he is near, at the very gates" (Matthew 24:32-33). Jesus indicates that God has prophetically revealed certain things, and people who know the Bible should understand that a prophecy is being fulfilled—or perhaps the stage is being set for a prophecy to eventually be fulfilled. Jesus is encouraging His followers to be accurate observers of the times so that when biblical prophecies are fulfilled, they will recognize what is happening (see also Luke 21:25-28). All of this is simply to say that we should not be ignorant of what the prophetic Scriptures teach about the antichrist, one of the central figures of end-times biblical prophecy.

YOU CAN TRUST BIBLICAL PROPHECY

Can we really trust what the Bible reveals about the person, words, and works of the antichrist in the future? Absolutely, yes! I say this because biblical prophecy originates in God Himself, and God has the ability to foretell the future.

Christians have often referred to prophecy as history written in advance. I think it is more accurate to say that prophecy is God's revelation regarding history in advance. We cannot leave God out of the equation, for only God in His omniscience knows the future.

Some Christian do not believe that God is all-knowing or knows the future (this is called *open theism*). Such a view is contrary to the Bible. God transcends time—He is above time—so He can see the past, present, and future in a single intuitive act. God's knowledge of all things is from the vantage point of eternity, so all events in the past, present, and future are encompassed in one ever-present "now" to Him.

God knows all things, both actual and possible (Matthew 11:21-23). He knows all things past (Isaiah 41:22), present (Hebrews 4:13), and future (Isaiah 46:10). Because He knows all things, His knowledge cannot increase or decrease. Psalm 147:5 affirms that God's understanding is beyond measure. His knowledge is infinite (Psalm 33:13-15; 139:11-12; Proverbs 15:3; Isaiah 40:14; Acts 15:17-18; 1 John 3:20).

We can trust Bible prophecy, for it comes from the God who knows the end from the beginning.

> I am God, and there is no other; I am God, and there is
> none like me, declaring the end from the beginning and
> from ancient times things not yet done, saying, "My coun-
> sel shall stand, and I will accomplish all my purpose"...I
> have spoken, and I will bring it to pass; I have purposed,
> and I will do it (Isaiah 46:9-11).

God's ability to foretell future events separates Him from all the false gods of paganism. He confronted the polytheism* of Isaiah's time:

- "Who is like me? Let him proclaim it. Let him declare and set it before me...Let them declare what is to come, and what will happen. Fear not, nor be afraid; have I not told you from of old and declared it? And you are my witnesses! Is there a God besides me? There is no Rock; I know not any" (Isaiah 44:7-8).

- "Who told this long ago? Who declared it of old? Was it not I, the Lord? And there is no other god besides me, a righteous God and a Savior; there is none besides me" (Isaiah 45:21).

- "The former things I declared of old; they went out from my mouth, and I announced them; then suddenly I did them, and they came to pass...I declared them to you from of old, before they came to pass I announced them to you, lest you should say, 'My idol did them, my carved image and my metal image commanded them'" (Isaiah 48:3,5).

Of course, anyone can make predictions—that is easy. But fulfilling them is another story altogether. The more statements you make about the future and the greater the detail, the better the chances that you will be wrong. But God has never been wrong. In fact, more than 100 prophecies in the Old Testament refer to the Messiah's first coming, and all of them were literally fulfilled. For example, Scripture prophesies that the Messiah would be...

> from the seed of a woman (Genesis 3:15)
>
> the offspring of Abraham (Genesis 12:3)
>
> from the tribe of Judah (Genesis 49:10)
>
> the son of David (Jeremiah 23:5-6)
>
> conceived of a virgin (Isaiah 7:14)
>
> born in Bethlehem (Micah 5:2)

---

* Polytheism is the belief in many gods.

the heralded Messiah (Isaiah 40:3)

the coming King (Zechariah 9:9)

wounded and crushed for our sins (Isaiah 53)

pierced in His side (Zechariah 12:10)

killed about AD 33 (Daniel 9:24-25)

raised from the dead (Psalm 2; 16)

All of these prophecies and a multitude of others were precisely fulfilled to the crossing of the *t* and the dotting of the *i*, so you can absolutely trust what the prophetic Scriptures reveal about the antichrist and the end times. God knows the future, and He reveals it to us in Scripture (see Isaiah 42:9; Ezekiel 12:26-28; 2 Peter 1:20-21).

INTERPRETING PROPHECY LITERALLY

Because I am an author, I am interviewed by various publications when a new book comes out—some of them secular newspapers. Some secular reporters express surprise that many Christians in modern America take biblical prophecy literally. They are often also surprised to learn that there are substantial rational reasons for doing so.

Because the more than 100 prophecies regarding the first coming of Christ were literally fulfilled, the precedent has been set. We may expect that all the prophecies dealing with the second coming and the events that lead up to it—including the manifestation of the antichrist—will be fulfilled literally as well. Besides, there are other reasons for interpreting Scripture (including prophecy) literally.

- A literal interpretation honors the normal use of all languages.
- The Bible makes more sense when taken literally.
- A literal approach leaves room for a metaphorical interpretation whenever it is appropriate, such as when Jesus said He was the door (John 10:7).
- A literal interpretation is the only sane and safe check on the human imagination, which is prone to be subjective.
- Only a literal approach is in line with the nature of inspiration.

Every word of Scripture is "breathed out by God" (2 Timothy 3:16).

The Scriptures themselves call for a literal method of interpretation. For example...

- Later biblical texts interpret earlier ones literally, including the accounts of the creation of the world (Genesis 1–2; Exodus 20:10-11), the creation of Adam and Eve (Matthew 19:6; 1 Timothy 2:13), the fall of Adam and his resulting death (Romans 5:12,14), Noah (Matthew 24:38), Jonah (Matthew 12:40-42), Moses (1 Corinthians 10:2-4,11), and numerous other historical figures.

- By specifically indicating the presence of a parable (Matthew 13:3) or allegory (Galatians 4:24), the Bible clearly implies that the ordinary meaning is a literal one.

- By giving the interpretation of parables, Jesus revealed that there is a literal meaning behind them (Matthew 13:18-23).

- Jesus rebuked those who did not interpret the resurrection literally (Matthew 22:29-32; see also Psalm 16:10).

- By interpreting prophecy literally (Luke 4:16-21), Jesus indicated His acceptance of the literal interpretation of the Old Testament.

Many years ago, Bible scholar David L. Cooper set out what he called the golden rule of interpretation: "When the plain sense of Scripture makes common sense, seek no other sense; therefore, take every word at its primary, ordinary, usual, literal meaning unless the facts of the immediate context, studied in the light of related passages and axiomatic and fundamental truths, indicate clearly otherwise."[3]

In view of all this, I do not take scriptural teachings regarding the antichrist to be allegorical or metaphorical descriptions of evil, as some secular reporters and liberal Christians do. No, the antichrist is a literal person who will emerge on the world scene during the future seven-year tribulation period. The rest of this book will provide convincing evidence for this view.

THE CENTRALITY OF THE BOOK OF REVELATION

As we study the doctrine of the antichrist, the majority of the focus will be on the book of Revelation. To be sure, we will also examine the teachings of other biblical books, but the book of Revelation is central to a study on the antichrist.

The book of Revelation is the only apocalyptic book in the New Testament. The author is the apostle John, who had been imprisoned on the isle of Patmos, in the Aegean Sea, for the crime of sharing the good news about Jesus Christ (Revelation 1:9). This island is where John received the revelation. He wrote the book in approximately AD 95.

The recipients of the book of Revelation were suffering severe persecution, and some were even killed (see Revelation 2:13). Things were about to get even worse. John wrote this book to give his readers a strong hope that would help them patiently endure in the midst of suffering. At the time, evil seemed to be prevailing at every level. However, Revelation indicates that evil will one day come to an end. At the second coming, Christ will overthrow wicked personages (such as the antichrist) and wicked governments, cast the wicked into a place of horrible suffering, and establish His 1000-year millennial kingdom on earth. Following this will be an eternal state where Satan will be forever banished. There will be no further sin, sorrow, or death, and fellowship with God will be perpetual and uninterrupted.

God gave John a prophetic vision of the end times. John affirmed, "I was in the Spirit on the Lord's day," and as he experienced a prophetic vision, he heard a loud voice (Revelation 1:10) and received God's revelation regarding what the future holds.

Prophets and apostles had previously received messages from God in various ways, including visions, dreams, and hearing God's voice (Hebrews 1:1; see also Luke 24:23; Acts 26:19; 2 Corinthians 12:1). Visions are especially characteristic of apocalyptic literature, such as the books of Daniel and Revelation. The term *vision* comes from the Latin word *visio*, which means "to see." Through visions, God showed His prophets and apostles things normally hidden from human eyes. Visions were typically related in the first person, as the visionary often described his experience by saying, "I saw…" John recorded all that he saw in the book of Revelation.

Revelation 1:19 provides an outline of the book: "Write therefore the things that you have seen, those that are and those that are to take place after this." "The things that you have seen" is a reference to Revelation 1, where we find a description of Jesus in His present glory and an introduction to the book of Revelation. "Those that are" refers to the circumstances of the seven churches of Asia Minor recorded in Revelation 2–3. "Those that are to take place after this" refers to futuristic prophecy of the tribulation period, the antichrist and the false prophet, the second coming, the millennial kingdom, and the eternal state (Revelation 4–22).

The book promises a special blessing to all who study it. "Blessed is the one who reads aloud the words of this prophecy, and blessed are those who hear, and who keep what is written in it, for the time is near" (Revelation 1:3). This is yet another reason that we ought to study end-time prophecy!

So strap on your seat belt, and let's embark on an eye-opening tour of Scripture with a special focus on the antichrist—his person, his words, and his works.

A ROAD MAP OF THE END TIMES: NOTABLE EVENTS AND PERSONALITIES

I travel a lot. When I visit a new city where I will be speaking at a conference, sometimes navigating around town is a little difficult because everything is new to me. But once I have been there for a short time and have gotten the lay of the land, I can more easily find my way around.

The same can be true when going on a tour through prophetic Scripture. If you do not know the prophetic lay of the land, it might seem a little difficult to navigate through some of the concepts. The rapture, the tribulation, the antichrist, the false prophet, the abomination of desolation, the millennial kingdom, the two witnesses, the 144,000 Jews, Armageddon, the second coming, the great white throne judgment, the eternal state…unless you are familiar with such language, navigating through prophecy can be a little confusing.

To make things easier for you, this chapter provides a basic road map of notable events and personalities of end-times prophecy. Once you become acquainted with the road map, the rest of the book will be much easier to navigate.

THE TRIBULATION PERIOD

The Greek word for *tribulation* (*thlipsis*) literally means "to press" (as grapes), "to press together," "to press hard upon," and it refers to times of oppression, affliction, and distress. It is translated variously as *tribulation*, *affliction*, *anguish*, *persecution*, *trouble*, and *burden*. The word has been used in relation to...

- those hard-pressed by the calamities of war (Matthew 24:21)
- a woman giving birth to a child (John 16:21)
- the afflictions of Christ (Colossians 1:24)
- those pressed by poverty and lack (Philippians 4:14)
- great anxiety and burden of heart (2 Corinthians 2:4)
- a period of unparalleled tribulation in the end times (Revelation 7:14)

All Christians can expect a certain amount of general tribulation in their lives. Jesus Himself said to His disciples, "In the world you will have tribulation" (John 16:33). Paul and Barnabas warned, "Through many tribulations we must enter the kingdom of God" (Acts 14:22). But such general tribulation is to be distinguished from the tribulation period of the end times.

- Scripture refers to a definite period of tribulation at the end of the age (Matthew 24:29-35).
- It will be of such severity that no period in history—past or future—will equal it (Matthew 24:21).
- It will be shortened for the sake of the elect (Matthew 24:22). Otherwise, no one could survive it.
- It is called the time of Jacob's trouble or distress, for it is a judgment on Messiah-rejecting Israel (Jeremiah 30:7; Daniel 12:1-4).
- The nations will also be judged for their sin and rejection of Christ during this period of tribulation (Isaiah 26:21; Revelation 6:15-17).
- This tribulation period will last precisely seven years (Daniel 9:24,27).
- This period will be so bad that people will want to hide and even die (Revelation 6:16).

The tribulation period will be characterized by wrath (Zephaniah 1:15,18), judgment (Revelation 14:7), fury (Isaiah 26:20-21), trial (Revelation 3:10), distress (Jeremiah 30:7), destruction (Joel 1:15), darkness (Amos 5:18), desolation (Daniel 9:27), overturning (Isaiah 24:1-4), and punishment (Isaiah 24:20-21). Simply put, no Bible passage alleviates at all the severity of this time to come on the earth.

Scripture reveals that this tribulation will envelop the entire world, not just part of it. Revelation 3:10 describes this period as "the hour of trial that is coming on the whole world, to try those who dwell on the earth." Isaiah likewise describes this tribulation: "Behold, the LORD will empty the earth and make it desolate, and he will twist its surface and scatter its inhabitants...Terror and the pit and the snare are upon you, O inhabitant of the earth!" (Isaiah 24:1,17).

As to the source of the tribulation, Scripture mentions both divine wrath and satanic wrath—but especially divine wrath. We are told that the tribulation is a "day of the wrath of the LORD" (Zephaniah 1:18). The earth will experience "the wrath of the Lamb" (Revelation 6:16-17). "The LORD will empty the earth" (Isaiah 24:1), and "the LORD is coming out from his place to punish the inhabitants of the earth for their iniquity" (Isaiah 26:21). Satan's wrath is evident in Revelation 12:4,13,17.

THE RAPTURE

The rapture is that glorious event in which the dead in Christ will be resurrected, living Christians will be instantly translated into their resurrection bodies, and both groups will be caught up to meet Christ in the air and be taken back to heaven (John 14:1-3; 1 Corinthians 15:51-54; 1 Thessalonians 4:13-17). This means that one generation of Christians will never pass through death's door. They will be alive on earth one moment, and the next moment they will be instantly translated into their resurrection bodies and caught up to meet Christ in the air. What a moment that will be!

Christians seem to love to debate end-time issues. Perhaps the hottest debate relates to when the rapture occurs. These are the four primary views:

Partial rapturism is the view that only spiritual Christians will be raptured prior to the beginning of the tribulation period. Carnal Christians will be left behind. Throughout the tribulation period, as more Christians become spiritual, they too will be raptured. Such raptures may continue to occur throughout the tribulation. (This view is not widely held today.)

Pretribulationism is the view that Christ will rapture the entire church before any part of the tribulation begins. This means the church will not go through the judgments prophesied in Revelation 4–18.

Posttribulationism is the view that Christ will rapture the church after the tribulation at the second coming of Christ. This means the church will go through the time of judgment prophesied in the book of Revelation, but believers will be kept or preserved through such judgments.

Midtribulationism is the view that Christ will rapture the church in the middle of the tribulation period. In this view, the two witnesses of Revelation 11, who are caught up to heaven, are representative of the church.

Most Christians today are either "pretribs" or "posttribs." I believe the pretrib position—the majority view among evangelicals—is most consistent with the biblical testimony. For one thing, Revelation 3:10 indicates that believers will be kept from the actual hour of trial that is coming on the whole world. Further, no Bible passage on the tribulation mentions the church, either in the Old Testament (Deuteronomy 4:29-30; Jeremiah 30:4-11; Daniel 8:24-27; 12:1-2) or in the New (Matthew 13:30,39-42,48-50; 24:15-31; 1 Thessalonians 1:9-10; 5:4-9; 2 Thessalonians 2:1-11; Revelation 4–18).

Granted, Scripture does say there will be believers who live during the tribulation period (for example, Revelation 6:9-11). But in pretribulationism, these people become believers sometime after the rapture. Perhaps they become convinced of the truth of Christianity after witnessing millions of Christians supernaturally vanish off the planet at the rapture. Or perhaps they become Christians as a result of the ministry of the 144,000 Jewish followers of Christ introduced in Revelation 7 (who themselves apparently come to faith in Christ after the rapture). Many people could become believers as a result of the miraculous ministry of the two witnesses of Revelation 11, prophets who apparently have the same powers as Moses and Elijah.

In any event, Scripture assures us that the church is not destined for wrath (Romans 5:9; 1 Thessalonians 1:9-10; 5:9). This means the church cannot go through the great day of wrath in the tribulation period (Revelation 6:17).

Throughout Scripture, God protects His people before judgment falls (see 2 Peter 2:5-9). Enoch was transferred to heaven before the judgment of the flood. Noah and his family were in the ark before the judgment of the flood. Lot was taken out of Sodom before judgment was poured out there. The firstborn among the Hebrews in Egypt were sheltered by the blood of the Paschal lamb before judgment fell. The spies were safely out of Jericho and Rahab was secured before judgment fell on Jericho. So too will the church be secured safely (by means of the rapture) before judgment falls in the tribulation period.

Note that Scripture portrays the rapture and the second coming as distinct events. For example, at the rapture the translated saints return with Christ to heaven (John 14:1-3), whereas at the second coming Christ returns to earth (Zechariah 14:4; Acts 1:11). The nations are not judged at the rapture, but they are judged at the second coming (Matthew 25:31-46). The rapture could happen any moment (1 Thessalonians 5:1-3), whereas many prophetic signs will precede the second coming (Luke 21:11,25). The rapture takes place before the "day of wrath" (1 Thessalonians 1:10; 5:9), but the second coming occurs after the day of wrath. At the rapture Christ comes *for* His own (1 Thessalonians 4:17; John 14:3), whereas at the second coming Christ comes *with* His own (Revelation 19:6-14). The tribulation period follows the rapture, whereas the millennial kingdom follows the second coming.

Key verses on the rapture. John 14:1-3; Romans 8:19; 1 Corinthians 1:7-8; 15:51-53; 16:22; Philippians 3:20-21; 4:5; Colossians 3:4; 1 Thessalonians 1:10; 2:19; 4:13-18; 5:9,23; 2 Thessalonians 2:1,3; 1 Timothy 6:14; 2 Timothy 4:1,8; Titus 2:13; Hebrews 9:28; James 5:7-9; 1 Peter 1:7,13; 5:4; 1 John 2:28–3:2; Jude 21; Revelation 2:25; 3:10.

Key verses on the second coming. Daniel 2:44-45; 7:9-14; 12:1-3;

Zechariah 12:10; 14:1-15; Matthew 13:41; 24:15-31; 26:64; Mark 13:14-27; 14:62; Luke 21:25-28; Acts 1:9-11; 3:19-21; 1 Thessalonians 3:13; 2 Thessalonians 1:6-10; 2:8; 1 Peter 4:12-13; 2 Peter 3:1-14; Jude 14-15; Revelation 1:7; 19:11–20:6; 22:7,12,20.

THE ANTICHRIST

I will obviously address the antichrist in great detail throughout this book. As a way of introduction, however, the apostle Paul called him a "man of lawlessness" (2 Thessalonians 2:3,8-9). He will perform counterfeit signs and wonders and deceive many people during the future tribulation period (2 Thessalonians 2:9-10). The apostle John describes this anti-God individual in the book of Revelation as a hideous beast who will rise to political prominence in the tribulation period, seek to dominate the world, attempt to destroy the Jews, persecute all true believers in Jesus Christ, set himself up as God in a rebuilt Jewish temple, and set up his own kingdom (Revelation 13). He will glorify himself with arrogant and boastful words (2 Thessalonians 2:4). He will eventually rule the whole world (Revelation 13:7) from his headquarters in Rome (Revelation 17:8-9). He will be defeated and destroyed by Jesus at His second coming (Revelation 19:11-16) and is destined for the lake of fire (Revelation 19:20).

THE FALSE PROPHET

The false prophet is like the first lieutenant of the antichrist. He will be motivated by Satan (Revelation 13:11), promote the worship of the antichrist (verse 12), execute those who refuse to worship the antichrist (verse 15), control economic commerce on the earth in order to enforce worship of the antichrist (verse 17), perform apparent signs and miracles (verse 13), and bring deception and false doctrine upon the whole world (verse 14).

SEAL, TRUMPET, AND BOWL JUDGMENTS

Human suffering will steadily escalate during the tribulation period. First are the seal judgments, involving bloodshed, famine, death, economic upheaval, a great earthquake, and cosmic disturbances

(Revelation 6). Then come the trumpet judgments, involving hail and fire mixed with blood, the sea turning to blood, water turning bitter, further cosmic disturbances, affliction by demonic scorpions, and the death of a third of humankind (Revelation 8:6–9:21). Then come the bowl judgments, involving horribly painful sores on human beings, more bodies of water turning to blood, the death of all sea creatures, people being scorched by the sun, total darkness engulfing the land, a devastating earthquake, and much more (Revelation 16). The tribulation period will be a horrible time to live.

ARMAGEDDON

Worse comes to worst when these already traumatized human beings find themselves in the midst of a catastrophic series of battles called Armageddon. The name Armageddon literally means "Mount of Megiddo" and refers to a location about 60 miles north of Jerusalem. This is the location of Barak's battle with the Canaanites (Judges 4) and Gideon's battle with the Midianites (Judges 7). This will be the site for the final horrific battles of humankind just prior to the second coming (Revelation 16:16).

Napoleon is reported to have once commented that this site is perhaps the greatest battlefield he had ever witnessed. Of course, the battles Napoleon fought will dim in comparison to Armageddon. So horrible will Armageddon be that no one would survive if it were not for Christ coming again (Matthew 24:22).

THE SECOND COMING

The second coming is that event when Jesus Christ—the King of kings and Lord of lords—will return to earth in glory at the end of the tribulation period and set up His kingdom. The very same Jesus who ascended into heaven will come again at the second coming (Acts 1:9-11).

The second coming will involve a visible, physical, bodily return of the glorified Jesus. One key New Testament Greek word used to describe the second coming of Christ is *apokalupsis*. This word carries the basic meaning of "revelation," "visible disclosure," "unveiling," and "removing the cover" from something that is hidden. The word is used of Christ's second coming in 1 Peter 4:13: "Rejoice insofar as you share Christ's sufferings, that you may also rejoice and be glad when his glory is revealed."

Another New Testament Greek word used of Christ's second coming is *epiphaneia*, which carries the basic meaning of "to appear," or "to shine forth." In Titus 2:13 Paul speaks of "our blessed hope, the appearing of the glory of our great God and Savior Jesus Christ." In 1 Timothy 6:14 Paul urges Timothy to "keep the commandment unstained and free from reproach until the appearing of our Lord Jesus Christ."

The second coming will be a universal experience in the sense that every eye will see it. Revelation 1:7 says, "Behold, he is coming with the clouds, and every eye will see him, even those who pierced him, and all tribes of the earth will wail on account of him." Moreover, at the time of the second coming, there will be magnificent signs in the heavens (Matthew 24:29-30). Christ will come as the King of kings and Lord of Lords with many crowns on His head—crowns that represent absolute sovereignty. His eyes will be like blazing fire (Revelation 19:11-16).

THE MILLENNIAL KINGDOM

Following Christ's second coming, He will personally set up His millennial kingdom on earth. This is another one of those doctrines that Christians seemingly love to debate, and there are three theological views.

Premillennialism teaches that following the second coming, Christ will institute a kingdom of perfect peace and righteousness on earth that will last for 1000 years. After this reign of true peace, the eternal state begins (Revelation 20:1-7; see also Isaiah 65:17-25; Ezekiel 37:21-28; Zechariah 8:1-17). The reason I subscribe to this view is that it recognizes that just as the Old Testament messianic prophecies were literally fulfilled in the first coming of Christ, so the prophecies of Christ's second coming and millennial kingdom will be literally fulfilled.

Amillennialism, a spiritualized view, teaches that when Christ comes, eternity will begin with no prior 1000-year (millennial) reign on earth. Amillennialists generally interpret the 1000 years metaphorically and say it refers to Christ's present (spiritual) rule from heaven.

The postmillennial view, another spiritualized view, teaches that through the church's progressive influence, the world will be "Christian-ized" before Christ returns. Immediately following this return, eternity will begin (with no 1000-year kingdom). Of course, a practical prob-lem for postmillennialism is that the world seems to be getting worse and worse instead of better.

A literal and plain reading of Scripture leads effortlessly to premil-lennialism. As we saw in the introduction, when the plain sense of Scripture makes good sense, we need not seek another sense. I see no reason to spiritualize Bible prophecies relating to the millennium. The Bible plainly teaches a literal 1000-year kingdom over which Christ will rule on the earth. The antichrist will be in the lake of fire by the time the millennial kingdom begins.

SIGNS OF THE TIMES

Scripture reveals that no one can know the day or the hour of spe-cific end-time events. Matthew 24:36 tells us, "Concerning that day and hour no one knows, not even the angels of heaven, nor the Son, but the Father only." Likewise, Acts 1:7 instructs us, "It is not for you to know times or seasons that the Father has fixed by his own author-ity." However, the Lord Jesus did indicate in the parable of the fig tree that we can know the general time of His coming (see Matthew 24:33).

The term *signs of the times* (Matthew 16:3) describes specific charac-teristics and conditions that warn people that we are living in the end times. Jesus provides this explanation in the Olivet Discourse:

> See that no one leads you astray. For many will come in my name, saying, "I am the Christ," and they will lead many astray. And you will hear of wars and rumors of wars…Nation will rise against nation, and kingdom against king-dom, and there will be famines and earthquakes in various places…Many will fall away and betray one another and hate one another. And many false prophets will arise and lead many astray. And because lawlessness will be increased, the love of many will grow cold (Matthew 24:4-12).

The apostle Paul offers a similar alert.

> In the last days there will come times of difficulty. For people will be lovers of self, lovers of money, proud, arrogant, abusive, disobedient to their parents, ungrateful, unholy, heartless, unappeasable, slanderous, without self-control, brutal, not loving good, treacherous, reckless, swollen with conceit, lovers of pleasure rather than lovers of God, having the appearance of godliness, but denying its power (2 Timothy 3:1-5).

He likewise warns in 1 Timothy 4:1, "The Spirit expressly says that in later times some will depart from the faith by devoting themselves to deceitful spirits and teachings of demons." We see this in the kingdom of the cults.

All of these, then, are signs of the times. They clue us in to the reality that we are living in the end times and that the emergence of the antichrist cannot be far off. I will address these signs further at the end of the book.

DIFFERING CONCEPTS
OF THE ANTICHRIST

Things would be nice and neat if everyone throughout church history agreed on one interpretation of the Scriptures about the antichrist. But such is not the case. Far from it! In fact, throughout church history, a number of different interpretive options have been suggested. We will see below that a lot of this has to do with one's overall approach to Scripture. Let's briefly consider the primary options.

A MYTH

Liberal Christian scholars hold that the concept of the antichrist is rooted in mythology. Scholars in this tradition teach that the Bible does not contain the words of God but rather is a fallible human document. They approach Scripture with an antisupernatural bias and dismiss all miracles as the fantasies of ignorant people in biblical times who did not understand the laws of nature. It is not surprising that these scholars, with their low view of the Bible, dismiss biblical teachings on the antichrist.

Some of these scholars believe that the idea of an antichrist was carried over from Judaism into Christianity but holds no basis in reality. One such scholar claims, "It is evident that the early Christians made use of traditions regarding eschatological opponents that depended upon Jewish apocalyptic and earlier prophetic traditions."[1] He asserts, "Modern research has uncovered similar concerns about eschatological foes in the Qumran community (e.g., War Rule 17.6 and the fragments known as 4 Q 186)."

Of course, a notable problem for the liberal Christian view of prophecy is that messianic prophecies referring to the first coming of Christ were precisely and literally fulfilled. Regardless of how many bad things liberal Christian scholars may say about the Bible, more than 100 Old Testament prophecies concerning the coming Messiah were dead-on accurate. People cannot predict the future, so the Bible clearly contains God's revelation and not mere human words, as claimed.

Some of these liberal scholars rebut that these messianic prophecies were made after Jesus lived, not before. They maintain that the books of the Old Testament were written close to the time of Christ and that the messianic prophecies were merely Christian inventions. But to make this type of claim is to completely ignore the historical evidence, as Norman Geisler and Ron Brooks point out.

> Even the most liberal critics admit that the prophetic books were completed some 400 years before Christ, and the book of Daniel by about 167 B.C. Though there is good evidence to date most of these books much earlier (some of the psalms and earlier prophets were in the eighth and ninth centuries B.C.), what difference would it make? It is just as hard to predict an event 200 years in the future as it is to predict one that is 800 years in the future. Both feats would require nothing less than divine knowledge.[2]

These messianic prophecies were literally fulfilled in Christ, and they predate the time of Christ by between 167 and 800 years, so the divine nature of the Bible seems more than obvious to the unbiased observer. And therein lies the relevance for the prophetic Scriptures related to the coming antichrist: The words in the Bible about the antichrist are not mere myths borrowed from ancient Jewish traditions but are rather direct "thus saith the Lord" revelations that will prove to be just as reliable as the prophecies of Christ's first coming.

A PRINCIPLE OF EVIL

Another view held by some is that the term *antichrist* is a metaphor for the principle of evil, or perhaps a personification of the evil in the world. Bible scholar Walter K. Price, who himself does not hold to this view, illustrates the concept this way: "Just as Uncle Sam is the personification of all that is American, so the Antichrist will be the personification of all that is evil."[3] Seen in this light, *antichrist* is a broad term inclusive of a variety of forms of evil in the world. It is a personification of "some evil principle, power(s), or idea(s) of the world, always until the end of time in opposition to the kingdom of God."[4] So, for example, ideologies like communism and fascism would be categorized as antichrist.

AN INSTITUTION OF EVIL

Still other interpreters have concluded that perhaps the term *antichrist* points to some kind of institution that propagates evil in the world. Different institutions have been suggested at different times in church history.

For example, many preterists hold to this viewpoint. The word *preterism* derives from the Latin *preter*, meaning "past." In this view, the biblical prophecies in the book of Revelation and Matthew 24–25 (Christ's Olivet Discourse) have already been fulfilled. This approach to interpreting prophecy appeared in the early writer Eusebius (263–339) in his *Ecclesiastical History*. Later writers who incorporated this approach include Hugo Grotius of Holland (seventeenth century), and in modern times, David Chilton. In this view, the book of Revelation was written specifically to encourage the persecuted saints of the first century who were suffering under Roman tyranny. The institution of the Roman Empire is seen as the antichrist.

During the time of the Reformation, some people believed the Roman Catholic Church was the antichrist. Others have pointed out that Islam not only denies the biblical concepts of God, Jesus Christ, and the gospel of salvation, but also—at least in the case of extremist Muslims—can be life-threateningly hostile to Christians and their beliefs.[5]

A PERSON

Another view is that the antichrist will be an actual person—which, I am sure you have surmised, is my personal view. This is also the view of most Christians who interpret literally the end-times prophecies we have already referenced.

Some claim that one problem with this view is that various persons—some prior to the founding of the church in New Testament times—have been seen as the antichrist, and none of them panned out. As one theologian explains, "Some contemporary man who seems particularly dangerous to Christianity in the opinion of the interpreter has frequently been held to be the man of sin of 2 Thessalonians 2 or the Beast of Revelation and Daniel."[6]

The Roman general Pompey was claimed to be the "anti-Messiah" in *The Psalms of Solomon* (written about 60 BC). Other suggested antichrist candidates included various Roman emperors, Islam's prophet Muhammad, various popes of the Roman Catholic Church, famous heretics throughout church history, Napoleon, Kaiser Wilhelm II, and Mussolini. (More on these misidentifications in the next chapter.) Despite such misidentifications, the biblical evidence is both massive and persuasive that the antichrist is a person—but he will not be revealed until the future seven-year tribulation period that precedes the second coming of Christ. I will substantiate this view throughout the rest of the book.

PARALLEL DEVELOPMENT

A view closely associated with the "real person" view above points out that good and evil have a parallel development throughout church history. These parallel developments will allegedly reach a consummation in the end times in a personal Christ and a personal antichrist. These two will meet in a final conflict at the second coming.[7] Obviously, Christ will be the Victor.

THE DYNAMIC VIEW

There is yet another view that includes the three previous views and combines them into what has been called the "dynamic view of the antichrist."[8] As a backdrop, the apostle John said in 1 John 2:18, "Children, it is the last hour, and as you have heard that antichrist is coming, so now many antichrists have come. Therefore we know that it is the last hour." John likewise said, "Every spirit that does not confess Jesus is not from God. This is the spirit of the antichrist, which you heard was coming and now is in the world already" (1 John 4:3).

Proponents of the dynamic view note that in the original Greek of 1 John 2:18, there is no definite article (*the*) in the phrase "the last hour." It is more properly translated, they suggest, as "a last hour." It is argued that John seems to be referring to *an* hour of crisis that has similarities to *the* future end-time hour of crisis.

> The crisis of John's day is not *the* last hour, merely *a* last hour. Just as the last hour is preceded in history by various hours of crisis, so the Antichrist will be preceded in history by many persons and institutions that will have some or many, but not all, of his characteristics...Only the Antichrist will consummate in himself, at the end of the age, all the evil that has appeared periodically in various historical institutions and persons.[9]

According to this view, the term *antichrist* refers more than to just one person. Even though there will be a definitive antichrist in the end times who will dominate the world scene, there are also many partial manifestations of the antichrist throughout church history that share some of his characteristics.

> In many historical instances, when some person or institution has been identified as Antichrist, this identification was not totally false. Such attempts were in error when they said that a certain historical person was *the* Antichrist—which most of them did. However, there was a measure of truth in these identifications when we recognize that these historical persons actually did have some of the characteristics of the Antichrist.[10]

CONCLUSION

Having thoroughly studied not only the biblical text but also countless books and articles on the subject, I have no doubt that the antichrist is a real person who will come into global power in the end times. Personal names and titles are consistently ascribed to him in Scripture. He engages in personal relationships with other persons. He performs personal actions, talks like a person, is consistently addressed with personal nouns and pronouns, and is treated like a person by others. A plain reading of the biblical text leaves no doubt that the antichrist is a person.

This evil person will stand against the person of Jesus Christ and all that is holy. He will be the archenemy of God's people. He will force the entire world to submit to him and make a choice: worship him or suffer death. His doom and defeat will come only at the hands of the divine Messiah Himself, Jesus Christ. Christ will then cast this diabolical person into the lake of fire, where he will spend all eternity.

HISTORICAL IDENTIFICATIONS OF THE ANTICHRIST

I could fill a book with stories about people who have been labeled as the antichrist, but I will provide a concise overview instead.

ANCIENT JEWISH EXTRABIBLICAL LITERATURE

The Testament of the Twelve Patriarchs refers to Beliar ("worthless one"), a king who embodies evil and will be the end-time opponent of God and the Messiah. Other ancient Jewish extrabiblical books refer to him as well. Bible scholar Randall Price notes that Beliar "serves as a portent of the imminent conclusion of the age and its cataclysmic end (see Testament of Joseph 20:2; Testament of Simeon 5:3; Testament of Naphali 2:6; Testament of Issachar 6:1; 7:7; Testament of Reuben 2:1; Testament of Dan 5:10; Testament of Levi 18:12; Testament of Judah 25:3)."[1] Those who sin are said to be doing Beliar's bidding (Testament of Naphali 2:8). Both evil spirits and sinful human beings follow his lead (see Testament of Reuben 2:1; Testament of Issachar 6:1; 7:7). Israel will reportedly find no deliverance in the end times until Beliar is defeated and destroyed by the Messiah (Testament of Dan 5:10; cf. 5:3-7), who will cast him into eternal punishment (Testament of Dan 5:10; Testament of Issachar 6:1; Testament of Levi 18:12; Testament of Judah 25:3).

There are a number of allusions to an antichrist figure in the Dead Sea Scrolls, discovered at Qumran in 1947. For example, Beliar is viewed as an end-times seducer and corrupter of Israel. Some literature distinguishes between a "son of Beliar" and a "blasphemous/boastful king" who will emerge to oppress the Jewish people in the end times.

One ancient Jewish text describes the antichrist figure this way: "He shall be great on earth...[All] will worship and all will serve [him]" (4Q246 1:8-10). Israel will find its deliverance only in a Messiah figure whose "kingdom will be an eternal kingdom and its/his ways will be in righteousness; he will judge the earth in righteousness, and all will have/make peace; the sword will cease from the earth and every nation will submit to/worship him" (verses 9-12).[2] There are obvious parallels here to Daniel's prophecies about the antichrist (see also 2 Thessalonians 2:4).

The Oracles of Hystaspes speak of an evil king who "shall arise out of Syria, born from an evil spirit," and be "the over-thrower and destroyer of the human race...That king will not only be the most disgraceful in himself, but he will also be a prophet of lies, and he will constitute, and call himself God and will order himself to be worshipped as the son of God" (*Lactantius Divinae Institutiones* 7.17:2-4). Much ancient Jewish extrabiblical literature mentions the divine claims of the antichrist figure.

The Assumption of Moses speaks of an evil end-times king who will persecute the Jews, speak blasphemy against God, violate God's holy law, and desecrate the Jewish temple by entering into the Holy of Holies and offering pagan sacrifices on the altar. This bears striking resemblance to the abomination of desolation that Daniel (Daniel 12:11) and Jesus (Matthew 24:15) describe.

Some in ancient times held that the antichrist would emerge out of the Jewish tribe of Dan. They alleged that evil spirits were active in this tribe (Testament of Dan 5:5) and that Satan was their prince (5:6). They believed that this tribe would be hostile to other Jewish tribes in the future (5:6-7).

Another Jewish tradition, recorded in the Jerusalem Talmud, ascribes the name Armilus to the antichrist figure. Other Jewish works referring to Armilus include *Sefer Zerubbavel* and *Saadiah Gaon*. According to these and other such works, the antimessiah will emerge out of Rome, have miraculous powers, deceive the world into believing he is God, and reign supreme over the world. He will persecute the Jews and banish them into the wilderness. God Himself will make war against Armilus and his forces.

Jewish literature also speaks of the downfall of the antichrist. The Psalms of Solomon, for example, affirm that the Messiah—the "Son of David"—will deliver Israel, destroying the "lawless one" with the "word of his mouth." Similarities to the New Testament are quite obvious (Matthew 24:30-31; Mark 13:26-27; Luke 21:27-28; 2 Thessalonians 2:8; Revelation 19:14-21).

ANTIOCHUS EPIPHANES

Many people, as far back as the days of the Jewish historian Josephus (AD 37–100), have held that Antiochus Epiphanes was the antichrist. Antiochus ruled the Seleucid Empire from 175 BC until his death in 164 BC. He opposed the worship of Yahweh, defiled the Jewish temple by slaughtering a pig in the Holy of Holies, set up a graven image of himself, and treated the Jews cruelly. However, Bible scholar Arthur W. Pink thoroughly debunks this view.

> There are many conclusive reasons to prove that Antiochus Epiphanes could not possibly be the Antichrist, though undoubtedly he was, in several respects, a striking *type** of him, inasmuch as he foreshadowed many of the very things which this coming Monster will do. It is sufficient to point out that Antiochus Epiphanes had been in his grave for more than a hundred years when the apostle [Paul] wrote 2 Thess. 2.[3]

Paul, in 2 Thessalonians 2:1-9, warns of the coming of the antichrist, whose appearance was yet future.

---

* A type is an Old Testament institution, event, person, object, or ceremony that has reality and purpose in biblical history but that also by divine design foreshadows something yet to be revealed.

THE EARLY CHURCH

Roman emperors. In New Testament times, a number of Rome's emperors were identified as the antichrist. Such leaders claimed to be God, demanded to be worshipped, and were relentless persecutors of God's people. Naturally, then, some of the early believers saw them as antichrist figures.[4]

The emperor Caligula began his reign in AD 37. He made a bold attempt to put his image in the Jewish holy sanctuary. This caused many to believe that Caligula was the antichrist, for this seemed to be a fulfillment of the abomination of desolation predicted by Daniel the prophet (Daniel 12:11) and by Jesus in the Olivet Discourse (Matthew 24:15). He died in AD 41, but some believed he would rise from the dead and place his image in the temple.

Another Roman emperor alleged to have been the antichrist was the infamous Nero, who reigned from AD 54 to 68. The *Sibylline Oracles* claimed that Nero would reappear in the end times. Randall Price explains: "Here the eschatological Anti-Messiah is cast in the mold of the worst of the deified Roman emperors, Nero, who was expected to reappear in the end-time as *Nero redivivus* ('Nero risen [from the dead]')."[5] This idea persisted for a long time. Interestingly, after Nero died by suicide in AD 68, impostors claimed to be Nero in AD 69, 80, and 88, throwing many people into great terror (see Suetonius, *Nero* 57; Tacitus, *History* 1.2, 2.8-9; Dio Cassius 64.9). Unbelievably, the idea that Nero would return was still circulating in the fifth century AD.

> Others, again suppose that he [Nero] is not even dead, but that he was concealed that he might be supposed to have been killed, and that he now lives in concealment in the vigor of that same age which he had reached when he was believed to have perished, and will live until he is revealed in his own time and restored to his kingdom.

Augustine wrote these words between AD 412 and 426, some 350 years after Nero's death.[6] Pink puts such lore and legend into perspective.

> This man of infamous memory, Nero, did nothing more

than foreshadow that one who shall far exceed him in satanic malignity. Positive proof that Nero was not the Antichrist is to be found in the fact that he was in his grave before John wrote the thirteenth chapter of the Revelation.[7]

The Epistle of Barnabas. The Epistle of Barnabas (early second century) suggested that the Roman Empire was the fourth beast of Daniel's vision and would be followed by ten kingdoms out of which the antichrist would arise. In fact, many of the church fathers in the second century agreed that the fourth kingdom in Daniel's vision was the contemporary Roman Empire. They also believed this empire would come to its demise by fragmenting into ten kingdoms, setting the stage for the emergence of the antichrist. Christians were thus warned to "take heed in these last days." Bible scholar Walter Price explains the history of early Christian thought this way:

> Since we have a much larger historical perspective, we now see that the ancient Roman empire and the revived Roman empire are separated by the age of the church, already of two thousand years' duration. However, in this early age, prophetic interpreters believed that the next form of world government would immediately follow the fall of Rome. Therefore, they taught that when the Roman empire fell it would be followed immediately by the ten-toed kingdom, out of which the Antichrist, the "little horn" of Daniel 7, would arise. As long as Rome stood, therefore, the ten-kingdom confederation remained in the future, and the advent of the Antichrist was forestalled. Hence the Roman empire was seen as the restrainer of 2 Thessalonians 2:7.[8]

This created an interesting situation. Because early Christians believed that the Roman Empire was restraining the emergence of the antichrist, they prayed for its continuance and preservation. As long as the empire stood fast, they reasoned, the antichrist could not emerge on the world scene.

At the same time, many Christians were suffering persecution by various Roman emperors. Still, many believed things would be even worse if the Roman Empire collapsed into ten kingdoms and the antichrist arose. The Roman Empire was the lesser of two evils—it was indeed bad, but not nearly as bad as things would be under the antichrist. The conclusion was that all should hope for the Roman Empire's continuance.

Irenaeus. Irenaeus (AD 200) believed the antichrist would be a Jew from the tribe of Dan.* This was reasonable to him because Scripture seemed to indicate that this tribe had fallen from God's favor. It was the first of Israel's tribes to indulge in gross idolatry, and it is not mentioned in the list of tribes in Revelation 7:5-8.

Irenaeus also held that the antichrist would emerge three and a half years before Christ's second coming and His subsequent millennial reign on earth. He thought this would occur in the near future. Like others of his time, he had no idea that the first and second comings of Christ would be separated by a long period of time. He thus believed the rise of the antichrist was imminent.

Tertullian. Tertullian (AD 150–225) identified the heretic Marcion as having the spirit of antichrist. But he also believed that a Gentile antichrist would emerge in the near future. His delay was due only to the continued existence of the Roman Empire. He believed that when Rome fragmented into ten kingdoms, the rise of the antichrist would quickly occur. Understandably, Tertullian claimed, "[We are] lending our aid to Rome's duration."

Hippolytus. Hippolytus (AD 160–235) wrote a work titled *Treatise on Christ and Antichrist* in which he expressed the view that the first beast of Revelation 13 was the then-existent Roman Empire. The second beast, however, would be a separate kingdom—the kingdom of the antichrist. He believed that the original Roman Empire would experience a fatal wound, after which it would be revived (see Revelation 13:3). He also perceived that there would be a time gap between the sixty-ninth and seventieth weeks of Daniel, and that the seventieth week would directly precede Christ's second coming.

Cyprian. Cyprian (AD 200–258) was a bishop of Carthage who lived during a time of intense Roman persecution under Emperor

---

* I will evaluate the claim that the Antichrist will be a Jew later in the book.

Decius. Martyrdom was common among Christians. During this time, Cyprian was hidden, and during his concealment he wrote letters for Christian clergy. Roman persecution continued under other emperors, including Gallus (251–253) and Valerian (253–260). Cyprian interpreted such nonstop persecution to mean that history was drawing to a close and that the rise of the antichrist was imminent (Epistle 55). Cyprian was martyred in AD 258 and expressed thanks to God for setting him free from the "chains of the body."

THE POST-NICENE ERA

Rome becomes Christian. Things changed radically under Constantine, emperor of Rome from AD 306 to 337. Whereas Rome had formerly persecuted the Christian church, Christianity was now officially recognized and even given preference by the Roman state. Roman emperors were no longer identified with the coming antichrist.

During this time, however, doctrinal disputes gave rise to speculations about the antichrist. The Council of Nicaea (AD 325), which convened during Constantine's rule, sided with Athanasius in upholding the absolute deity of Jesus Christ.

> Constantine's son, Constantius, who followed his father upon the throne, favored the Arian view which had been denounced by the Nicaean council, over which Constantine had presided. (The Arians denied the full absolute deity of Jesus Christ.) This caused Athanasius to believe that Constantius was the forerunner of the Antichrist.[9]

Later, some would continue to believe that the antichrist would emerge out of Arianism.

Millennial madness. Fast-forward several hundred years. As AD 1000 loomed on the horizon, many believed that the end of the world was near and that the antichrist would emerge just before the end came. Because of such strong expectations, many people gave all their possessions to the church. Churches were filled with worshippers, and a religious revival erupted. People forgave debts and freed prisoners as they prepared for the end.

One of Augustine's key teachings contributed to the belief that the antichrist would appear soon. He had taught that Satan was bound at the death of Jesus Christ and that his activities would be curtailed for the 1000 years that followed (this was his view of the millennial kingdom and his interpretation of Revelation 20:2). Christians thus speculated that the antichrist would appear 1000 years after the crucifixion.

Gerberga, queen of France, became enamored with this teaching and instructed her court chaplain, Adso, to research the matter. He wrote a pamphlet titled *Little Work on Antichrist* in AD 954, suggesting that the spirit of antichrist had been already manifested in such leaders as Antiochus, Nero, and Domitian but that a personal antichrist was yet to appear from Babylon and the tribe of Dan. However, he said, the antichrist would not emerge until after the Roman Empire passed away. He believed the antichrist would reign for three and a half years either in the Jewish temple or the Christian church and would be killed by Christ at His coming.

The Crusades. The Crusades, which lasted from AD 1095 to 1291, represented the church's attempt to regain control of the Holy Land from the Muslims. During this time, the Muslims were identified with the spirit of antichrist. The Roman Catholic pope urged, "It is the will of God that through the labors of the crusaders Christianity shall flourish again at Jerusalem in these last times, so that when antichrist begins his reign there—as he shortly must—he will find enough Christians to fight!"[10] The relentless advances of Islam had caused many to conclude that the antichrist would emerge out of the Muslim religion.

The Roman Catholic pope. Throughout church history, popes have been targeted as being the antichrist. For example, a Christian bishop in AD 991 wrote with fervor, "What, in your eyes reverend fathers, is that Pontiff, seated on a throne, and clad in purple and gold? If he hath not charity, and be puffed up with his learning only, he is Antichrist sitting in the temple of God, and demeaning himself as a god; he is like unto a statue in the temple, like a dumb idol, and to ask of him a reply, is to appeal to a figure of stone."[11] This statement was representative of the views of many. Pope Leo in the twelfth century and Pope

Gregory IX in the thirteenth century were both branded as antichrist, as were others in other centuries.

During the time of the Reformation, we witness a shift from belief in a personal antichrist to a corporate one in the papacy of the Roman Catholic Church. Indeed, most Reformers tended to see the successive popes and the Roman Church as antichrist. Historians note that Martin Luther and other reformers often utilized antichrist rhetoric in their battle against Rome.[12]

During Reformation times the papal system was consistently identified as the antichrist. Imminent writers that held to this viewpoint include Martin Luther (1483–1546), Philip Melanchthon (1497–1560), John Calvin (1509–1564), Ulrich Zwingli (1484–1531), Nicholas Ridley (1500–1555), Hugh Latimer (1485–1555), William Tyndale (1492–1536), Thomas Cranmer (1489–1556), John Foxe (1516–1597), and John Knox (1505–1572). Never in the history of the church were so many responsible scholars, preachers, linguists, theologians, and Bible expositors convinced that the antichrist was alive and living in Rome.

Even the Westminster Confession of Faith called the pope the antichrist: "There is no other head of the church but the Lord Jesus Christ: nor can the Pope of Rome in any sense be the head thereof; but is that Antichrist, that man of sin and son of perdition, that exalteth himself in the church against Christ, and all that is called God" (25.6).

The Roman Catholic Church retaliated by branding the Reformers and their movement as antichrist. Catholics also began arguing—with some urgency—that the antichrist would be a Jew. If that one point could be convincingly proven, there would consequently be no way the pope or the papacy could be the antichrist.

Puritan leaders of the seventeenth century continued to identify the papacy with antichrist. Such men as John Carter, William Ames, John Trapp, Thomas Goodwin, John Cotton, and Jeremiah Burroughs added the weight of their names to this identification. Spiritual leaders of the Great Awakening, beginning in the early eighteenth century, continued to hold this position—including John Wesley.

Even today there are many who continue to believe the pope or papacy may be the antichrist described in the Bible. For example, at present a billboard near the Oregon–California border calls the pope the antichrist.

A.W. PINK'S ASSESSMENT OF THE POPE-ANTICHRIST CONNECTION

Reformed Bible scholar A.W. Pink—no fan of Roman Catholicism—provides a number of arguments against the idea that the Roman Catholic papacy is the antichrist.

- The term *antichrist* refers to a person and not a system, such as the papacy.

- The antichrist will sit in the temple of God (2 Thessalonians 2:4). By no stretch of the imagination can St. Peter's at Rome be called that. The temple in Scripture is Jewish, not Catholic. The antichrist also opposes and exalts himself above all that is called God or that is worshipped. He sets himself in the place of God. No pope has ever engaged in such an action.

- The antichrist will make a covenant with the Jews (Daniel 9:27). No pope in history has ever made a seven-year covenant with the Jews. The antichrist will also cause sacrifices to cease. If the papacy is the antichrist, how can this be made to square with the continued sacrifice of the Mass?

- The antichrist cannot be revealed until the body of Christ, in whom the Holy Spirit dwells, has been removed from earth at the rapture (see 2 Thessalonians 2:6). If the antichrist cannot appear before the rapture, the antichrist has not yet appeared.

- If the papacy is the antichrist, who or what is the false prophet?

- The papacy may exercise authority over the Catholics of the world, but the papacy does not exercise authority over the rest of the world. The antichrist, by contrast, will have authority over all the world (Revelation 13:3,7). Further, what pope has ever required everyone to receive a mark, without which one cannot buy or sell (13:17)?

- The antichrist's career is limited to forty-two months (Daniel 7:25; see also Revelation 12:6,14; 13:5). This cannot be made to square with the long history of the Roman Catholic papacy.[13]

To clarify, Pink is not defending Roman Catholicism. He is a staunch Calvinist, and the furthest thing from his mind would be to defend Roman Catholicism. He simply wants to dispel the idea that the papacy is the antichrist. In fact, Pink says, the antichrist is yet future, and he will be a person who will engage in all the activities we find described in such passages as Daniel 9, 2 Thessalonians 2, and Revelation 13.

JUDAS ISCARIOT

According to one theory that refuses to die, the antichrist will be Judas Iscariot brought back from the grave. Advocates of this position cite Luke 22:3, where we are told that "Satan entered into Judas called Iscariot." Moreover, in John 6:70-71 we read, "Jesus answered them, 'Did I not choose you, the Twelve? And yet one of you is a devil.' He spoke of Judas the son of Simon Iscariot, for he, one of the Twelve, was going to betray him." Then, in John 17:12, Jesus referred to Judas as "the son of destruction," also sometimes translated "son of perdition." This same phrase is used of the antichrist in 2 Thessalonians 2:3. Finally, in Acts 1:25, we are told that when Judas died, he went "to his own place"—that is, a special place where Judas would await his resurrection as the final antichrist.[14]

Frankly, such a fanciful view involves more *eisogesis* (reading a meaning into the text) than *exegesis* (deriving the meaning out of the text). The biblical evidence is simply not there for the Judas–antichrist connection. Most scholars today say this view makes unwarranted assumptions and involves wild leaps of logic.

MORE RECENT ANTICHRIST IDENTIFICATIONS

Many people in recent history have been labeled as the antichrist. Such attempts at identifying the antichrist have always proved to be utterly futile. Here is a brief list of candidates:

Emperor Frederick II

Napoleon

Kaiser Wilhelm

Adolf Hitler

Joseph Stalin

Benito Mussolini

Boris Yeltsin

Nikita Khrushchev

John F. Kennedy (targeted by anti-Catholics)

Henry Kissinger

Margaret Thatcher

Mikhail Gorbachev

Ronald Wilson Reagan (he had six letters in each of his
     three names)

Bill Clinton (Hillary was claimed to be the false prophet)

Prince William

BARAK OBAMA

Even president Barak Obama has been targeted as the antichrist. According to a Harris poll, 24 percent of Republicans and 14 percent of Americans overall thought Mr. Obama was the antichrist.[15]

So popular has this theory been that Daniel Wallace, a distinguished New Testament professor at Dallas Theological Seminary, found it necessary to write an article debunking the idea. Wallace notes that a video that has gone viral on YouTube provides alleged hard evidence that Barak Obama is the antichrist. The narrator of the video cites Luke 10:18: "I saw Satan fall like lightning from heaven." It is argued that even though this verse was written in Greek, Jesus initially spoke it in Aramaic. Wallace then explains how the narrator arrives at his conclusion (it's a bit technical, but I think you'll pick up the gist of it):

> First, he claims that Luke 10:18 was written originally in
> Greek, but that Jesus spoke these words in Aramaic, "which

is the most ancient form of Hebrew." Second, he observes that the Old Testament was written in Hebrew and claims that the Aramaic that Jesus spoke would have been quite similar to the Hebrew that is spoken today and, presumably, similar to the Hebrew of the Old Testament. Third, he then says that Jesus spoke these words in Hebrew, and retranslates the text as follows: "I saw Satan falling as lightning from the heights, or from the heavens." Fourth, he discusses the Hebrew words for 'lightning' and 'heights.' He notes that the word for 'lightning' is *baraq*. Fifth, he claims that Isaiah is the source of the Christian understanding of Satan or 'Lucifer' (Isa. 14:12 in the KJV). Sixth, Isaiah 14:14 has Satan say, "I will ascend above the heights of the clouds; I will be like the Most High." Seventh, the Hebrew word in Isa. 14:14 for 'heights' is *bamaw*, and this is surely what 'heavens' means in Luke 10:18. Eighth, the Hebrew letter *waw* is sometimes transliterated as a *u* or *o*. Ninth, the *waw* is used in Hebrew as a conjunction. Tenth, in Hebrew poetry *baraq obamah* literally is translated "lightning and the heights" or "lightning from the heights." Eleventh, if Jesus' words in Luke 10:18 were spoken in Hebrew by a Jewish Rabbi today he would say, "And I saw Satan as *baraq ubamah*." He concludes his narration by asking, "Did Jesus reveal the name of the Antichrist? I report; you decide."[16]

Wallace then seeks to answer the narrator.

> What can we say about these videos and the linguistic argument used? Of the eleven points noted above, the fourth and eighth are the only ones that are indisputable: The Hebrew word for lightning is *baraq*; and the *waw* is sometimes transliterated as a *u* or *o*. The seventh point comes close to being correct: the Hebrew word for height is *bamah*, but the plural is used in Isa 14:14, *bamot* (pronounced baw-moat). As for the rest of the points, some are debatable, while others are factually wrong.[17]

Wallace then makes a number of other points that undermine the Obama–antichrist connection:

- It is debatable whether Jesus spoke most of the time in Aramaic.

- The narrator first said Jesus spoke in Aramaic and then said He spoke in Hebrew. Which is it? Similarity in languages does not mean they are identical.

- Is Isaiah really the source for the Christian view of Satan? Such is grossly simplistic.

- The narrator's thesis has a number of linguistic problems— problems that take a lot of wind out of the sails of his arguments: "A linguistic leap from Greek to Aramaic to Hebrew, with the grammar and vocabulary changing along the way, is required to make Luke 10:18 mean what the narrator wants it to mean. This is hardly a case of 'I report; you decide.' It is rather a case of 'I'll tell you only part of the evidence, and will use some fancy exegetical gymnastics to make everything fit; and based on the skewered evidence, you decide.'"[18]

After a detailed analysis, Wallace concludes, "When all is said and done, the evidence is simply bogus."

WARNING TO THE WISE

In each case above, people have read the prophetic Scriptures through the cultural lenses of their own times. They have practiced "newspaper exegesis." Later in the book, I will demonstrate that Christians will not know the identity of the antichrist, for the rapture will take place *prior* to his manifestation. I will also demonstrate that when the antichrist actually appears on the world scene, he will have clearly definable characteristics that rule out all of the people mentioned above. Thomas Ice and Timothy Demy provide us with some wise advice:

> Misidentifications of the Antichrist throughout church history should be a lesson to contemporary students of prophecy. Biblical prophecy must be interpreted consistently and

carefully, always maintaining a futurist perspective...What is perhaps most significant is the belief in the person and work of the Antichrist. Although many Christians have been wrong in their *identification*, they were not wrong in their *anticipation*.[19]

UNDERSTANDING OUR TERMS

What do we mean by the term *antichrist*? What is *the spirit of the antichrist*? Are these terms identical, or do they refer to different things? Moreover, were there antichrists in John's day that are distinct from the future and final antichrist that is yet to come? It makes good sense to seek a biblical understanding of these terms early in the book.

THE SPIRIT OF ANTICHRIST

Scripture reveals that in addition to a future person known as the antichrist who will come to power in the future seven-year tribulation period (2 Thessalonians 2:1-9; Revelation 13), there is also a "spirit of the antichrist" that is already at work, promoting heretical and cultic doctrine.

> Beloved, do not believe every spirit, but test the spirits to see whether they are from God, for many false prophets have gone out into the world. By this you know the Spirit of God: every spirit that confesses that Jesus Christ has come in the flesh is from God, and every spirit that does not confess Jesus is not from God. This is the spirit of the antichrist, which you heard was coming and now is in the world already (1 John 4:1-3).

In 2 John 7, John reveals that those who hold to such false doctrines are antichrists: "Many deceivers have gone out into the world, those who do not confess the coming of Jesus Christ in the flesh. Such a one is the deceiver and the antichrist."

By the time the aging apostle John wrote these epistles in about AD 90, Christianity had already been around for some 50 years. Plenty of time had passed for spiritual and doctrinal errors to develop. John seems to be dealing with an early strain of the Gnostic heresy. Apparently some Gnostic teachers were conducting an itinerant ministry in John's congregations, seeking converts. John wrote his epistles to warn true followers of Jesus Christ against such heresies.

John was most concerned about the Gnostic view of Jesus. The primary error related to whether Jesus was both human and divine. The root of the problem was the Greek idea that the spiritual and material realms are entirely separate and have nothing to do with each other. Some false teachers argued that the spiritual Christ did not actually become human but rather entered into the human Jesus at the time of the baptism and left the human Jesus before the crucifixion. This scenario avoids the idea that the spiritual became material when Jesus came into the world.

For example, the Gnostic Cerinthus drew a distinction between the human Jesus and the Christ, who was viewed as a cosmic spirit. We learn of the unique views of Cerinthus from the writings of a defender against heresies, Irenaeus (AD 130–200), who studied under Polycarp, who himself was a disciple of the apostle John.

> [Cerinthus] represented Jesus as having not been born of a virgin, but as being the son of Joseph and Mary according to the ordinary course of human generation, while he nevertheless was more righteous, prudent, and wise than other men. Moreover, after his baptism, Christ descended upon him in the form of a dove from the Supreme Ruler, and that then he proclaimed the unknown Father, and performed miracles. But at last Christ departed from Jesus, and that then Jesus suffered and rose again, while Christ remained impassible [inaccessible to harm or pain], inasmuch as he was a spiritual being.[1]

According to Cerinthus, when Jesus was taken captive in order to be crucified, "Christ ascended up on high" so that Jesus alone was subject to the pain of crucifixion. This "ascension" of "the Christ" is hardly that described in the Bible. Irenaeus goes on to tell us that the apostle John specifically directed his Gospel against Cerinthus.

John's writings also refute the closely related heresy of Docetism. Because of the dualistic belief that matter is evil and spirit is good, Docetists believed Jesus could not have had a real material human body because that would have involved a union of spirit and matter (good and evil). Jesus therefore must have had a phantomlike body— that is, He only had the appearance of flesh without substance or reality. (The word *Docetism* comes from the Greek word *dokeo*, meaning "to seem" or "to appear.") Jesus' suffering and death on the cross were therefore not real, for it is inconceivable that a Supreme God (who is spirit) would give Himself up to the destructive power of evil (in the form of matter).

John effectively refutes such false views of Christ in his Gospel and his epistles, providing convincing proof of Christ's full humanity (John 1:1,14; 1 John 4:2; 2 John 7). John also provided evidence for the bodily, physical resurrection of Christ (John 20:5-6,20,27). In essence, John's writings were aimed straight at the spirit of antichrist. Based on John's writings, we can conclude that the spirit of antichrist involves deception (2 John 7), denies that Christ came in the flesh (1 John 4:2-3), denies the Father and the Son (1 John 2:22), was prevalent in apostolic times (1 John 2:18; 4:3), and is closely related to false prophets (1 John 4:1).

Many theologians believe that "the spirit of the antichrist" refers to demonic spirits who promulgate anti-Christian teachings. In keeping with this, the apostle Paul had earlier warned, "The Spirit expressly says that in later times some will depart from the faith by devoting themselves to deceitful spirits and teachings of demons" (1 Timothy 4:1).

In any event, John was likely not limiting the manifestation of the spirit of antichrist to Gnosticism and Docetism alone, but these heretical systems were indicators of the spirit of antichrist in his day. Theologians suggest that "this anti-Christian spirit does everything it can to reject, deny, and undermine the truth about Jesus Christ."[2] In this sense, "an antichrist is any false teacher who denies the person and work of Jesus Christ."[3] Demonic spirits hate Jesus Christ and are delighted when they can entice someone away from the true doctrine of Christ in the Bible.

In their book *Global Warning*, Tim LaHaye and Ed Hindson note that the spirit of antichrist has been active in every century of church history.

> The New Testament authors assure us that the "spirit of antichrist" was active in their day over 20 centuries ago. It has remained active throughout the whole of church history, expressing itself in persecutions, heresies, spiritual deceptions, false prophets, and false religions. Satan has battled the church at every turn throughout its long history, waiting for the right moment to indwell the right person— the Antichrist—as his final masterpiece.[4]

MANY ANTICHRISTS

The apostle John warned, "Children, it is the last hour, and as you have heard that antichrist is coming, so now many antichrists have come. Therefore we know that it is the last hour" (1 John 2:18). What does John mean by this statement?

Many scholars suggest that the entire time span between the first and second comings constitute "the last hour" (see 1 Timothy 4:1; James 5:3; 1 Peter 4:7; 2 Peter 3:3; Jude 18). During this time span, various manifestations of antichrist take place.

For example, as one who has written many books on the kingdom of the cults, I can tell you with some authority that without exception, the various cults all present heretical views of Jesus Christ—His person, His words, His works, and His resurrection. All such false religious groups throughout church history are the work of antichrists, just as Gnostic antichrists were active in John's day. Such individuals may be considered wolves in sheep's clothing, proliferating damaging lies (see Matthew 7:15).

With this backdrop in mind, the lexical meaning of the term *anti-christ* makes good sense. It is a compound word composed of two Greek words—*anti* and *christos*. *Anti* can mean "instead of" or "against" or "opposed to." So *antichrist* can literally mean "instead of Christ" or "against Christ" or "opposed to Christ." The false Christ proposed by the Gnostic and Docetic antichrists of John's day were offered instead of the true Christ, against the true Christ, and opposed to the true Christ.

THE ANTICHRIST

As opposed to the many antichrists of church history, Scripture reveals that there is a single individual known as *the* antichrist who is yet to come and who will emerge into power during the future tribulation period (see Daniel 8:9-11; 11:31-38; 2 Thessalonians 2:1-12; Revelation 13:1-5; 19:20; 20:10). This individual will be the embodiment of all that is anti-God and anti-Christian. He will be the supreme antichrist of human history. More than any other, he will position himself as instead of Christ, against Christ, and opposed to Christ. He will set himself up against Christ and the people of God in the last days before the second coming. More than 100 passages in Scripture speak of this diabolical being, and this book touches on every one of them.

Some theologians relate the doctrine of the antichrist to warnings in the New Testament about false Christs.[5] For example, Jesus Himself warns, "Many will come in my name, saying, 'I am the Christ,' and they will lead many astray" (Matthew 24:5). Likewise, He warns that "false christs and false prophets will arise and perform great signs and wonders, so as to lead astray, if possible, even the elect" (24:24). This would be in keeping with one of the meanings of *anti* in the word *antichrist*: "instead of."

Some Bible scholars argue against this idea. For example, Bible expositor J. Dwight Pentecost, suggests that "a study of the five usages of antichrist in John's epistles seems clearly to indicate the idea of *opposition* rather than *exchange*."[6] Greek scholar R.C. Trench likewise notes, "To me St. John's words seem decisive that *resistance* to Christ, and *defiance* of Him—and not any treacherous assumption of his character and offices—is the essential mark of the Antichrist."[7] Consequently, they say, it is probably not correct to relate the idea of false Christs to the antichrist.

Despite my great respect especially for Professor Pentecost, I can see no good lexical or theological reason for denying that this end-times antichrist will be instead of Christ, against Christ, and opposed to Christ. All meanings of *anti* seem appropriate in this case.

The antichrist will mimic the true Christ in several ways.

Christ	Antichrist
Performs miracles, signs, and wonders (Matthew 9:32-33; Mark 6:2)	Performs miracles, signs, and wonders (Matthew 24:24; 2 Thessalonians 2:9)
Appears in the millennial temple (Ezekiel 43:6-7)	Sits in the tribulation temple (2 Thessalonians 2:4)
Is God (John 1:1-2; 10:36)	Claims to be God (2 Thessalonians 2:4)
Is the Lion from Judah (Revelation 5:5)	Has a mouth like a lion (Revelation 13:2)
Makes a peace covenant with Israel (Ezekiel 37:26)	Makes a peace covenant with Israel (Daniel 9:27)
Causes men to worship God (Revelation 1:6)	Causes men to worship Satan (Revelation 13:3-4)
Seals followers on their forehead (Revelation 7:4; 14:1)	Seals followers on their forehead or right hand (Revelation 13:16-18)
Has a worthy name (Revelation 19:16)	Has blasphemous names (Revelation 13:1)
Is married to a virtuous bride (Revelation 19:7-9)	Is married to a vile prostitute (Revelation 17:3-5)
Is crowned with many crowns (Revelation 19:12)	Is crowned with ten crowns (Revelation 13:1)
Is the King of kings (Revelation 19:16)	Is called "the king" (Daniel 11:36)

Sits on a throne (Revelation 3:21; 12:5; 20:11)	Sits on a throne (Revelation 13:2; 16:10)
Has a sharp sword in His mouth (Revelation 19:15)	Has a bow in his hand (Revelation 6:2)
Rides a white horse (Revelation 19:11)	Rides a white horse (Revelation 6:2)
Has an army (Revelation 19:14)	Has an army (Revelation 19:19)
Suffered a violent death (Revelation 5:6; 13:8)	Suffered a violent death (Revelation 13:3)
Was resurrected (Matthew 28:6)	Appeared to be resurrected (Revelation 13:3,14)
Will return from heaven (Revelation 19:11-21)	Will return from the bottomless pit (Revelation 17:8)
Will rule over a 1000-year worldwide kingdom (Revelation 20:1-6)	Will rule over a three-and-a-half-year worldwide kingdom (Revelation 13:5-8)
Is part of the Holy Trinity—Father, Son, and Holy Spirit (2 Corinthians 13:14)	Is part of an unholy trinity—Satan, antichrist, and false prophet (Revelation 13)[8]

Reformed scholar A.W. Pink draws even more parallels between Christ and the antichrist.

1. Christ was the subject of Old Testament prophecy; so also is the Antichrist. Many are the predictions which describe this coming one; see especially Daniel 11:21-45.

2. The Lord Jesus was typified by many Old Testament characters such as Abel, Joseph, Moses, David, etc. So also will the Antichrist be: such characters as Cain, Pharaoh, Absalom, Saul, etc., foreshadow the man of sin...

3. Christ was revealed only at God's appointed time; such will also be the case with the Antichrist. Of the one we read, "But when *the fullness of time was come*, God sent forth His Son" (Galatians 4:4); of the other it is said, "And now we

know what withholdeth that he might be *revealed in his time*" (2 Thessalonians 2:6).

4. Christ was a Man, a real Man, "the Man Christ Jesus" (1 Timothy 2:5); so also will the Antichrist be—"that man of sin" (2 Thessalonians 2:3).

5. But Christ was more than a man: He was the God-Man; so also will the Antichrist be more than a man: the Super-man...

6. Christ is entitled "the Morning Star" (Revelation 22:16); so also is the Antichrist (Isaiah 14:12).

7. Christ is referred to as Him "which was, and is, and is to come" (Revelation 4:8); the Antichrist is referred to as him that "was, and is not; and shall ascend out of the bottomless pit" (Revelation 17:8).[9]

When you think about it, it is not surprising that the antichrist mimics Christ, for he is inspired by Satan, and other Scriptures reveal that Satan himself is a great counterfeiter.

- Satan has his own church—the "synagogue of Satan" (Revelation 2:9).
- Satan has his own ministers—ministers of darkness that bring false sermons (2 Corinthians 11:4-5).
- He has formulated his own system of theology—called "teachings of demons" (1 Timothy 4:1; Revelation 2:24).
- His ministers proclaim a counterfeit gospel—Paul called it "a gospel contrary to the one we preached" (Galatians 1:7-8).
- Satan has his own throne (Revelation 13:2) and his own worshippers (13:4).
- He inspires false christs and self-constituted messiahs (Matthew 24:4-5).
- He employs false teachers who bring in "destructive heresies" (2 Peter 2:1).

- He sends out false prophets (Matthew 24:11) and sponsors false apostles who imitate the true (2 Corinthians 11:13).

So we see that the antichrist takes on the character of the one who empowers him, the devil of old. But of course, there are also many significant dissimilarities between Christ and the antichrist. Here are some of the more important.

- One is called the Christ (Matthew 16:16); the other, the antichrist (1 John 4:3).
- One is called the man of sorrows (Isaiah 53:3); the other, the man of lawlessness (2 Thessalonians 2:3).
- One is called the Son of God (John 1:34); the other, the son of destruction (2 Thessalonians 2:3).
- One is called the Lamb (Isaiah 53:7); the other, the beast (Revelation 11:7).
- One is called the Holy One (Mark 1:24); the other, the lawless one (2 Thessalonians 2:8).
- Christ came to do the Father's will (John 6:38); the antichrist will do his own will (Daniel 11:36).
- Christ was energized by the Holy Spirit (Luke 4:14); the antichrist will be energized by Satan, the *un*holy spirit (Revelation 13:4).
- Christ submitted Himself to God (John 5:30); the antichrist defies God (2 Thessalonians 2:4).
- Christ humbled Himself (Philippians 2:8); the antichrist exalts himself (Daniel 11:37).
- Christ honored the God of His fathers (Luke 4:16); the antichrist refuses to (Daniel 11:37).
- Christ cleansed the temple (John 2:14,16); the antichrist defiles the temple (Matthew 24:15).
- Christ was rejected by men (Isaiah 53:3); the antichrist will force people to accept him (Revelation 13:4).

- Christ was slain for the people (John 11:51); the antichrist slays the people (Isaiah 14:20).

- Christ was received up into heaven (Luke 24:51); the antichrist goes down into the lake of fire (Revelation 19:20).[10]

This Satan-inspired individual will rise to prominence in the tribulation period, initially making a peace treaty with Israel (Daniel 9:27). But then he will dominate the world, double-cross the Jews and attempt to destroy them, persecute believers, and set up his own kingdom (Revelation 13). He will speak arrogant and boastful words, glorifying himself (2 Thessalonians 2:4). His assistant, the false prophet, will entice the world to worship him (Revelation 13:11-12). He will control the global economy by forcing people around the world to receive his mark in order to buy or sell (Revelation 13:16-17). However, to receive this mark ensures one of being the recipient of God's wrath. The antichrist will eventually rule the whole world (Revelation 13:7) from his headquarters in Rome (Revelation 17:8-9). This beast will be defeated and destroyed by Jesus at His second coming (Revelation 19:11-16). I will discuss all this in great detail throughout the rest of the book.

IS THE ANTICHRIST A MUSLIM?

In recent days, for understandable reasons, many have concluded that the antichrist will be a Muslim. This has become the focus of a variety of books, articles, radio shows, television shows, and Internet discussions.

Is it really possible that the biblical references to the antichrist are referring to an end-times Muslim leader? A growing chorus of people think so. I will evaluate this hypothesis from a biblical perspective and test whether this is truly a viable interpretive option.

Right up front, let me say that I have studied the various arguments offered in favor of this position and found some of the arguments compelling, but in the end I concluded that the position is untenable. Let's keep in mind something that Solomon—the wisest man who ever lived (1 Kings 4:29-31)—once said: "The one who states his case first seems right, until the other comes and examines him" (Proverbs 18:17). When one examines the Muslim-antichrist hypothesis against the specific affirmations of Scripture, it is found wanting.

AN OVERVIEW OF ISLAMIC ESCHATOLOGY

Before examining why some Christians believe the antichrist predicted in the Bible will be a Muslim, let's first examine what Muslim eschatology broadly teaches on these matters.[1] Then we will be in a better position to note comparisons and contrasts.

The Islamic view of the antichrist. In Muslim theology, the antichrist is called the *Dajjal.* Muslim literature reveals that he will...

- be a Jew born in Iran
- be born to parents childless for 30 years
- have only one eye
- claim to be a prophet
- claim to be divine
- seek to be worshipped
- deceive people by seemingly miraculous acts
- conquer the world (except Mecca and Medina) with a large army
- reign for 40 days, each day being like a year

The Islamic view of the Messiah. The Messiah, according to Muslim theology, is called the *Mahdi.* He will...

- be a descendent of Muhammad
- ride on a white horse
- bring global deliverance from the reign of the antichrist, the Dajjal
- conquer and slaughter the Jews
- establish his headquarters in Jerusalem
- reign for seven (or more) years

The Islamic view of Jesus. The Jesus of Islam is substantially different from the Jesus of biblical Christianity. According to Muslim theology, Jesus...

- was one of the foremost prophets of Allah
- was a lesser prophet than Muhammad

- was a sinless man who was a messenger of God
- was not the Son of God or God in human flesh
- was not crucified or resurrected but was raised directly to heaven by Allah
- was not a sacrifice to atone for the sins of humankind
- will come back to earth to the Mount of Olives, meet up with the Mahdi and submit himself to him, slay all who do not accept Islam as the one true religion, kill the Dajjal, and see to the annihilation of the Jews
- will reign for 40 years after the death of the Mahdi, assume control of the Islamic global kingdom, bring global blessing, bring peace on earth, and marry and have children
- will die and be buried next to Muhammad in Medina
- will then be resurrected with all other men and women on the last day

THE CASE FOR A MUSLIM ANTICHRIST

To fairly represent the full Muslim-antichrist hypothesis would require a substantially long treatment. Here we have room only for a basic summary. Resources are available for those who wish to study the hypothesis in detail.[2]

Keep in mind what was said previously about the Islamic interpretation of the antichrist (Dajjal), the Messiah (Mahdi), and Jesus. In a capsule, the Muslim-antichrist hypothesis argues that...

- The Islamic Mahdi (Islamic Messiah) will be the antichrist described in the Bible.
- The Muslim Jesus will be the false prophet of the Bible, who will render service to the antichrist (or Mahdi).
- Both of these individuals will be destroyed when the true biblical Jesus returns at the end of the tribulation period.

Advocates of this position draw support for it by noting significant similarities between the biblical antichrist and the Muslim Mahdi. Joel Richardson, the author of *The Islamic Antichrist*, makes the following points in his book:[3]

- The Bible reveals that the antichrist will emerge in the last days as an unparalleled political, military, and religious leader, and Islam describes the Mahdi in the same way.

- The Bible indicates that the false prophet will emerge to support the antichrist, and Muslim eschatology teaches that the Muslim Jesus will emerge to support the Mahdi.

- The Bible reveals that the antichrist and the false prophet will seek to subdue the earth by a powerful army. Muslim eschatology teaches the same thing about the Mahdi and the Muslim Jesus.

- The Bible reveals that the antichrist and the false prophet will establish a new world order. Muslim eschatology teaches the same about the Mahdi and the Muslim Jesus.

- The Bible reveals that the antichrist and the false prophet will institute new laws for the whole earth. Muslim eschatology teaches that the Mahdi and the Muslim Jesus will institute Sharia law all over the earth.

- The Bible reveals that the antichrist "shall think to change the times" (Daniel 7:25). Muslim eschatology teaches that the Mahdi—after conquering the globe for Islam—will seek to change Christianity's rest days of Saturday and Sunday to Friday, the holy day of Islam.

- The Bible reveals that the antichrist and the false prophet will institute a world religion. Muslim eschatology teaches that the Mahdi and the Muslim Jesus will make Islam the world religion.

- The Bible reveals that the antichrist and the false prophet will execute anyone who does not submit to their world religion. Muslim eschatology teaches that the Mahdi and the Muslim Jesus will execute anyone who does not submit to Islam.

- The Bible reveals that the antichrist and the false prophet will behead those who refuse to submit to them (Revelation 20:4). Muslim eschatology teaches that the Mahdi and the Muslim Jesus will behead those who refuse to submit to Islam.

- The Bible reveals that the antichrist and the false prophet will seek to kill Jews, and Muslim eschatology teaches the same thing about the Mahdi and the Muslim Jesus.

- The Bible reveals that the antichrist and the false prophet will attack to conquer and seize Jerusalem. Muslim eschatology teaches that the Mahdi and the Muslim Jesus will do the same thing for Islam.

- The Bible reveals that the antichrist will set himself up in the Jewish temple in a position of authority. Muslim eschatology teaches that the Mahdi and the Muslim Jesus will establish the Islamic caliphate from Jerusalem.

- The biblical antichrist and the Muslim Mahdi both ride on a white horse.

- The Bible reveals that the antichrist will make a peace treaty with Israel for seven years. Muslim eschatology teaches that the Mahdi and the Muslim Jesus will make a peace treaty through a Jew (a Levite) for exactly seven years.

- The spirit of antichrist denies key doctrines of Christianity (such as the Incarnation). Islam does this.

Richardson draws this conclusion:

> We see that several of the most unique and distinguishing aspects of the biblical Antichrist's person, mission, and actions are matched to quite an amazing degree by the descriptions of the Mahdi as found in the Islamic traditions. And now, even further, we see that Muslim scholars actually apply Bible verses about the Antichrist to their awaited savior, the Mahdi. This must be seen as quite ironic, if not entirely prophetic.[4]

THE CASE AGAINST A MUSLIM ANTICHRIST

A scriptural analysis emboldens me to say that the antichrist will *not* be a Muslim, despite the case made by Joel Richardson and others. Here are some of the reasons why I believe the Muslim-antichrist view is fallacious.

The Contradictory Nature of Islamic Eschatology

Many of the passages in the Hadith (Islamic tradition) that deal with the end times are contradictory.[5] This makes it difficult to construct a detailed Muslim eschatology that all Muslims would agree with. As one Bible prophecy expert put it, "It is extremely difficult to piece together the Islamic concept of the end times. The information is greatly disjointed, being spread throughout the Hadith."[6] Books and articles written by proponents of the Muslim-antichrist hypothesis avoid addressing this reality.

The Dependency of Islamic Eschatology

David Reagan points out that Muhammad "got most of his ideas concerning the end times from discussions with Christians and Jews. And these ideas were later embellished by his followers who were even better acquainted with biblical prophecies concerning the end times."[7] Dr. Samuel Shahid, the director of Islamic studies at Southwestern Baptist Theological Seminary in Fort Worth, Texas, agrees, noting that the major concepts of Islamic eschatology were borrowed from the Hebrew Scriptures, the Christian New Testament, and various concepts of Zoroastrianism.[8] In fact, much of this information was derived by Muhammad before he became a prophet—when he was a businessman traveling in caravans, often encountering people of different faiths.

Further, many of the teachings recorded in the Hadith (literature that documents Muslim traditions) were heavily influenced by Christian sources. Academics who study Islam in detail have often noted such theological dependency. For example, the Islamic signs of the times, which point to the end times, include an increase in false prophets, apostasy, natural calamities, and wars, events all found in the

Christian Scriptures, which far predate the time of Muhammad (see, for example, Matthew 24).

Consider also the role of Satan, the father of lies. Scripture is clear that Satan can inspire false religions and cults (see, for example, 1 Timothy 4:1; 1 John 4:1). Further, we infer from Satan's temptation of Christ (Matthew 4:1-11) that Satan has knowledge of Scripture, because he quotes from Scripture in seeking to tempt Christ. Thus Satan, who knows biblical prophecy, may have sought to give credence to the false religion of Islam by inspiring similar prophecies (a one-world religion, a rider on a white horse, a false prophet, and the like) in that religion. Satan is a great deceiver.

Muslim Disagreements on the Mahdi

Christian prophecy scholars have also pointed out that the entire world of Muslims would not be likely to accept the coming of a so-called Mahdi. After all, this is a primary area of doctrinal conflict between Shi'ite and Sunni Muslims. These two varieties of Muslims hold to different views on the Mahdi. Shi'ite Muslims believe the Mahdi is now on earth but is in hiding and will soon emerge. Sunni Muslims, by contrast, believe that the Mahdi has yet to emerge in history. Or, as one historian put it, Shi'ite Muslims believe in a "coming out" of the Mahdi, whereas Sunni Muslims believe in a "coming back" of the Mahdi. Proponents of the Muslim-antichrist hypothesis seem to ignore such conflicting views.

The Spirit of Antichrist

We might agree that Islam's denials of key Christian doctrines such as the Incarnation is a representation of the spirit of antichrist. But Islam is not distinct or unique in this regard. After all, many religious groups and cults deny the Incarnation and other key Christian doctrines. Therefore, the "spirit of antichrist" argument lends no real support to the Muslim-antichrist hypothesis.

The Antichrist Will Be a Roman

Scripture reveals that the antichrist will be a Roman. Daniel 9:26, speaking of the 70 weeks of Daniel, tells us, "After the sixty-two weeks, an anointed one shall be cut off and shall have nothing. And the people of the prince who is to come shall destroy the city and the sanctuary. Its end shall come with a flood, and to the end there shall be war. Desolations are decreed." This passage tells us that Jerusalem and its temple will be destroyed by the "people of the prince who is to come." Who destroyed Jerusalem and its temple in AD 70? It was Titus and his Roman army. The Roman people are the people of "the coming prince," the antichrist. In view of this, it seems impossible to argue that the antichrist will be a Muslim.

The Antichrist's Covenant with Israel

The tribulation period will begin when the antichrist signs a covenant with Israel. In Daniel 9:27 we read that the antichrist "shall make a strong covenant with many for one week" (that is, one week of years—seven years).

Discerning interpreters wonder why a Muslim leader would sign a covenant with Israel guaranteeing its protection. After all, most Muslims today hate Israel and want the land back.

Related to this, many prophecy scholars have believed that this covenant is what allows Israel to dwell securely (Ezekiel 38:8,11) so that it can rebuild the Jewish temple. It seems hard to believe that a Muslim leader would protect Israel in this regard. Muslims would certainly not want what they would consider to be a pagan temple to be built in the holy city of Jerusalem.

And just as no Muslim leader would want to sign a covenant protecting Israel, Israel would never trust its security to a Muslim leader (see Daniel 9:27). Israel couldn't possibly dwell securely under a covenant with a Muslim leader, especially with today's rhetoric about how Muslims want to "wipe Israel off the face of the earth."[9]

Still further, the Muslim population in Muslim countries around the world would never follow a Muslim leader who made such a covenant with Israel. The Muslim-antichrist hypothesis assumes that Muslims will universally submit to such a covenant. I cannot believe it. Based on a long historical precedent, it seems clear that Muslims would strongly react against such a covenant made by a Muslim leader.

In addition, in Muslim eschatology, the covenant is made with the Romans, not the Jews. This cannot be reconciled with the biblical account in any way.

The Changing of the Calendar

As for changing the times, or changing the calendar, nothing in Daniel 7:25 supports the Muslim-antichrist hypothesis. The calendar we now use is a Christian calendar that dates from the time of the birth of Jesus Christ, so it is not surprising that the antichrist would change the calendar so that it would not honor or point to Jesus Christ in any way. The idea that the rest days of Saturday or Sunday will be changed to the Islamic holy day of Friday is nothing more than reading a meaning into the text of Scripture (eisogesis).

Beheading in the End Times

The same is true regarding the argument about beheading as a means of execution. Advocates of the Muslim-antichrist hypothesis assume that beheading is an automatic indicator of Islam, but such is not the case. We read about beheadings in both the Old Testament (2 Samuel 4:7) and the New Testament (Matthew 14:10), and they predate the emergence of Islam as a religion by many centuries. Reading Islam into end-time prophecies (Revelation 20:4) is thus not legitimate.

The Antichrist Claims to Be God

Daniel 11:36 tells us the antichrist "shall exalt himself and magnify himself above every god." We also read in 2 Thessalonians 2:4 that the antichrist ultimately "opposes and exalts himself against every so-called god or object of worship, so that he takes his seat in the temple of God, proclaiming himself to be God." To say the very least, a Muslim antichrist claiming to be God would be trashing the Muslim creed: "There is one God named Allah, and Muhammad is his prophet." I cannot imagine a true Muslim making any claim that he was God. Just as it is anathema to Muslims to call Jesus "God incarnate" or the "Son of God," so it would be anathema to Muslims for any human to claim he was God. (Keep in mind that Muslims are radical monotheists.) A

Muslim antichrist would thus be viewed as an infidel among Quran-believing Muslims.

In addition, Muslims teach that "God can have no partners." They generally say this as a means of arguing against the doctrine of the Trinity. But it is certainly applicable to human leaders on earth who claim to be God.

Still further, Muslims believe Allah is so radically unlike any earthly reality—so utterly transcendent and beyond anything in the finite realm—that he can scarcely be described using earthly terms. So how could a human Muslim (the antichrist) claim to be God described in earthly terms?

Not unexpectedly, proponents of the Muslim-antichrist hypothesis have an answer for all this. They claim that in the middle of the tribulation period, the antichrist will become self-absorbed and claim to be God. As Richardson explains it, "The Mahdi throws the ultimate curveball. In the same way that Christians view Jesus to be the incarnation of God, so the Mahdi now declares himself an incarnation of Allah, and as such, he demands worship."[10]

There are several suggested explanations for what may happen next. Some Muslims may be too embarrassed to admit they have been duped. They will not want to admit they were wrong all along. As Richardson puts it, "For many...an utter determination to believe in the legitimacy of the Mahdi and Islam will overwhelm them. These would rather be swept up into a great deception with an Islamic nature than acknowledge having been wrong all along."[11]

Such a scenario is impossible to believe. If true Muslims—firmly committed to Muhammad, the Quran, the Muslim creed, and Allah—discovered another Muslim who claimed to be God, they would want to behead the infidel. No true Muslim would allow such a claim to go unanswered.

Another scenario suggested by Richardson is that when the antichrist claims to be God, "it is quite likely that at this time multitudes of Muslims will see the evil person that the antichrist really is and will turn to the true Jesus for salvation. Who knows?"[12] This scenario sounds inviting, for all Christians want as many people as possible to be saved—including Muslims. The problem is, this is a speculative interpretation with no genuine biblical support. It seems more eisogesis than exegesis.

The Antichrist's Domain Is Worldwide

Some proponents of the Muslim-antichrist hypothesis argue that the domain of the antichrist will be regional and not global. They suggest that the antichrist's domain includes several Muslim nations and not the whole world. "The Bible abounds with proofs that the antichrist's empire will consist only of nations that are, today, Islamic," says Richardson.[13] He believes that the Mahdi's empire will be a revived Ottoman Empire.

Such an interpretation seems foreign to the pages of prophetic Scripture. Revelation 13:7, for example, affirms that the antichrist will gain authority "over every tribe and people and language and nation." How can such words mean anything less than global authority? It will not do to claim that such language involves a hyperbole (an obvious and benign exaggeration). Such words are elsewhere used in the book of Revelation in reference to people being saved all over the world. In the praise song celebrating Jesus the Lamb of God, we read, "You ransomed people for God from every tribe and language and people and nation" (Revelation 5:9). Just as the redeemed will come from all over the globe, so also will the antichrist gain authority over the whole globe during the tribulation period.

Moreover, Daniel 7:23 informs us that the antichrist "shall devour the whole earth, and trample it down, and break it to pieces." Notice our text says not "earth" but "whole earth." The qualifying word *whole* leaves no doubt that the antichrist's reach and influence will be global.

Revelation 6–9 describes horrific destruction around the entire globe that leads to half the world's population dying. Such could not possibly be the case if the antichrist's domain were merely regional. The book of Revelation points to worldwide catastrophes.

Richardson must engage in hermeneutical gymnastics in his treatment of Daniel 2:31-45 to arrive at the conclusion that the antichrist will emerge out of a revived Ottoman Empire instead of the traditionally understood revived Roman Empire. Richardson suggests that the Roman Empire existed in the form of the Byzantine Empire until 1453, when it was overcome by the Ottoman Empire. Thus, he says, it will be the Ottoman Empire—which fell from power in the early 1900s—that will be revived in the end times and not the Roman Empire. This means that the antichrist will rise out of the Ottoman Empire—a Muslim Empire.

This view ignores the fact that the actual Roman Empire fell and ceased to exist in the fifth century AD. What remained might loosely be called Roman geographically, but Rome as a political entity—the people who destroyed Jerusalem and its temple—was dead and gone. The antichrist is specifically predicted to come from the actual people who destroyed Jerusalem and its temple (Daniel 9:26)—that is, the Roman Empire that fell in the fifth century AD.

Richardson's scenario cannot be made to fit in the context of the prophecy in Daniel 2. This prophecy contains no specific symbol for the Ottoman Empire the way it does for the other empires mentioned—a head of gold representing the Babylonian Empire, a chest of silver representing the Medo-Persian Empire, thighs of bronze representing the Greek Empire, and legs of iron representing the Roman Empire. The final form of the Roman Empire is represented by feet of iron mixed with clay. There are no symbols in the context that can be made to fit the Ottoman Empire here (see also Revelation 17:10-11). Richardson seems to engage in forced exegesis.

The Ezekiel Invasion

I wonder how the Muslim-antichrist hypothesis would be feasible with the Ezekiel invasion! As I argue in my book *Northern Storm Rising*, some 2600 years ago Ezekiel prophesied that the Jews will be gathered from many nations to the land of Israel in the end times (Ezekiel 36–37). He then prophesied that sometime later there would be an all-out invasion of Israel by a massive northern assault force, with Russia heading up a coalition of Muslim nations, including modern Iran, Sudan, Turkey, and Libya. This invasion will likely take place either prior to or at the beginning of the tribulation period. The goal of the

Muslim invaders will be to utterly obliterate the Jews. With the sheer size of this assault force, Israel will seem to have no chance of defending itself. God, however, will intervene and supernaturally annihilate the Islamic invaders (38–39).

The description in Ezekiel 38–39 also seems to indicate that Muslim countries will thus be reduced to ashes. This raises the question of how a Muslim leader could emerge into great prominence on the world scene out of the ashes of the destroyed Muslim coalition. Such a scenario seems impossible to fathom.

What makes better sense is that once Christians are removed from the earth at the rapture (which precedes the tribulation period), and once the Muslims are largely destroyed by God during the Ezekiel invasion (which either precedes the tribulation or takes place at the beginning of the tribulation), it will be much easier for the Roman antichrist to emerge into power along with the false prophet, who will promote a false one-world religion and bring about a one-world government.

Not surprisingly, Richardson departs from traditional interpretations in arguing that the list of nations in Ezekiel 38, with a heavy emphasis on Turkey, fits well with his scenario of the Turkish/Ottoman Empire.[14] In making his case, he entirely removes Russia from Ezekiel's prophecy, claiming that the case for Russia being involved in this northern military coalition is weak at best. He makes this claim about the interpretation of the word *Rosh* as Russia:

> [It] is based on a bogus principle. One cannot simply take a word from an ancient Semitic language (in this case Hebrew) and find a correlation to a modern name from a drastically different language…simply because the two words "sound the same"…The notion that Ezekiel specifically mentioned Russia is a strong, if not irresponsible, stretch—mere speculation built on a very weak foundation.[15]

He also asserts, "It is fair to say that the entire argument for a primary Russian involvement is based on weak scholarship and actually requires a violation of basic linguistic norms."[16]

Of course, it is easy to see why Richardson would not want Russia to be mentioned in Ezekiel's list of nations. Russian involvement would not mesh well with his claim that the antichrist will be a Muslim who emerges out of a revived Turkish/Ottoman Empire—which Russia was never a part of.

We can make a number of observations in response. First, no Bible prophecy interpreter I know bases his view that Rosh is Russia on the mere fact that the terms sound alike. Richardson is creating a straw man—that is, he fabricates a feeble argument allegedly held by those who believe in a Rosh-Russia connection, and then he knocks that feeble argument down. If the view that Rosh is Russia were based solely on the similarity of sound between the two, I would not hold to this position either. Here is a summary of the more substantive reasons for taking the term as referring to Russia.

First, highly respected Hebrew scholars have taken the term as referring to Russia. This should not be taken lightly. A notable example is Wilhelm Gesenius, whose original Latin version of his lexicon titled *Thesaurus Linguae Hebraeae et Chaldaeae Veteris Testamenti* contains nearly a page of notes dealing with the word *Rosh* and the Rosh people mentioned in Ezekiel 38–39.

There is considerable historical evidence that a place known as Rosh—sometimes using alternate spellings such as Rus, Ros, and Rox—was familiar in the ancient world and was located in the territory now occupied by modern Russia.

Related to this, the Septuagint, the Greek translation of the Hebrew Old Testament that predates the time of Christ, translates *Rosh* as *Ros*. It is noteworthy that the Septuagint is not much more than three centuries removed from Ezekiel's time. Moreover, there is evidence of a people named Rosh/Rashu in the ninth through seventh centuries BC in Assyrian sources that predate the book of Ezekiel. So quite early, we find evidence of a Ros people that was geographically located in today's Russia.

Rosh also appears as a place name in Egyptian inscriptions as *Rash* from as early as 2600 BC. One inscription that dates to 1500 BC refers to a land called Reshu that was located to the north of Egypt (as is the case with modern Russia). Rosh (or its equivalent) is found in a variety of other ancient documents as well.

Placing Rosh in the area today known as Russia has long been a tradition in the Christian church, as early as AD 438.

Finally, Ezekiel 39:2 says Rosh is "from the remotest parts of the north." The term *north* is to be understood in relation to Israel. Russia is due north of Israel.

For these and other reasons, there is good evidence to include Russia in the northern military coalition of nations described in Ezekiel 38. This chapter indicates that Russia will join a number of Muslim nations in an all-out attack against Israel.

There is already historical precedence for Russia joining with Muslim nations against Israel. In 1973, Russia showed indisputable military aggression toward Israel. Egypt, Syria, and some other Arab/Islamic countries initially launched an attack against Israel, but it soon became clear that Russia was providing the military muscle behind the attack—including weaponry, ammunition, intelligence, and military training to assist this Arabic coalition to destroy Israel. Because Russia has joined forces with Muslims before, the coalition described in Ezekiel 38 is entirely feasible in terms of current events.

Even today, one can observe alliances between Russia and Iran and other Muslim nations. The northern military coalition prophesied by Ezekiel is slowly but surely coming together in our day, with alliances or strategic agreements forming between Russia, Iran, Turkey, Libya, Syria, various former Soviet republics, and others.

The implication of all this for Richardson's scenario is significant. If Rosh is indeed Russia, and if Russia was never a part of the Ottoman Empire (as history proves), then Ezekiel 38 can hardly be cited as a support for his Ottoman Empire hypothesis.

Lone-Ranger Interpretations

David Reagan responds to the Muslim-antichrist hypothesis with a warning against lone-ranger interpretations. He says that "God does not reveal the meaning of prophecy only to a person or two" (see 2 Peter 1:20). Those who are writing and defending this hypothesis are few, and they go against the great majority of biblical prophecy scholars. At the very least, this ought to give one pause when considering novel theories. Reagan warns that "the current rush to identify the antichrist as a Muslim is a classic example of newspaper exegesis—of reading the news headlines into the Bible rather than letting the Bible speak for itself." I think Reagan is correct.

IS THE ANTICHRIST A JEW?

In early 1999, the Reverend Jerry Falwell caused a worldwide stir when he said at a pastors' conference that the antichrist would be a Jew and was alive somewhere in the world. "Since Jesus came to Earth the first time 2,000 years ago as a Jewish male, most evangelicals believe the Antichrist will, by necessity, be a Jewish male."[1]

Jewish leaders around the world immediately took great offense. Abraham H. Foxman, director of the Anti-Defamation League, responded: "In identifying the antichrist as a living Jewish man, Reverend Falwell draws from an especially vicious tradition of Christian theological anti-Judaism...It appears clear that after years of Christian-Jewish dialogue, Reverend Falwell hasn't learned a thing."[2] Foxman commented that Falwell's comments give "license to bigots and anti-Semites" to continue in their prejudices and feelings of superiority.[3] Lauren Levin, also of the Anti-Defamation League, commented that Falwell's statements were "greatly disappointing."[4]

Rabbi James Rudin, director of interreligious affairs for the American Jewish Committee in New York, affirmed that he was surprised by the comment because he was aware of Falwell's strong support of Israel. He then said, "To single out any one man and particularly to identify him as Jewish plays into some latent and historical anti-Semitism from the past...This is very, very radioactive material. I think

Christian leaders have to exercise great care because this can produce negative responses among people who are not educated in the New Testament."[5] Rabbi David Wolfman, regional director of the Union of American Hebrew Congregations, likewise said Falwell's statement was an "insult to the Jewish community."[6]

Jewish people weren't the only ones who were offended. Bishop Walter F. Sullivan, bishop of the Catholic Diocese of Richmond, Virginia, said that Falwell's remarks "put into motion" exactly what "the antichrist embodies...hatred, prejudice, discrimination, [and] bigotry...[It is] but one more instance of blaming the Jews for the world's trouble...again [making] the Jews the scapegoat for our fears and insecurities."[7]

Falwell quickly became the target of pundits on national television talk shows, radio shows, and political commentary programs. He was also widely denounced in newspaper editorials throughout the country. As a result of the firestorm ignited by Falwell's comment, he issued a public apology.

Most people failed to realize at the time that far before Falwell made his comment, certain Roman Catholic leaders of the past argued that the antichrist would be a Jew. Their motivation was to disarm claims that the pope was the antichrist. In fact, the idea of a Jewish antichrist has been held by many for thousands of years, even in biblical times.

THE CASE FOR A JEWISH ANTICHRIST

Let's examine the evidence for the theory that the antichrist will be a Jew. Then we can evaluate this idea from a biblical perspective.

Anti-Semitism

Some have tried to argue that the Jews are responsible for most of the world's problems. They conclude that the antichrist must be Jewish because he will cause the worst problems of all. Clearly, this is simply uninformed and hateful anti-Semitism.

The Tribe of Dan

Some have believed the antichrist would be a Jew because of an early tradition that the antichrist would come from the tribe of Dan (one of the 12 tribes of Israel). Some relate this to the fact that the tribe of Dan fell into deep apostasy and idolatry, setting up a graven image (Judges 18:30). In the Testament of Dan (5:6), Satan is called the prince of the tribe. Irenaeus, writing in the latter part of the second century, noted that the omission of Dan in the list of the 144,000 (Revelation 7:4-8) was due to a tradition that the antichrist was to come from that tribe (*Against Heresies,* book 5, 30.2).

Genesis 49:17 is occasionally cited in support of this idea: "Dan shall be a serpent in the way, a viper by the path, that bites the horse's heels so that his rider falls backward." Stated in the form of a syllogism, the argument goes as follows:

Major premise: The tribe from whom the antichrist would come would not be listed among the 144,000.

Minor premise: Dan is not among the 144,000.

Conclusion: The antichrist is from the tribe of Dan.[8]

The Church Fathers

Some important church fathers held that the antichrist would be a Jew. This includes not only Irenaeus, mentioned above, but also Hippolytus, a disciple of Irenaeus. Indeed, Hippolytus wrote that the "Antichrist is a Jewish false messiah whose coming is still some time in the future."[9] Others who held that the antichrist would be a Jew include Origen, Chrysostom, Jerome, and Augustine.

The Little Horn

It is sometimes argued that the antichrist is specifically referred to as "the little horn" (Daniel 7:8) because Israel is a comparatively small nation. Despite the fact that the antichrist will emerge out of a small nation, he will subdue one nation after another until he attains global dominion.

John 5:43

In John 5:43, Jesus stated, "I have come in my Father's name, and you do not receive me. If another comes in his own name, you will receive him." It is argued that the Jews would never receive anyone as a leader who himself was not a Jew, so the antichrist must be a Jew. A.W. Pink says, "He will ape Christ. He will pose as the real Messiah of Israel. In such case he must be a Jew."[10] Grant Jeffery puts it this way:

> The Jews would one day accept for a time the false claims of the Antichrist as their promised Messiah...Since the prophecies tell us that the Antichrist will present himself to Israel as the Messiah many scholars have concluded that he must be Jewish. Certainly no religious Jew would dream of accepting a Gentile as the Messiah of Israel.[11]

Revelation 11:8

It is sometimes argued from Revelation 11:8 that the seat of the antichrist's dominion will be the "great city" were the "Lord was crucified." This being the case, the antichrist must be a Jew, for only a Jew could reign from this city.

The God of His Fathers

Appeal is sometimes made to Daniel 11:37, which, in the King James Version, says the antichrist will not "regard the God of his fathers." A.W. Pink comments, "This passage, it is evident, refers to and describes none other than the coming antichrist...What are we to understand by this expression? Why, surely, that he is a Jew, an Israelite, and that his fathers after the flesh were Abraham, Isaac and Jacob."[12]

THE CASE AGAINST THE ANTICHRIST BEING A JEW

There are quite a number of arguments that militate against the idea that the antichrist will be a Jew. I have found the following arguments convincing.

No Explicit Statement

Let's begin with the recognition that the Bible never says the antichrist will be a Jew. This should at least give one pause in subscribing to this theory.

Invalidity of Anti-Semitism

This argument is really not worthy of response, for it is nothing more than a form of racism. Biblically, all human beings are completely equal—equal in terms of their creation (Genesis 1:27), the sin problem (Romans 3:23), God's love for them (John 3:16), and God's provision of salvation for them (Matthew 28:19). The apostle Paul affirmed that God "made from one man every nation of mankind to live on all the face of the earth, having determined allotted periods and the boundaries of their dwelling place" (Acts 17:26). Moreover, Revelation 5:9 tells us that God's redeemed will be "from every tribe and language and people and nation." There is no place for racial discrimination, for all people are equal in God's sight. One will find no biblical support for the idea that the antichrist will be a Jew simply because the Jews are troublemakers.

Rising Up out of the Sea

Revelation 13:1 speaks of the "beast rising out of the sea." Later in the book of Revelation, we are told, "The waters that you saw...are peoples and multitudes and nations and languages" (17:15). Since the antichrist is said to rise up out of the sea, and the sea is a reference to the Gentile nations around the earth, it seems clear that the antichrist will be a Gentile, and not a Jew.

A Roman

We can also infer that the antichrist will be of Roman descent (see Revelation 17:9-12). Daniel 9:26 warns us that "the people of the prince who is to come shall destroy the city and the sanctuary." Romans, under Titus, destroyed the city of Jerusalem and the Jewish temple in AD 70. The antichrist will be of this same people, so he will be Roman.

Cruel Persecutor of Jews

The prophetic Scriptures reveal that the antichrist will be a great and cruel persecutor of the Jews (Matthew 24:16-21; Revelation 12:6). He will trample on Jewish laws and traditions and desolate the Jewish temple (Daniel 9:27; 11:31; 12:11). It therefore hardly seems possible that the antichrist could himself be a Jew.

Parallel to Antiochus Epiphanes

It seems clear that Antiochus Epiphanes was an Old Testament type* of the antichrist (see Daniel 11). Antiochus was a great persecutor of the Jews who also desolated the Jewish temple—and he was a Gentile. It therefore stands to reason that the antichrist will also be a Gentile.

Anti-Jewish Messiah

Some theologians note that the antichrist will be an "anti" Jewish messiah. In other words, because he will truly be "anti" Christ, it stands to reason that he will "oppose the very concept of a promised Jewish Messiah."[13]

Jerusalem Under Siege

The argument that the antichrist will have a seat of power in Jerusalem does not necessarily demand that he be a Jew. After all, the Scriptures are clear that in the middle of the tribulation period, the antichrist becomes the great persecutor of the Jews, and the Jews flee out of Jerusalem (Matthew 24:16-21; Revelation 12:6). The antichrist overturns Jewish traditions and sacrifices and desolates the Jewish temple (Daniel 9:27; 11:31; 12:11). His strong stand against the Jews enables him to take over and have a seat of power in Jerusalem. Put another way, the antichrist becomes elevated in Jerusalem not because of Jewish support but because of cruel persecution of Jewish people.

No Jewish Acceptance

Arnold Fruchtenbaum makes note of the false logic involved in the line of argumentation that says the antichrist will be Jewish because the Jews would not accept anyone other than a Jewish leader (see John 5:43). The argument, in syllogism form, is as follows:

Major premise: The Jews will accept the antichrist as the Messiah.
Minor premise: The Jews will never accept a Gentile as the Messiah.
Conclusion: The antichrist will be a Jew.[14]

---

* A type is an Old Testament institution, event, person, object, or ceremony that has reality and purpose in biblical history but that also by divine design foreshadows something yet to be revealed.

The conclusion is built on false premises. The simple fact that the Jewish people sign a covenant with the antichrist (Daniel 9:26) does not in any way mean they are accepting him as their Messiah. David Reagan agrees: "The Bible does not teach that the Jews will receive the antichrist as their Messiah. It teaches they will accept him as a great political leader and diplomat and that they will put their trust in him as the guarantor of peace in the Middle East."[15] Because of this, there is no support here for the idea of a Jewish antichrist.

Tribe of Dan

The argument regarding the tribe of Dan is completely unconvincing. At the outset, we must note that the Old Testament has "no fewer than twenty variant lists of the tribes, and these lists include anywhere from ten to thirteen tribes, though the number twelve is predominant (cf. Gen. 49; Deut. 33; Ezek. 48)."[16] No list of the twelve tribes of Israel must be identical. However, twelve seems to be the ideal number in terms of listing Israel's tribes, so it seems clear that John in Revelation 7 and 14 wanted to maintain this ideal number.

Most scholars today agree that Dan's tribe was omitted because that tribe was guilty of idolatry on many occasions and, as a result, was largely obliterated (Leviticus 24:11; Judges 18:1,30; see also 1 Kings 12:28-29). Bible scholar Robert H. Mounce explains: "When the tribe of Dan migrated to the north and settled at Laish, they set up for themselves the graven image (Judg. 18:30). Later Dan became one of the two great shrines in the northern kingdom (1 Kings 12:29)."[17] To engage in unrepentant idolatry is to be cut off from God's blessing.

The fact that Dan's tribe succumbed to idolatry, however, does not constitute evidence that the antichrist will come from this tribe. That is a mere assumption without real evidence. It requires a leap of logic for which there is no true justification.

Times of the Gentiles

Many prophecy scholars believe that the nature of the "times of the Gentiles" (Luke 21:24) supports a Gentile antichrist. Fruchtenbaum provides this explanation:

82

> It is agreed by all premillennialists that the period known as the Times of the Gentiles does not end until the second coming of Christ. It is further agreed that the Antichrist is the final ruler of the Times of the Gentiles...If this is so, how then can a Jew be the last ruler at a time when only Gentiles can have the preeminence? To say the Antichrist is to be a Jew would contradict the very nature of the Times of the Gentiles.[18]

Gods of His Fathers

I noted previously that appeal is sometimes made to Daniel 11:37, which, in the King James Version, says the antichrist will not "regard the God of his fathers." This allegedly indicates a Jewish antichrist who will have no regard for the God of Abraham, Isaac, and Jacob.

Unfortunately, the King James Version mistranslates this verse. Most English translations render it as does the English Standard Version: "He shall pay no attention to the gods of his fathers." This is referring not to the one true God of Abraham, Isaac, and Jacob, but to false pagan deities. In view of this, the verse offers no support for the idea of a Jewish antichrist who has abandoned the Jewish God.

CONCLUSION

In view of the foregoing arguments, we must conclude that the antichrist will not be a Jew, but rather will be a Gentile. More precisely, he will be a Roman Gentile who will emerge in a revived Roman Empire and rule in the last phase of the times of the Gentiles.

IS THE ANTICHRIST "GOG"?

The word *Gog* refers to the military leader who will head up the northern military coalition—composed of Russia, Iran, Sudan, Turkey, Libya, and other Muslim nations—against Israel in the end times (Ezekiel 38–39). Gog is specifically referred to as the "prince of Rosh, Meshech and Tubal" (Ezekiel 38:2 NASB). He is the leader of these nations, the one in charge. These nations follow his lead in moving against Israel. The word *Gog* appears 11 times in Ezekiel 38–39, thereby indicating that he plays a significant role in this end-times invasion.

Gog may or may not be a proper name. There is reference to an altogether different Gog in 1 Chronicles 5:4, where we read that among the sons of Joel were "Shemaiah his son, Gog his son, Shimei his son," and others. This verse at least indicates that the term *can* be used as a proper name.

It would seem, however, that the term is not intended as a proper name in the context of Ezekiel 38–39. Numerous prophecy experts have suggested that the term may refer to a king-like role—such as *Pharaoh, caesar, czar,* or *president*.[1] The term literally means "high," "supreme," "height," or "a high mountain."[2] Apparently, then, this czar-like military leader will be a man of great political stature who commands tremendous respect.

Some in church history have come to the conclusion that *Gog* is one of several scriptural titles for the antichrist. Earlier in the book, I discussed Joel Richardson's theory that the antichrist will be a Muslim. Richardson also believes that the antichrist is Gog.

For example, Richardson says, "I personally reject the idea that Gog is anyone other than the Antichrist."[3] He believes that the antichrist heads up the northern coalition of Muslim nations that will invade Israel.

> The Prophet Ezekiel lists the nations of this final empire quite specifically as he prophesies the future attack of the Antichrist against Israel. In the thirty-eighth chapter of his book, Ezekiel begins by directly addressing the Antichrist, whom the Lord refers to by the unusual name of "Gog."[4]

In terms of both role and function, Gog and the antichrist are viewed as the same. Further, Richardson says, Gog is a puppet of Satan.[5]

THE CASE AGAINST GOG BEING THE ANTICHRIST

In my view, the Bible interpreter will end up in prophetic chaos if he or she tries to make the identification between Gog and the antichrist. There are a number of scriptural factors that militate against this identification.

Different Domains

First and foremost, Gog and the antichrist rule over different domains. The nations Gog rules over are specifically listed in Ezekiel 38:1-6. Who are these nations?

Magog. Magog, mentioned in the table of nations in Genesis 10:2, probably constitutes the geographical area in the southern portion of the former Soviet Union. Many scholars take Magog to generally refer to the mountainous area near the Black and Caspian Seas, the former domain of the Scythians. More specifically, it likely refers to the area that is today occupied by the former southern Soviet republics of Kazakhstan, Kyrgyzstan, Uzbekistan, Turkmenistan, Tajikistan, and possibly even northern parts of modern Afghanistan. Significantly, this entire area is dominated by Muslims and has more than enough religious motivation to move against Israel.

Rosh. As we have seen, Rosh apparently refers to Russia. To summarize my previous discussion, some highly respected Hebrew scholars are convinced the term refers to Russia, including Wilhelm Gesenius in his *Thesaurus Linguae Hebraeae et Chaldaeae Veteris Testamenti.* Further, a people named Rosh/Rashu appear in the ninth through seventh centuries BC in Assyrian sources that predate the book of Ezekiel, and these people were geographically located in today's Russia. Rosh also appears as a place name in Egyptian inscriptions, referring to a people located to the north of Egypt (as is the case with modern Russia). Finally, in Ezekiel 39:2 Rosh is said to be "from the remotest parts of the north." The term *north* is to be understood in relation to Israel. Russia is due north of Israel.

Meshech and Tubal. Meshech and Tubal were the sixth and fifth sons of Japheth, the son of Noah (Genesis 10:2). Often mentioned together in Scripture, the names appear to refer to the geographical territory to the south of the Black and Caspian Seas of Ezekiel's day, which is today modern Turkey, though there may be some overlap with some neighboring countries. Meshech and Tubal are identified with the Mushki and Tabal of the Assyrians, and the Moschi and Tibareni of the Greeks. The ancient historian Herodotus confirms that these groups inhabited the territory that is now modern Turkey.

Persia. A look at an ancient map of Persia shows that this same territory is occupied by modern Iran. In fact, in 1935 Persia became modern Iran. During the Iranian Revolution in 1979, the name changed to the Islamic Republic of Iran.

Ethiopia. This term refers to the geographical territory just south of Egypt on the Nile River—what is today known as Sudan. Sudan is a hardline Islamic nation and a kindred spirit with Iran in its venomous hatred of Israel. In fact, these nations are already such close allies that a mutual stand against Israel would be expected. This nation is infamous for its ties to terrorism and its harboring of Osama bin Laden from 1991 to 1996.

Put. Scholars agree that Put, a land to the west of Egypt, is modern-day Libya. However, ancient Libya is larger than the Libya that exists today, so the boundaries of Put as referenced in Ezekiel 38–39 may extend beyond modern Libya, perhaps including portions of Algeria and Tunisia.

Gomer. Identifying Gomer is difficult. No clear consensus exists among Bible scholars. The best guess is that it refers to modern Turkey. In support of this hypothesis, the ancient historian Josephus said Gomer founded those whom the Greeks called the Galatians. The Galatians of New Testament times lived in the region of central Turkey, so there is a direct connection of ancient Gomer to modern Turkey. Moreover, many claim Gomer may be a reference to the ancient Cimmerians or Kimmerians. History reveals that from around 700 BC, the Cimmerians occupied the geographical territory that is modern Turkey.

Beth-togarmah. In Hebrew, *Beth* means "house." Beth-togarmah is a Hebrew term that literally means "the house of Togarmah." Ezekiel 38:6 says Beth-togarmah is from the remote parts of the north, so Beth-togarmah must be located to the north of Israel.

Some expositors believe Beth-togarmah is a reference to modern Turkey, which is to the far north of Israel. This is in keeping with the geography of Ezekiel's time, for in that day there was a city in Cappodocia (modern Turkey) known as Tegarma, Tagarma, Til-garimmu, and Takarama. If this identification is correct, this means that Turkey will be one of the nations in the northern military coalition that will invade Israel in the end times (Ezekiel 38:1-6).

In view of this brief analysis, it seems clear that the domain of Gog will be Russia, Iran, Turkey, Libya, and Sudan. This is clearly a limited domain—a coalition of nations who unite against Israel.

The domain of the antichrist. By contrast, the initial domain of the antichrist will be a revived Roman Empire, as discussed elsewhere in this book. The wild imagery in Daniel 2:7-8 refers to the Roman Empire. Rome already existed in ancient days, but it fell apart in the fifth century AD. It will be revived, however, in the end times, apparently comprised of ten nations ruled by ten kings (the ten horns). An eleventh horn—a little horn (the antichrist)—emerges from within this ten-nation confederacy. He apparently starts out in an insignificant way but grows powerful enough to uproot (overtake) three of the existing horns (or rulers). He eventually comes into power and dominance over this revived empire.

Not long after this, the domain of the antichrist broadens to a global scale. For example, we read in Revelation 13:7 that the antichrist will gain authority "over every tribe and people and language and nation." Such words point to worldwide authority. Moreover, Daniel 7:23 informs us that the antichrist "shall devour the whole earth, and trample it down, and break it to pieces."

Gog has no such global domain. Therefore, Gog and the antichrist are two distinct rulers.

Different Time Frames

Gog and the antichrist have different time frames as well as different domains. Gog's moment in the limelight is relatively short-lived. He moves all his forces—including Russia, Iran, Turkey, Sudan, and Libya—against Israel from the north, and it is all over when God destroys the invading force (Ezekiel 39). The destruction described in Ezekiel 39 is so thorough, it takes seven months to bury all the dead bodies. Following that destruction, Gog is no longer in the limelight.

By contrast, the book of Revelation indicates that the antichrist is in power throughout the seven-year tribulation (Revelation 4–18). Keep in mind that the tribulation period begins when the antichrist signs a covenant with Israel (Daniel 9:26-27). The career of the antichrist continues until the second coming of Jesus Christ, after which he and the false prophet will be thrown into the lake of fire (Revelation 19:20). So again, whereas the antichrist is in power for seven years, Gog's time in power is much shorter—entailing only the time it takes to invade Israel and be destroyed by God. As I argue in my book *Northern Storm Rising*, this destruction of Gog and his forces will take place either before the tribulation period or right at the very beginning of it.

Gog Challenges the Antichrist

As we have seen, the tribulation period begins when the antichrist signs a covenant with Israel (Daniel 9:26-27). This covenant allows Israel to dwell securely (see Ezekiel 38:8,11). Some prophecy experts believe that the northern invasion against Israel will constitute a direct challenge to the antichrist's covenant with Israel. That would require that Gog and the antichrist are two different leaders.

CONCLUSION

It would seem impossible to say that Gog and the antichrist are one and the same, as Joel Richardson and others have suggested. It is better to see these as distinct leaders who rule over different domains during different time frames. Further, it is best to see Gog's actions against Israel as a challenge to the antichrist.

FORESHADOWING THE ANTICHRIST

I have alluded to *types* a few times earlier in the book. Many scholars believe that significant typological Old Testament references are related to the antichrist.

A *type* is a figure or representation of something to come.[1] Theologian Donald K. Campbell says that a type is "an Old Testament institution, event, person, object, or ceremony which has reality and purpose in biblical history, but which also by divine design foreshadows something yet to be revealed."[2] Types are therefore prophetic.

Many of the types we find in the Old Testament speak prophetically of Christ in some way. Theologian John F. Walvoord tells us that "a study of Christological typology includes about fifty important types of Christ—about half of the recognized total in the entire field of typology."[3] Yet as we will see in this chapter, there are also types that foreshadow the antichrist in some way.

It is important to distinguish types and prophecies. In his book *The Interpretation of Prophecy*, Paul Lee Tan explains that "a *type* prefigures coming reality; a *prophecy* verbally delineates the future. One is expressed in events, persons, and acts; the other is couched in words and statements."[4] Types and prophecies may have different forms, but they complement each other. We study both in order to fully understand God's revelation.

Two extremes must be avoided in the study of typology. Some interpreters see too much as being typical in the Old Testament. Directly opposite to this group are those who see all alleged types as cases of forced exegesis. These extremes are unbalanced and should be avoided. A number of good sources are available for those interested in a balanced approach to interpreting types.[5]

Types in the Old Testament are legitimate not because interpreters have said so but rather because God is sovereign in the revelatory process. Some Old Testament persons or things foreshadow someone or something in the New Testament because God planned it that way.[6] So as we consider types of the antichrist in the Old Testament, remember that they foreshadow the antichrist *under God's sovereign direction* and that God wants to teach us something through these types.

ANTIOCHUS EPIPHANES

Antiochus Epiphanes (215–164 BC) ruled the Seleucid Empire from 175 BC until his death. He was a son of King Antiochus III the Great and the brother of Seleucus IV Philopator. He was vile, vengeful, and cruel. That Antiochus Epiphanes was a type of the antichrist is clear from the following factors:[7]

- Both persecute the Jewish people, even seeking to exterminate them.

- Both are self-exalted and demand worship.

- Both set up an image in the Jewish temple, causing an abomination of desolation. Antiochus Epiphanes erected an altar to Zeus on the altar of burnt offering in the temple at Jerusalem and sacrificed a pig (an unclean animal) on it. He thereby dedicated a holy temple to a pagan deity.

- Both impose their own belief systems and codes of conduct on the Jewish people. Antiochus Epiphanes sought to impose Hellenism upon the Jews of his day, and the antichrist will seek to impose the religion of the beast upon the Jews of his day.

- Both express respect to the Roman Empire. Theologian Walter Price provides this summary:

  > There is no doubt that Antiochus IV had healthy respect for Roman society and for Roman political life, and especially for Roman military power. This is the only way to explain his action when he immediately backed away from the conquest of Egypt at the word of the Roman Senate. There is no doubt that Roman policy and power greatly influenced Antiochus—as it will greatly influence the Antichrist in the future.[8]

- Both are assisted by a religious leader—the priest Menelaus assisted Antiochus Epiphanes, and the false prophet will assist the antichrist.

- Both are resisted by a faithful remnant.

  > Antiochus IV was opposed by a pious remnant called the Hasidim, while the Antichrist will be opposed by the 144,000. It was the faithful remnant in Antiochus' day that kept him from completely conquering the Jews, and it will be the 144,000 who preach the gospel who will keep the Antichrist from complete success in his day.[9]

- Both are reported dead but then appear alive again (see 2 Maccabees 5:5; Revelation 13:3,12,14).

  > This does not suggest that Antiochus IV experienced a resurrection, for he was actually not dead when the rumor of his death was circulating. However, the fact that he was reported dead, and then appears alive to reap vengeance upon the Jews, is significant, especially since the same thing seems to occur during the career of the Antichrist.[10]

- Both are active in the Middle East for about seven years.
- Both are defeated by the coming of a deliverer. Judas

Maccabeus defeated Antiochus Epiphanes, and Jesus Christ will defeat the antichrist.

Clearly, Antiochus Epiphanes is an idolatrous prototype of the final antichrist (see Daniel 11:31; 24:15).

LESSER TYPES

Aside from Antiochus Epiphanes, many Bible interpreters have identified other lesser types of the antichrist, including these:

- The devilish serpent in the garden of Eden that sought to corrupt God's paradise, instigating rebellion against God in the first man and woman (Genesis 3).

- Nimrod, the blasphemous ruler who sought to bring about worldwide, organized rebellion against God (Genesis 10:8; 11:1-9).

- Amalek, the son of Esau (Genesis 36:12,16), whose descendants opposed Israel during the wilderness sojourn (Exodus 17:8-16; Deuteronomy 25:19; 1 Samuel 15:2-3).

- Balaam, a foreign prophet who stood against Israel (Numbers 22–24).

- The pharaoh of the exodus, who harshly oppressed the Israelites in Egypt and openly defied the one true God (Exodus 1:11,22; 5:2).

- The Assyrian king Sennacherib, who oppressed the northern kingdom and arrogantly sought to capture Jerusalem (2 Kings 18:13–19:37).

- The Babylonian king Nebuchadnezzar, who destroyed the temple in Jerusalem, persecuted Israel in exile, and usurped divine prerogative (2 Kings 24:13-14; Daniel 4:30).

- The Roman Caesars, who ruled the world and promoted emperor worship (see John 19:12,15).

- The Roman general Titus, who destroyed Jerusalem and the temple in AD 70.

CONCLUSION

By studying these types of the antichrist, we find evidences that the antichrist in the end times will…

- oppose the divine program
- impose a foreign (anti-God) belief system upon people
- oppose and oppress the people of God
- seek to be worshipped
- desecrate the Jewish temple
- be assisted by a religious leader
- appear to be dead and then be seen alive again
- be resisted by a faithful remnant of Jews
- and be defeated in the end by a Deliverer—Jesus Christ

THE RESTRAINER OF
THE ANTICHRIST

The mystery of lawlessness is already at work. Only he who now restrains it will do so until he is out of the way. And then the lawless one will be revealed" (2 Thessalonians 2:7-8). This passage clearly reveals that the antichrist cannot be revealed until the one who restrains lawlessness is taken out of the way.

But who is this restrainer? And how does the restrainer relate to the "mystery of lawlessness"? What *is* the mystery of lawlessness?

The Bible Knowledge Commentary points us toward answers to these questions.

> A mystery in the New Testament is a new truth previously unknown before its revelation in the present dispensation. In this case the mystery is the revelation of a future climax of lawlessness in the world. Then and now a movement against divine law directed by Satan was and is operative. But it is being restrained somewhat, and this restraining will continue until the time appointed for revealing the man of sin and the climax of lawlessness.[1]

The man of sin, of course, is the antichrist. He will embody sin and will promote sin as it has never been promoted before. Everything about him will be rooted in sin. Truly he is the definitive man of sin.

There has been significant debate through the centuries of church history regarding who this restrainer is. I will briefly explain the primary viewpoints.

ROME

Some of the church fathers believed that the restrainer mentioned in 2 Thessalonians 2:7-8 was the Roman Empire. They thought the restraining power was embodied in the Roman emperor. Eventually, as time passed, Roman civil authorities began to clash with the Roman Catholic Church. Some at that time came to interpret 2 Thessalonians 2:7-8 as meaning that Rome's government would restrain the papacy until the Lord came, after which the papacy would be destroyed.

It was suggested that the apostle Paul was purposefully vague about the identity of the restrainer. After all, if he explicitly identified the restrainer as Rome, and his epistle fell into the hands of Roman authorities, his statement about Rome being removed might be considered seditious.

Such a view may have made some sense to people living at that time, but we now see multiple problems with this interpretation. First and foremost, the Roman Empire fell from power in the fifth century, and the antichrist is yet to be revealed. So whoever the restrainer of 2 Thessalonians 2:7-8 is, it is surely not the Roman Empire. Moreover, another explanation for Paul's vagueness makes good sense. Paul had already spoken to the Thessalonians verbally about the restrainer, so they would have readily understood his brief allusion to it in 2 Thessalonians 2 without him having to explain it in detail again.

The antichrist will be a powerful figure in himself, exercising authority over the whole world, but he will also be empowered by Satan. Consequently, many interpreters say the restrainer must be powerful enough to stand against Satan. They suggest that no human being or human government has the power to restrain the work of Satan.

Scripture reveals that the antichrist will rule over a revived Roman Empire (Daniel 2; 7). It hardly makes sense to say that the Roman Empire—itself a bastion of false religion—would restrain the coming of the antichrist.

HUMAN GOVERNMENT IN GENERAL

A similar view proposes that human government in general will restrain the antichrist. The idea is that "restraint through the rule of law [by the government] is the opposite of the man of sin and the mystery of lawlessness."[2] In other words, lawlessness is restrained by the enforcement of law by the government. In this view, the antichrist will one day overthrow human government so that he can work his lawless will in the world.

Perhaps the most cogent argument for this view comes from prophecy scholar Arnold G. Fruchtenbaum. This is from his book *Footsteps of the Messiah*:

> The task of restraining evil was given to human government under the Noahic Covenant in Genesis 9:1-17, and this basic doctrinal truth was reiterated by Paul in Romans 13:1-7. On one hand, human government is even now restraining lawlessness. On the other hand, the government of the last of the three kings will restrain the Antichrist, the lawless one, until the middle of the Tribulation.[3]

Fruchtenbaum is here referring to Daniel 7:7-8, which speaks of the rise of the antichrist.

> Behold, a fourth beast, terrifying and dreadful and exceedingly strong. It had great iron teeth; it devoured and broke in pieces and stamped what was left with its feet. It was different from all the beasts that were before it, and it had ten horns. I considered the horns, and behold, there came up among them another horn, a little one, before which three of the first horns were plucked up by the roots. And behold, in this horn were eyes like the eyes of a man, and a mouth speaking great things.

This wild imagery refers to the Roman Empire. Rome already existed in ancient days, but it fell apart in the fifth century AD. It will be revived, however, in the end times, apparently comprised of ten nations ruled by ten kings (ten horns). An eleventh horn (a little horn—the antichrist) starts out apparently in an insignificant way but grows powerful enough to uproot three of the existing horns (kings), who apparently resist the rise of the antichrist. He eventually comes into absolute power and dominance over this revived Roman Empire.

> It is only when the last of these three kings has been killed, leading to complete submission by the other seven kings, that the Antichrist will be free to take over full global dictatorship…Consequently, the last restrainer of the Antichrist will be the last of the three kings and the government which he represents.[4]

Fruchtenbaum certainly may be right. If there is a weakness to the view, it is that human beings and human governments may not be strong enough to stand against the antichrist, who will be energized by Satan. Indeed, Satan is much more powerful than humans, so some Bible interpreters reject the possibility of any form of human government restraining him. "It would seem that a person is required to restrain a person, and a supernatural one to restrain this man of lawlessness who is motivated by Satan himself."[5]

Some Bible expositors also point out that both Scripture and modern empirical evidence reveal that not all human governments restrain sin. Some actually encourage it. To say that the restrainer is human government may therefore be unrealistic. But this view still remains a possibility.

THE HOLY SPIRIT INDWELLING THE CHURCH

Who is powerful enough to restrain the antichrist? Who is omnipotently powerful enough to restrain Satan? Only one person—God. For this reason, many Bible expositors (perhaps the majority) believe the restrainer is the Holy Spirit, who indwells the church. The view that the Holy Spirit is the restrainer was held by many in the early church, including Theodoret of Cyrus, Theodore of Mopsuestia, and Chrysostom.[6]

Many believe that only God the Holy Spirit has sufficient power to engage in this restraining. Bible expositor Thomas Constable is representative: "The Holy Spirit of God is the only Person with suffi-cient [supernatural] power to do this restraining...The removal of the Restrainer at the time of the rapture must obviously precede the day of the Lord."[7]

In keeping with this, 1 John 4:4 tells us, "He who is in you is greater than he who is in the world." "He who is in" Christians is the Holy Spirit, who is more powerful than the devil.

The Popular Bible Prophecy Commentary points out the grammar of 2 Thessalonians 2 in support of this view.

> The word "restrain" (Greek, *katecho*, "to hold down") in both verses 6 and 7 is a present active participle, but in verse 6 it appears in the neuter gender ("*what* restrains") while in verse 7 it is in the masculine ("*he* who restrains, holds down"). Such usage also occurs in reference to the Spirit of God. The Greek word for "spirit," *pneuma*, is a neuter gender word, but the masculine pronoun is used when referring to the person of the Holy Spirit.[8]

Note also that the word *restrain* in the Greek carries the idea, "to hold back from action, to keep under control, to deprive of physical liberty, as by shackling."[9] This is what the Holy Spirit does in our day to prevent the antichrist from arising.

Prophecy expert Mark Hitchcock notes, "The Holy Spirit is spoken of in Scripture as restraining sin and evil in the world (see Genesis 6:3) and in the heart of the believer (see Galatians 5:16-17)."[10] Mal Couch agrees. "By divine providence, and by all the evidence of the Scriptures, the Holy Spirit characteristically restrains and strives against sin (Gene-sis 6:3). The Spirit presently abides in the world in a special way in this age through the church."[11] Once this special abiding is removed, the antichrist will manifest himself.

TAKEN OUT OF THE WAY AT THE RAPTURE

When will the Holy Spirit, who dwells within all members of the church, be taken out of the way so that the antichrist can be revealed? It seems clear that the rapture must take place prior to the beginning of the tribulation period (see 1 Corinthians 15:50-52; 1 Thessalonians 1:10; 4:13-17; 5:9). More specifically, the antichrist's signing of a covenant with Israel marks the actual beginning of the seven-year tribulation period (Daniel 9:26-27), so the rapture of the church must take place *prior* to the signing of this covenant. At that moment, the Holy Spirit—who indwells the church—will be "taken out of the way" so that the antichrist can be revealed.

Many Scriptures provide evidence that the rapture takes place before the tribulation period. This is important to understand, for some Christians place the rapture in the middle of the tribulation, or at the latter part of the tribulation, or at the very end of the tribulation. Let's briefly review what Scripture says in this regard.

First, we know that when the rapture occurs, the church—the universal body of believers in Christ from the day of Pentecost right on up to the present (Ephesians 1:3; 2:5; see also Acts 1:5; 1 Corinthians 12:13)—will be caught up to be with Christ in the air.

Second, we know that all Christians (which is to say, those who make up the church) are indwelt by the Holy Spirit.

- "Do you not know that you are God's temple and that God's Spirit dwells in you?" (1 Corinthians 3:16).

- "Do you not know that your body is a temple of the Holy Spirit within you, whom you have from God?" (1 Corinthians 6:19).

- "In one Spirit we were all baptized into one body—Jews or Greeks, slaves or free—and all were made to drink of one Spirit" (1 Corinthians 12:13; see also 1 John 3:24).

This means that if the church is taken from the earth at the rapture, the Holy Spirit will be taken out of the way. This removal of the Holy Spirit's restraint allows the antichrist, energized by Satan, to come into power during the tribulation period.

How do we know this rapture takes place before the tribulation period? We have seen that a number of Scripture passages provide evidence:

- Revelation 3:10 indicates that believers will be kept from the actual hour of testing that is coming on the whole world.

- No Old Testament passage on the tribulation mentions the church (Deuteronomy 4:29-30; Jeremiah 30:4-11; Daniel 8:24-27; 12:1-2). Its absence would seem to indicate that it is not on earth during the tribulation.

- Likewise, no New Testament passage on the tribulation mentions the church (Matthew 13:30,39-42,48-50; 24:15-31; 1 Thessalonians 1:9-10; 5:4-9; 2 Thessalonians 2:1-11; Revelation 4–18).

- A pretribulational rapture best explains the sudden apostasy that comes upon the world by the removal of the restrainer, who is apparently the Holy Spirit (2 Thessalonians 2:3-7).

- The Bible indicates that the rapture involves Christ coming *for* His saints in the air prior to the tribulation, whereas at the second coming He will come *with* His saints to the earth to reign for a thousand years (Revelation 19; 20:1-6). The fact that Christ comes with His holy ones (redeemed believers) at the second coming presumes they've been previously raptured.

- Scripture assures us that the church is not appointed to wrath (Romans 5:9; 1 Thessalonians 1:9-10; 5:9). This means the church cannot go through the "great day of…wrath" in the tribulation period (Revelation 6:17).

- Throughout Scripture, God protects His people before judgment falls (see 2 Peter 2:5-9). Enoch was transferred to heaven before the judgment of the flood. Noah and his family were in the ark before the judgment of the flood. Lot was taken out of Sodom before judgment was poured out on Sodom and Gomorrah. The firstborn among the Hebrews in Egypt were sheltered by the blood of the Paschal Lamb before judgment fell. The spies were safely out of Jericho and Rahab was secured before judgment fell on Jericho. So, too, will the church be secured safely (by means of the rapture) before judgment falls in the tribulation period.

- The term *imminent* means "ready to take place" or "impending." The New Testament teaches that the rapture is imminent—that is, nothing must be prophetically fulfilled before the rapture occurs (see 1 Corinthians 1:7; 16:22; Philippians 3:20; 4:5; 1 Thessalonians 1:10; Titus 2:13; Hebrews 9:28; James 5:7-9; 1 Peter 1:13; Jude 21). No signs will precede the rapture—it can occur at any moment. This is in contrast to the second coming of Christ, which is preceded by many events in the seven-year tribulation period (see Revelation 4–18).

Here are more key verses on the rapture you may wish to consult:

John 14:1-3	1 Timothy 6:14
Romans 8:19	2 Timothy 4:1,8
1 Corinthians 15:51-53	1 Peter 1:7; 5:4
Colossians 3:4	1 John 2:28–3:2
1 Thessalonians 2:19; 4:13-18; 5:9,23	Revelation 2:25; 3:10
2 Thessalonians 2:1,3	

In view of such Scriptures, it seems clear that the rapture of the church will indeed take place prior to the beginning of the tribulation period. The Holy Spirit indwells the church, so when the church is removed from the earth at the rapture, the Holy Spirit will at the same time be "taken out of the way" so that the antichrist can emerge on the world scene.

THE HOLY SPIRIT DURING THE TRIBULATION

You may be wondering whether the Holy Spirit will be present during the tribulation period. Yes, He will. Bible scholar John Phillips explains it this way:

> The church age is a parenthesis in God's dealing with the world. The church, injected supernaturally into history at Pentecost and supernaturally maintained throughout the age by the baptizing, indwelling, and filling works of the Holy Spirit, will be supernaturally removed when this age

is over. What is to be removed then is the Holy Spirit's mighty working through the church. Until that happens, Satan cannot bring his plans to a head...After the rapture of the church, the Holy Spirit will continue His work in bringing people to salvation, but He will no longer baptize them into the mystical body of Christ, the church, nor will He actively hinder Satan from bringing His schemes to fruition. Once Satan has achieved his centuries-long goal, Christ will return and demolish the whole thing![12]

Bible scholar Paul Feinberg agrees.

There seems to be abundant evidence that the Holy Spirit will be active in the earth during the tribulation period. He will empower His witnesses (Mark 13:11). Evangelism will be more effective than it has ever been (Matt. 24:14; Rev. 7:9-14). It is reasonable to assume that as satanic activity increases, so will the activity of the Holy Spirit.[13]

THE 70 WEEKS
OF DANIEL

The prophet Daniel's prophecy of 70 weeks is especially important in a study of the antichrist, for during the final week—that is, a week of years, or seven years—the antichrist will be in power on the earth.

Like the book of Revelation, the book of Daniel is categorized as apocalyptic literature. It contains Bible prophecy of the end times. The book was written by Daniel in about 537 BC.

Daniel was a Jewish youth who had been deported to Babylon along with many other Jews in exile as a result of Nebuchadnezzar's siege of Jerusalem in 605 BC. In Babylon, Daniel rose to prominence through his commitment to God and through the skills God had given him.

Daniel's writing is filled with hope. Even though God's people were presently suffering great persecution in their exile in Babylon, God was nevertheless in control, and He had not abandoned them. One day He would deal with Israel's oppressors and set Israel free (Daniel 12:1-13). There would be justice in the end. God is sovereign over human history.

In Daniel 9:25, God provided a prophetic timetable for the nation of Israel. The prophetic clock began ticking at the command to restore and rebuild Jerusalem following its destruction by Babylon. According to this verse, Israel's timetable was divided into 70 groups of 7 years, totaling 490 years.

The first 69 groups of 7 years—or 483 years—counted the years "from the going out of the word to restore and build Jerusalem to the coming of an anointed one, a prince." The "anointed one" is Jesus Christ. *Anointed one* means "Messiah." The day Jesus rode into Jerusalem to proclaim Himself Israel's Messiah was exactly 483 years to the day after Cyrus, king of Persia, allowed the Jews to restore and rebuild Jerusalem.

At that point God's prophetic clock stopped. Daniel describes a gap between these 483 years and the final 7 years of Israel's prophetic timetable. According to Daniel 9:26, several events were to take place during this gap:

- The Messiah will be killed.
- The city of Jerusalem and its temple will be destroyed (which occurred in AD 70).
- The Jews will encounter difficulty and hardship from that time on.

SIGNING THE COVENANT

The seventieth and final "week" of seven years will begin for Israel when the antichrist confirms a covenant for seven years. "He shall make a strong covenant with many for one week, and for half of the week he shall put an end to sacrifice and offering. And on the wing of abominations shall come one who makes desolate, until the decreed end is poured out on the desolator" (Daniel 9:27). Aside from the reference to the signing of the covenant, this verse may contain phrases that you do not fully understand. Don't be concerned. In this chapter, I will give an overview of what is going on in this verse, especially as related to the activities of the antichrist.

The first thing to notice is that the signing of this peace pact signals the beginning of the tribulation period. That signature initiates the seven-year countdown to the second coming of Christ, which follows the tribulation period. As I have noted in the previous chapter, the church will have been raptured off planet Earth before the covenant is signed.

Some prophecy experts believe this covenant may relate to the future Ezekiel invasion in which Russia and a group of Muslim nations—including Iran, Sudan, Turkey, Libya, Kazakhstan, Kyrgyzstan, Uzbekistan, Turkmenistan, Tajikistan, Armenia, and possibly northern Afghanistan—invade Israel in the end times (Ezekiel 38:1-6). After all, Ezekiel's prophecy indicates that the invasion will take place when Israel is dwelling securely (Ezekiel 38:11). It is suggested that Israel will not have this strong sense of security and rest until the leader of the revived Roman Empire—the antichrist—signs a peace pact, guaranteeing Israel's protection (Daniel 9:27). Until the signing of this covenant, Israel will remain as it presently is—always on alert because of the possibility of attack. On any otherwise ordinary day, a Muslim suicide bomber could walk into a pizza parlor in Israel and blow everyone up. On any day, Palestinian militants might try to sneak in and take sniper shots at Israel's citizens. Without warning, missiles could fly in and destroy buildings in Israel. Many believe this will not stop until the peace pact is signed.

Whether or not this is so, this covenant is clearly a key event in the prophetic timetable. Indeed, the seven years that follow the signing of this agreement will be the seven worst years of human history and will lead to the second coming of Christ.

BUILDING THE TEMPLE

Look at Daniel 9:27 once again. "He shall make a strong covenant with many for one week, and for half of the week he shall put an end to sacrifice and offering. And on the wing of abominations shall come one who makes desolate, until the decreed end is poured out on the desolator." The fact that the antichrist will put an end to sacrifice and offering in the middle of the week (after three and a half years)—as well as desolate the Jewish temple—presupposes that the Jewish temple will have already been constructed by this time. Bible prophecy expert John F. Walvoord comments on these sacrifices.

This expression ["for half of the week he shall put an end to sacrifice and offering"] refers to the entire Levitical system, which suggests that Israel will have restored that system in the first half of the 70th seven. After this ruler gains worldwide political power, he will assume power in the religious realm as well and will cause the world to worship him (2 Thessalonians 2:4; Revelation 13:8). To receive such worship, he will terminate all organized religions. Posing as the world's rightful king and god and as Israel's prince of peace, he will then turn against Israel and become her destroyer and defiler.[1]

From a prophetic standpoint, all this is highly significant for several reasons. A key chronological prerequisite to the rebuilding of the temple—Israel back in her homeland as a nation—has been a reality since 1948. Moreover, the Jews have been streaming back to the holy land from around the world ever since (see Ezekiel 36–37).

The temple must be rebuilt at least by the middle of the seven-year tribulation, as is clear from the fact that Jesus in the Olivet Discourse warned of a catastrophic event that assumes the existence of the temple: "When you see the abomination of desolation spoken of by the prophet Daniel, standing in the holy place (let the reader understand), then let those who are in Judea flee to the mountains" (Matthew 24:15-16). This "abomination of desolation" is a desecration of the Jewish temple by the antichrist, who will set up an image of himself within the temple, as we have also seen in Daniel 9:27. The antichrist will actually set himself up to be God. (More on this shortly.)

In Matthew 24:1-2, Jesus had just positively affirmed that the great temple built by Herod (the Jewish temple of Jesus' day) would be utterly destroyed: "Truly, I say to you, there will not be left here one stone upon another that will not be thrown down." This prophecy was literally fulfilled in AD 70 when Titus and his Roman warriors overran Jerusalem and the Jewish temple.

The temple of Jesus' day was destroyed in the first century, so the abomination of desolation will occur in a yet-future temple. This latter temple will be built at least by the middle of the tribulation period (Daniel 9:27; 12:11).

Various individuals and groups are already working quietly to prepare various materials for the future temple: the menorah of pure gold, the pure gold crown worn by the high priest, fire pans and shovels, the mitzraq (a vessel used to transport the blood of sacrificial offerings), the copper laver, linen garments of the priests, stone vessels to store the ashes of the red heifer, and the like. These items are being prefabricated by the Temple Institute in Jerusalem so that when the temple is finally rebuilt, everything will be ready for it. I reiterate that the temple does not need to be rebuilt until the middle of the tribulation period, but the fact that many items are already being prefabricated is all the more exciting to many prophecy enthusiasts. The stage is even now being set for the eventual manifestation of the antichrist following the rapture of the church.

DIFFICULTY REBUILDING THE TEMPLE

The current impediment to rebuilding the Jewish temple in Jerusalem is that the Muslim Dome of the Rock, or the Mosque of Omar, stands right where the temple must be rebuilt. How will the Jews be able to rebuild the temple, with the Dome of the Rock on the same piece of real estate, without a major religious war breaking out? This is a difficult problem with no easy solution.

Most Bible prophecy experts believe the solution has to do with the covenant that the antichrist will sign with Israel at the beginning of the tribulation period. Perhaps this covenant will enforce some kind of peace treaty between the Arab Muslims and the Jews.[2] This would be a major strategic victory for the antichrist—one that would be hailed worldwide as a feat of a superpolitician.

The rebuilding of the Jewish temple may also relate to the aftermath of the Ezekiel invasion (Ezekiel 38). God's utter and complete destruction of the Muslim invaders (Ezekiel 39) may greatly weaken Muslim resistance to the rebuilding of the Jewish temple. If this invasion takes place either prior to or right at the beginning of the tribulation period, as I argue in my book *Northern Storm Rising* (Harvest House, 2008), this would make it much easier for the Jews to rebuild their temple.

THE ABOMINATION OF DESOLATION

I previously mentioned the abomination of desolation. The covenant the antichrist signs with Israel allegedly remains in effect for the full seven-year period (the seventieth week of Daniel). But the antichrist will double-cross Israel, for Daniel writes that "for half of the week he shall put an end to sacrifice and offering." In other words, after the covenant has been in effect for three and a half years, he will renege on the covenant and cause Israel's temple sacrifices to cease.

Daniel 11:45 seems to reveal that the antichrist will then move from Europe (the revived Roman Empire) into the land of Israel: "He shall pitch his palatial tents between the sea and the glorious holy mountain." Taking all this together, we infer that in the middle of the tribulation period, the antichrist will invade the Holy Land and prohibit sacrifices in the Jewish temple.

Why cause the sacrifices to cease? I previously noted that near the midpoint of the tribulation period, the antichrist—having already attained political power—will now seek to assume power in the religious realm as well. Setting up an image of himself in the temple amounts to enthroning himself in the place of deity, displaying himself as God (compare with Isaiah 14:13-14; Ezekiel 28:2-9). This blasphemous act will utterly desecrate the temple, making it abominable and therefore desolate. The antichrist will entice the world to worship him (see 2 Thessalonians 2:4; Revelation 13:8). In order for him to get all people on earth to worship him, he must necessarily destroy all competing religious systems—including the Jewish religion, with its Levitical sacrifices and offerings.

This means that the antichrist, once Israel's protector, will become Israel's persecutor. Israel's defender will become Israel's defiler by setting up an image of himself in the Jewish temple.

Understandably, all this is utterly detestable to the Jews. Note that the word *abomination* comes from a root term that means "to make foul" or "to stink." Thus it refers to something that makes one feel nauseous, and by implication, something morally abhorrent and detestable.[3]

An abomination took place on a lesser scale in 168 BC. Antiochus Epiphanies erected an altar to Zeus in the temple at Jerusalem and sacrificed a pig (an unclean animal) on it. Antiochus was thus a pro- totype of the future antichrist. (See chapter 8, "Foreshadowing the Antichrist.")

We should note that some Bible expositors—particularly of the amillennial and preterist persuasions—believe the abomination of des- olation spoken of in Matthew 24:15 was fulfilled when Titus and his Roman warriors overran Jerusalem and destroyed the Jewish temple. However, Paul's prophetic discussion of this event in 2 Thessalonians 2—with the antichrist positioning himself as God—demands that the abomination occur in reference to the future antichrist during the future tribulation period.

Scripture reveals that things get much worse after the abomina- tion of desolation takes place halfway through the tribulation period. Indeed, the events of the second half of the seven-year tribulation period are properly called "the great tribulation" (Revelation 7:14). As Matthew 24:21 puts it, "There will be great tribulation, such as has not been from the beginning of the world until now, no, and never will be." Daniel 12:1 likewise comments, "There shall be a time of trou- ble, such as never has been since there was a nation till that time." This time period largely deals with Israel, so Jeremiah 30:7 calls this period "a time of distress for Jacob" (Jacob is another name for Israel).

This means that in the middle of the tribulation period, things become traumatic for the Jewish people in Jerusalem. The antichrist will not only assume global political power but also declare himself to be God and exalt himself in the Jewish temple. To make matters worse, the antichrist will passionately persecute the Jewish people.

In the Olivet Discourse, Jesus points to how bad things will be and how Jews living in Jerusalem will need to flee for their lives.

> When you see the abomination of desolation spoken of
> by the prophet Daniel, standing in the holy place (let the
> reader understand), then let those who are in Judea flee to
> the mountains. Let the one who is on the housetop not
> go down to take what is in his house, and let the one who
> is in the field not turn back to take his cloak. And alas for

women who are pregnant and for those who are nursing
infants in those days! Pray that your flight may not be in
winter or on a Sabbath. For then there will be great tribulation, such as has not been from the beginning of the world
until now, no, and never will be (Matthew 24:15-21).

When these horrific circumstances unfold in Jerusalem, Jesus urges
that the Jews living there should have no concern whatsoever for personal belongings but rather should get out of town as quickly as possible. Time spent gathering personal belongings might mean the
difference between life and death. Jesus indicates that the distress will
escalate dramatically and rapidly (see also Jeremiah 30:7).

CONCLUSION

We have considered several important biblical teachings regarding
the coming of the antichrist. The tribulation period will begin when
the antichrist signs a covenant with Israel. The Jewish temple will exist
during these years, and in the middle of the tribulation, the antichrist
will cause offerings and sacrifices in the Jewish temple to cease. He will
desolate the temple by setting up an image of himself within it. Even
now preparations are being made for the eventual rebuilding of the
Jewish temple. Even now the stage is being set for the eventual manifestation of the man of sin, the antichrist.

THE CHARACTER OF
THE ANTICHRIST

The Bible reveals a great deal about the character of the antichrist. Even though he will be a human being, he will truly be unlike any human being who has ever lived. In fact, he will be so different that people living during the tribulation period will say, "Who is like the beast?" The implied answer is, no one.

The antichrist is even distinctive in terms of previous kings and kingdoms. "[The fourth beast] was different from all the beasts that were before it" (Daniel 7:7). His kingdom "shall be different from all the kingdoms," and he himself "shall be different from the former [kings]" (verses 23-24). The antichrist will be unique, one of a kind. Bible prophecy scholar Herman Hoyt puts it this way:

> The greatest person ever to appear on the earth, save One—the Lord Jesus Christ—is yet to come. This man will rise head and shoulders above men in general, calculated to earn him the designation of superman, in fact, the worship that belongs to deity. His appearance on the scene, his rise to power, his genius as a military leader, and his exploits will be nothing short of spectacular, colossal, and supernatural.[1]

Prophecy expert Ed Hindson likewise says, "The Antichrist will be the most incredible political leader the world has ever known. On the surface he will appear to be the epitome of human genius and power."[2]

Let's consider some of the primary characteristics of the antichrist.

STRONG APPEARANCE

Strong appearance is meaningful to many people. As one modern-day advertisement has said, "Image is everything!" We see this reality even in the pages of Scripture. Recall that in Old Testament times, Saul's appearance was part of the reason the people of Israel elected him as their king. "[He was] a handsome young man. There was not a man among the people of Israel more handsome than he. From his shoulders upward he was taller than any of the people" (1 Samuel 9:2).

The antichrist will seem greater than all others (Daniel 7:20) and will be a "king of bold face" (8:23). The whole world "will marvel to see the beast" (see Revelation 17:8; see also 13:3-4). One scholar infers from this that the antichrist "will be an exceptional physical specimen, possessing not only a large, well-proportioned body but also an attractive countenance and an impressive appearance."[3]

AN INTELLECTUAL GENIUS

The antichrist will be a man of great intellect. The Old Testament communicates this by referring to him as "one who understands riddles" (Daniel 8:23). That which may baffle other people of great intellect will be child's play for him. Of course, a man without substantial intellect could not possibly convince the other leaders of the world to submit to his authority (see Revelation 17:13). Scripture reveals that his intellect will be energized by Satan, who himself has a far greater intellect than mere human beings (Revelation 13:2).

> [The antichrist] will be possessed of extraordinary intelligence. He will be the devil's imitation of that blessed One "in whom are hid all the treasures of wisdom and knowledge" (Col. 2:3). This Son of Perdition will surpass Solomon in wisdom...His master mind will captivate the

educated world. His marvelous store of knowledge, his acquaintance with the secrets of nature, his superhuman powers of perception, will stamp him as an intellectual genius of the first magnitude.[4]

AN ORATORICAL GENIUS

The antichrist will also be an oratorical genius—a master of the spoken word. He will have "a mouth speaking great things" (Daniel 7:8, see also verse 20). He will have "a lion's mouth" (Revelation 13:2), which Bible interpreters believe means that his oratory skills will be majestic and awe-inspiring. "Most world dictators have proven to be persuasive speakers, able to motivate the masses to their political ideology. Like Adolf Hitler, who was able to mesmerize a whole nation by his inspiring speeches, the Antichrist will be no exception."[5]

Much that comes from the mouth of the antichrist will be blasphemous. The root meaning of the Greek word for *blasphemy* carries the idea of injuring the reputation of another. In the Bible, blasphemy can range from showing a lack of reverence for God to a more extreme attitude of contempt for either God or something considered sacred (see Leviticus 24:16; Matthew 26:65; Mark 2:7). It can involve speaking evil against God (Psalm 74:18; Isaiah 52:5; Romans 2:24; Revelation 13:1,6; 16:9,11,21). It can also involve showing contempt for the true God by making claims of divinity for oneself (see Mark 14:64; John 10:33). Those who deny the true identity of Jesus as Messiah also commit blasphemy (Luke 22:65; John 10:36). The most heinous blasphemy found in the pages of Scripture is attributed to the antichrist.

> I saw a beast rising out of the sea, with ten horns and seven heads, with ten diadems on its horns and blasphemous names on its heads…The beast was given a mouth uttering haughty and blasphemous words, and it was allowed to exercise authority for forty-two months. It opened its mouth to utter blasphemies against God, blaspheming his name and his dwelling, that is, those who dwell in heaven (Revelation 13:1,5-6; see also 17:3).

The antichrist's blasphemous words are in keeping with his blasphemous nature (see 2 Thessalonians 2:3-11).

> This man will be a blasphemer on an extraordinary scale. He will wear the name of blasphemy (Rev. 13:1); be given a mouth to speak blasphemy (Rev. 13:5); give expression to blasphemy (Rev. 13:6); and exalt himself above all that is called God or that is worshiped (2 Thess. 2:4).[6]

Some theologians suggest that as an oratorical master, the antichrist will try to mimic Jesus Christ. Crowds were astonished at His teaching (Matthew 7:28) and asked, "Where did this man get this wisdom?" (Matthew 13:54). The antichrist will have a perfect command and eloquent flow of language. His oratory will not only gain widespread attention but command respect from the masses.[7]

> As Satan's CEO, the Antichrist will also be his public voice. He will be able to sway crowds with his eloquence. He will, no doubt, be a superb television communicator. People will naturally want to follow him. Orators like Abraham Lincoln, Winston Churchill, John F. Kennedy, Martin Luther King Jr., and yes, even Adolf Hitler, were masters at captivating and moving large audiences. But even their best and most passionate speeches would be dull compared to the rhetoric of the Antichrist.[8]

Again, however, the antichrist will use all his oratory skills for blasphemous and anti-God purposes.

A PHILOSOPHICAL GENIUS

Many theologians believe the antichrist will also be a philosophical genius. He will be a master at presenting an anti-God philosophy that will sway the masses. This philosophy will be demon-driven (Revelation 16:13; see also 1 Timothy 4:1). Vast throngs of humanity will no doubt be deceived into believing his lies (see 1 John 4:1-6 and compare with John 8:44).

A POLITICAL GENIUS

The antichrist will undoubtedly be a political genius. He will have political savvy like no other.

> He will recognize the value and force of religion. So he will not hesitate to submit outwardly to the domination of the false religious system of the end time (Rev. 17:3,7). Once he has gained his end, he will turn and destroy the whore who is sitting upon him (Rev. 17:16-17). With craftiness, he will gradually rise to power among the ten kings in whose midst he first appears. At last he will convince them that they should form a confederation of which he will become the head (Rev. 17:12-13).[9]

The antichrist will emerge from apparent obscurity. By his profound diplomacy skills, however, he will win the admiration of the political world and compel others to follow his lead. Though he begins his political career as just a "little horn" (Daniel 7:8), he will be catapulted into global fame and power by means of brilliant statesmanship. He will quickly ascend to the topmost rung of the political world.[10] And once he gains ascendancy, none will challenge his political power. His political domain will be global.

A GOVERNMENTAL GENIUS

The antichrist will be not only a political genius but also a governmental genius. Because of his governing abilities, other world leaders will be inclined to be of "one mind…handing over their royal power to the beast" (Revelation 17:16-17). He will bring unity where there had been conflict, and all the world will marvel at his abilities.

A COMMERCIAL GENIUS

One cannot rise to global dominion and power without also being a commercial genius. During the tribulation period, no one will be able to buy or sell anything without receiving the mark of the antichrist (Revelation 13:17). All commerce will come under his absolute control. With today's technology—supercomputers, smart cards, RFID chips, biometrics, GPS technology, and the like—this policy will be easy to enforce.

A MILITARY GENIUS

It is not surprising that the antichrist will also be a man of great military genius. Keep in mind what we have learned earlier—that he will subdue and uproot three of the kings of the revived Roman Empire who resist his rise to power (Daniel 7:8). Revelation 6:2 tells us that the antichrist will come out "conquering, and to conquer." People living during that time will say, "Who is like the beast, and who can fight against it?" (Revelation 13:4). His military exploits will not be regional, but global. His military genius will be unparalleled.

A RELIGIOUS GENIUS

Scripture reveals that the antichrist will also be a religious genius. He will proclaim himself to be God and set up an image of himself in the Jewish temple (see 2 Thessalonians 2:4). He will seem to have succumbed to a mortal head wound, after which he shows himself alive again, mimicking Christ's resurrection from the dead (Revelation 13:3). People will readily pay him divine homage (Revelation 13:14-15).

A DEFIANT PERSONALITY

Closely related to the above, the antichrist will be utterly defiant. He will be the most arrogant, proud, and self-impressed person the world has ever known. "He shall exalt himself and magnify himself above every god, and shall speak astonishing things against the God of gods...He shall pay no attention to the gods of his fathers...He shall not pay attention to any other god, for he shall magnify himself above all" (Daniel 11:36-37). Indeed, he "opposes and exalts himself against every so-called god or object of worship, so that he takes his seat in the temple of God, proclaiming himself to be God" (2 Thessalonians 2:4).

FULL OF RELIGIOUS DECEPTION

The end times will be characterized by broad and penetrating deception. First Timothy 4:1 warns that "the Spirit expressly says that in later times some will depart from the faith by devoting themselves to deceitful spirits and teachings of demons." Second Timothy 4:3-4 likewise warns that "the time is coming when people will not endure sound teaching, but having itching ears they will accumulate for themselves teachers to suit their own passions, and will turn away from listening to the truth and wander off into myths."

A key verse pertaining to end-times deception is 2 Thessalonians 2:3, which speaks of the coming day of the Lord. "Let no one deceive you in any way. For that day will not come, unless the rebellion comes first, and the man of lawlessness is revealed, the son of destruction." The New American Standard Bible renders the critical part of this verse, "Let no one in any way deceive you, for it will not come unless the apostasy comes first." The King James Version puts it this way: "Let no man deceive you by any means: for that day shall not come, except there come a falling away first." These various translations give us insight into the apostle Paul's intended meaning. In the end times, there will be a great apostasy, a falling away from the truth, a rebellion against God and the truth of His Word (see also 1 Timothy 4:1-3; 2 Timothy 3:1-5; 4:3-4; James 5:1-8; 2 Peter 2; 3:3-6). Apparently, this rebellious apostasy will prepare the way for the emergence of the antichrist, who will be empowered by Satan, the father of lies (John 8:44). This falling away must take place before the man of sin is revealed.

Once the antichrist arrives on the scene, he will fan apostasy into flame, disseminating deception on a massive, lethal level. He will engage in "wicked deception" (2 Thessalonians 2:10). And, as noted above, he will be energized by Satan, the master deceiver of the nations (Revelation 20:3,8). (I will further address Satan's role in the life of the antichrist in chapter 14, "The Role of Satan.")

DIABOLICAL AT THE VERY CORE

The antichrist will be a diabolical person. In the first part of the tribulation period, he will give every appearance of being a world leader who truly cares about bringing about goodness and prosperity on earth. Many will marvel at him. Once he comes into full power, however, his true nature shines through. He will break the covenant he made with Israel (Daniel 9:27), persecute the saints (Daniel 7:21-25; Revelation 13:7), kill God's two witnesses (Revelation 11:7), force the world to worship him as God (Revelation 13:8), bring the world into economic bondage to himself (Revelation 13:16-17), cause all the nations to move against Jerusalem (see Zechariah 14:1-3), and much more.

A HOMOSEXUAL?

Some Bible expositors suggest the possibility that the antichrist may be a homosexual. Daniel 11:37 says of him: "He shall pay no attention to the gods of his fathers, or to the one beloved by women." The King James Version (KJV) of this verse says he will show no regard for "the desire of women." Largely based on the KJV rendering, many conclude that the antichrist will be a homosexual. It is suggested that this would be in keeping with his being energized by Satan, who is utterly vile, depraved, and sinful.

There are other possible meanings of this verse, however, as Bible expositor Thomas Constable explains.

> It may be a reference to the Messiah. Supposedly the supreme desire of every godly Jewish woman in Daniel's day was that she bear the Messiah. Another view is that the reference is to Tammuz (Adonis), a pagan goddess in Daniel's day that women found very attractive. Others believe that the meaning is that this king will have no desire for women. Some even speculate that he will be abusive toward women. In other words, he will be devoid of natural affection.[11]

It is certainly possible that this verse could indicate that the antichrist will be a homosexual. However, because this verse is widely disputed as to its correct meaning, it is not wise to be dogmatic and build one's theology upon it. The verse could actually mean that the antichrist will be so intoxicated by personal power and glory (see Daniel 11:38-39) that he will have no interest in women.

A WONDER OF THE WORLD

In view of all this, it seems clear that the antichrist will seem like a wonder of the world to many people. Many will be utterly and completely mesmerized. They will see him as an intellectual genius and unsurpassed master of oratory, philosophy, politics, government, commerce, military strategy, and religion. All this, combined with his impressive appearance, will cause many to marvel!

NAMES AND TITLES OF THE ANTICHRIST

Scripture includes many names and titles for the antichrist. In the ancient world, a name was not a mere label, as it is today. A name was considered equivalent to whomever or whatever bore it. The sum total of a person's thought and behavior was gathered up into his name. In fact, knowing a person's name amounted to knowing his essence. This is illustrated for us in 1 Samuel 25:25: "As his name is, so is he. Nabal is his name, and folly is with him." (Nabal means "folly.")

We also see this illustrated in the names of major Bible characters. The name Abraham, for instance, means "father of a multitude" and was fitting because Abraham was the father of the Jewish nation. The name David means "beloved," which is appropriate because David was a king specially loved by God. The name Solomon comes from a word meaning "peace," and Solomon's reign was characterized by peace. In each case, we learn something about the individual from his name.

The same is true of the antichrist. We learn much about this diabolical person from the names and titles ascribed to him in Scripture. I will summarize only his major names and titles and show how they demonstrate key aspects of his character.

THE ANTICHRIST

The term *antichrist* is a compound word composed of two Greek words—*anti* and *christos*. *Anti* can mean "instead of" or "against" or "opposed to." Therefore, *antichrist* can literally mean "instead of Christ," "against Christ," or "opposed to Christ."

We have seen that even though the spirit of antichrist has been around since biblical times, there is a single individual known as *the* antichrist who is yet to come and who will emerge into power during the future tribulation period (see Daniel 8:9-11; 11:31-38; 12:11; Matthew 24:15; 2 Thessalonians 2:1-12; Revelation 13:1-5; 19:20; 20:10). This individual will be the embodiment of all that is anti-God and anti-Christian. He will be the supreme antichrist of human history. More than any other, he will position himself as the one who is instead of Christ, against Christ, and opposed to Christ. He will set himself up against Christ and the people of God in the last days before the second coming.

THE BEAST

Revelation 13:1-3 refers to the antichrist as a beast. It is interesting to observe that *the beast* is the most frequently used title of the antichrist in the book of Revelation, being used there 32 times.

The Greek word for *beast* (*qhrion*) indicates a wild and rapacious animal. Theologian J. Hampton Keathley suggests that *qhrion* points out two things. "First, it portrays the brutal, bloody, uncontrolled, and wild character of the dictator and his system...Second, *qhrion* portrays this antichrist figure as the epitome and paramount outgrowth of the character of Satan who is himself called 'the great red dragon.'"[1]

God apparently chose the symbol of the beast to designate the beastly or animal nature of the antichrist. This does not mean that the term *beast* is just a personification of evil in the world, as some have tried to argue. Even though a symbol is used to describe this still-future human being, the symbol indicates that the antichrist will display an ungodly and anti-God character as a real historical person (2 Thessalonians 2:3-12).

We read of another beast in Revelation 13:11 who will serve as the antichrist's first lieutenant. This second beast—also known as the false prophet—will promote the worship of the antichrist by performing great and miraculous signs, such as bringing fire down from heaven (verse 13). Those who refuse receive a death sentence (verse 15). In those days no one will be able to buy or sell without having received the mark of the beast (verses 16-17). These three—Satan, the antichrist, and the false prophet—will form a counterfeit trinity.

The first beast—the antichrist—will be unlike any human being who has ever lived. "The whole earth marveled as they followed the beast...they worshiped the beast, saying, 'Who is like the beast?'" (Revelation 13:3-4).

The term *the beast* contrasts the antichrist from the true Christ, the Lamb of God. Interestingly, just as the term *the beast* is often used of the antichrist in Revelation, so *Lamb* is often used of Jesus Christ. Theologian A.W. Pink draws these contrasts:

- The Lamb is the Savior of sinners; the beast is the persecutor and slayer of the saints.

- *Lamb* calls attention to the gentleness of Christ; *beast* tells of the ferocity of the antichrist.

- *Lamb* reveals Christ as the harmless one (Hebrews 7:26); *beast* manifests the antichrist as the cruel and heartless one.

- Under the law, lambs were ceremonially clean and used in sacrifice, but beasts were unclean and unfit for sacrifices.[2]

We can make another interesting observation here. When Jesus the Lamb of God was baptized, the Spirit descended on him like a dove. The one who comes upon the beast (the antichrist) is the dragon, or Satan (see 2 Thessalonians 2:9). The imagery is stunning: a Lamb and a dove versus a beast and a dragon.

THE MAN OF LAWLESSNESS, OR MAN OF SIN

"Let no one deceive you in any way. For that day will not come, unless the rebellion comes first, and the man of lawlessness is revealed" (2 Thessalonians 2:3). The antichrist is likewise called "the lawless one" (verse 8). Why is the antichrist called "man of lawlessness" and "the lawless one"?

These descriptive terms indicate that the antichrist is full of sin. After all, 1 John 3:4 tells us, "Everyone who makes a practice of sinning also practices lawlessness; sin is lawlessness." So the antichrist, the man of lawlessness, is a man of sin.

Though sin and lawlessness are already at work in our own day (2 Thessalonians 2:7), Paul says a specific individual will come into power in the future tribulation period who will be the virtual embodiment of sin and lawlessness (compare with 1 John 2:18; Revelation 11:7; 13:1-10). This lawless one will lead the entire world into rebellion against God (2 Thessalonians 2:9-10). He will even exalt himself and oppose God by moving into the Jewish temple, declaring himself God and demanding to be worshipped as God.

We are elsewhere told that the antichrist will be a king who "shall do as he wills" (Daniel 11:36), not as God wills. He will therefore be lawless, for he stands against the law of God. "He is 'the lawless one' because he deliberately ignores and violates God's law. He is a ruthless rebel."[3]

> At last, the mystery of lawlessness will produce its fruit in this man (II Thess. 2:7). Sin is lawlessness (I John 3:4 ASV), but through the centuries there has been a certain restraint placed upon it because the Holy Spirit of God has exercised through God's people a hindrance to its full expression. Ultimately this Restrainer, the Holy Spirit, will lift His staying hand because the church in whom He dwells will have been translated [at the rapture] (II Thess. 2:6-7). Immediately this lawless one will be revealed (II Thess. 2:8). Intolerant of all restraint except the law of his own sinful desire, he will launch a career of the most high-handed tyranny the world has ever seen.[4]

The antichrist, as the man of lawlessness, contrasts with the true Christ in several significant ways:

- The Lord Jesus was the Righteous One; the man of sin will be the lawless one.

- The Lord Jesus was "born under the law" (Galatians 4:4); the antichrist will oppose all law, being a law unto himself.

- When the Savior entered this world, He came saying, "Behold, I have come to do your will" (Hebrews 10:9). But of the antichrist it is written, "And the king shall do as he wills" (Daniel 11:36).[5]

SON OF DESTRUCTION, OR SON OF PERDITION

Scripture also refers to the antichrist as the son of destruction, or the son of perdition (2 Thessalonians 2:3). The New Testament also describes Judas Iscariot, who did the bidding of Satan by betraying Jesus Christ, as the son of perdition. "Satan entered into Judas called Iscariot, who was of the number of the twelve. He went away and conferred with the chief priests and officers how he might betray him to them" (Luke 22:3-4). For this act, Judas was called "son of perdition" or "son of destruction" (John 17:12). The phrase carries the idea, "one who is now abandoned, one who is utterly lost and given over to evil."[6] This very phrase is used of the antichrist in 2 Thessalonians 2:3.

This term has been translated variously from the Greek. Aside from "son of destruction" and "son of perdition," the term has also been translated "that lost soul" (Twentieth Century New Testament), "the one who is doomed to destruction" (Williams), "the champion of wickedness...destined to inherit perdition" (Knox), "the man doomed to perdition" (New English Bible), and "the son of hell" (Living Letters).[7] Whichever translation is correct, it depicts a horrific person. Bible expositor Walter Price concludes, based on this term, that the antichrist is "a human personality who willfully gives himself to the complete dominion of Satan, and whom Satan transforms into the sinister world master and god he is destined to become."[8]

A.W. Pink says this name is frightful: "Not only a human degenerate, but the offspring of the Dragon. Not only the worst of humankind, but the incarnation of the Devil. Not only the most depraved of all sinners, but an emanation from the Pit itself...All the evil, malignity, cunning, and power of the Serpent will be embodied in this terrible monster."[9]

Tim LaHaye and Jerry Jenkins suggest that it should be obvious why both Judas and the antichrist are called the son of perdition.

> Judas openly revolted against Jesus and set himself against our Lord at His first advent; the Antichrist will openly revolt against Jesus and set himself against our Lord just before His second advent...Others during the days of Jesus' earthly ministry openly opposed Him—the Pharisees, the Sadducees, the scribes, the High Priest, Pilate, and the Romans—but the sin of these two is so awful and heinous and personal that their guilt is blatant—and so is their punishment. After Judas hanged himself, Scripture says, he went "to his own place" (Acts 1:25), and after the Antichrist is captured at the Battle of Armageddon, he will be thrown directly into the lake of fire (Revelation 19:20).[10]

It is interesting to observe that because both Judas and the antichrist are called the son of perdition, some Bible teachers of the past have concluded that the antichrist will be Judas. The theory is allegedly supported by the idea that Judas "turned aside to go to his own place" (Acts 1:25). It is inferred that Judas's own place is a special place where he has been held by Satan since the first century, ready to be revealed in the end times as the antichrist.

This novel view is fascinating but involves forced and even fanciful exegesis. It has very little to commend it and is rejected by most prophecy experts. Among other things, the biblical text tells us that Judas hanged himself and died (Matthew 27:5; Acts 1:18). I will demonstrate later in the book that Satan does not possess the power of resurrection from the dead.

VARIOUS OTHER NAMES AND TITLES

Scripture uses many other names and titles of the antichrist, including these:

the little horn (Daniel 7:7-8)

the prince who is to come (Daniel 9:26)

the one who makes desolate (Daniel 9:27)

the king [who] will do as he wills (Daniel 11:36-39)

a contemptible person (Daniel 11:21)

a king of bold face (Daniel 8:23)

a worthless shepherd (Zechariah 11:16-17)

a rider on a white horse (Revelation 6:2)

Such terms add even further insight regarding this diabolical, sinister world leader of the end times. Truly he will be anti-Christ in every way imaginable. As David Jeremiah put it, "There are more than twenty-five different titles given to the Antichrist, all of which help to paint a picture of the most despicable man ever to walk on the earth."[11] Woe to those who are on the earth during the time of his reign.

THE ROLE OF SATAN

We have already briefly looked at the role of Satan in the life and work of the antichrist, but now we will add some of the theological backdrop so we can fully grasp the significance of his role. Satan is a formidable presence in the antichrist.

SATAN'S NATURE REFLECTED IN THE ANTICHRIST

Satan, formerly known as Lucifer, is a fallen angel who is aligned against God and His purposes, and he leads a vast company of fallen angels, called demons, who are also aligned against God and His purposes. Though he possesses creaturely limitations—unlike God, he is not omnipresent, omnipotent, or omniscient—Satan is nevertheless extremely powerful and influential in the world. He is "the ruler of this world" (John 12:31) and "the god of this world" (2 Corinthians 4:4). He is "the prince of the power of the air" (Ephesians 2:2) and "the deceiver of the whole world" (Revelation 12:9, see also 20:3). He has power in the governmental realm (Matthew 4:8-9; 2 Corinthians 4:4), the physical realm (Luke 13:11,16; Acts 10:38), the angelic realm (Jude 9; Ephesians 6:11-12), and the ecclesiastical (church) realm (Revelation 2:9; 3:9). We learn much about Satan and his work by the various names and titles used of him.

The accuser of our brothers (Revelation 12:10). The Greek of this verse indicates that accusing God's people is a continuous, ongoing work of Satan. He never lets up. He brings charges against believers before God (Zechariah 3:1; Romans 8:33), and he accuses believers to their own conscience.

Our adversary (1 Peter 5:8). This word indicates that Satan opposes us and stands against us in every way he can.

Beelzebul (Matthew 12:24). This word literally means "lord of the flies," meaning "lord of filth." Satan corrupts everything he touches.

The devil (Matthew 4:1). This word carries the idea of "adversary" as well as "slanderer." The devil was and is the adversary of Christ, and he is also the adversary of all who follow Christ. Satan slanders God to man (Genesis 3:1-7) and man to God (Job 1:9; 2:4).

Our enemy (Matthew 13:39). This word comes from a root meaning "hatred." It characterizes Satan's attitude in an absolute sense. He hates both God and His children.

The evil one (1 John 5:19). He opposes all that is good and is the promoter of all that is evil. Indeed, he is the very embodiment of evil.

The father of lies (John 8:44). The word *father* is used here metaphorically of the originator of a family or company of persons animated by a deceitful character. Satan was the first and greatest liar.

A murderer (John 8:44). Hatred is the motive that leads to murder. Satan hates both God and His children, so he has a genuine motive for murder.

The god of this world (2 Corinthians 4:4). This does not mean that Satan is deity. It simply means that this is an evil world, and Satan is the head of it.

The prince of the power of the air (Ephesians 2:2). *Air* in this context seems to be the sphere in which the inhabitants of this world live. This sphere represents the very seat of Satan's authority.

The ruler of this world (John 12:31; 14:30; 16:11). The key word here is *world*. This word refers not to the physical earth but to an anti-God system that Satan has promoted and that conforms to his ideals, aims, and methods.

A roaring lion (1 Peter 5:8-9). This graphic simile depicts Satan's strength and destructiveness.

The tempter (Matthew 4:3). His constant purpose is to incite man to sin. He whispers the most plausible excuses and striking advantages of sinning against God.

A serpent (Genesis 3:1; Revelation 12:9). This word symbolizes the origin of sin in the Garden of Eden as well as the hatefulness and deadly effects of sin. The serpent is characterized by treachery, deceitfulness, venom, and murderous proclivities.

Based on what we learn about Satan from these titles, it is clear that the antichrist's character is directly related to his being energized by Satan. For indeed, the antichrist—like Satan—is an adversary, full of corruption, an enemy full of hatred, permeated with evil, a liar and deceiver, and a murderer. He will exercise extensive influence around the world, promoting an anti-God philosophy.

PRIDE AND SELF-EXALTATION

Many scholars believe Ezekiel 28 and Isaiah 14 provide insights regarding how Lucifer fell and became Satan. The being described in Ezekiel 28 has the nature of a cherub (verse 14), was initially blameless and sinless (verse 15), was on the holy mountain of God (verses 13-14), was cast out of the mountain of God and thrown to the earth (verse 16), and was full of wisdom, perfect in beauty, and having the seal of perfection (verse 12). Such things cannot be said of a mere human being, so many believe this is a reference to Lucifer.

Our text tells us that he was created in a state of perfection and remained perfect in his ways until iniquity was found in him (Ezekiel 28:12,15). What was this iniquity? We read in verse 17, "Your heart was proud because of your beauty; you corrupted your wisdom for the sake of your splendor." Lucifer apparently became so impressed with his own beauty, intelligence, power, and position that he began to desire for himself the honor and glory that belong to God alone. The sin that corrupted Lucifer was self-generated pride.

This relates directly to Isaiah 14:13-14, where we learn that Lucifer said in his heart, "I will ascend to heaven; above the stars of God I will set my throne on high; I will sit on the mount of assembly in the far reaches of the north; I will ascend above the heights of the clouds;

I will make myself like the Most High." Consider the implication of each of these statements:

"I will ascend to heaven." Apparently Lucifer wanted to abide in heaven and desired equal recognition alongside God Himself.

"Above the stars of God I will set my throne on high." The stars are likely the angels of God. Lucifer apparently desired to rule over the angelic realm with the same authority as God.

"I will sit on the mount of assembly in the far reaches of the north." Scripture elsewhere indicates that the "mount of assembly" is the center of God's kingdom rule (see Psalm 48:2; Isaiah 2:2). The phrase is sometimes associated with the Messiah's future earthly rule in Jerusalem during the millennial kingdom. Satan may have desired to rule over human beings in place of the Messiah.

"I will ascend above the heights of the clouds." Clouds often metaphorically represent the glory of God in the Bible (Exodus 13:21; 40:34; Job 37:15-16; Matthew 26:64; Revelation 14:14). Apparently Lucifer sought a glory equal to that of God Himself.

"I will make myself like the Most High." Scripture says God possesses heaven and earth (Genesis 14:18-19). Apparently Lucifer sought the supreme position of the universe for himself. Satan wanted to exercise the authority and control in this world that rightfully belongs only to God. His sin was a direct challenge to God's power and authority.

God rightfully judged this mighty angelic being: "I cast you to the ground" (Ezekiel 28:17). As a result of his heinous sin, Lucifer was banished from living in heaven (Isaiah 14:12). He became corrupt, and his name changed from Lucifer ("morning star") to Satan ("adversary"). His power became completely perverted (Isaiah 14:12,16-17). And his destiny, following the second coming of Christ, is to be bound in the bottomless pit during the 1000-year millennial kingdom over which Christ will rule (Revelation 20:3), after which he will be thrown into the lake of fire (Matthew 25:41; Revelation 20:10).

Like Satan, the antichrist will be prideful. He will engage in gross self-exaltation, and seek to take the place of God. First Timothy 3:6 informs us that Satan can "puff up" a human being with conceit in the heart so that he thinks more of himself than he ought. Satan will accomplish this in the antichrist to a measureless degree. The antichrist will be the epitome of conceit.

Indeed, 2 Thessalonians 2:4 tells us that the antichrist "opposes and exalts himself against every so-called god or object of worship, so that he takes his seat in the temple of God, proclaiming himself to be God." The antichrist will seek for all the world to worship him as God (see Revelation 13:8,12,15). Satan's influence on the antichrist is unmistakable and clear (see also Daniel 9:27; Matthew 24:15).

THE ANTICHRIST IS ENERGIZED BY SATAN

The antichrist's desires are not surprising. "The coming of the lawless one is by the activity of Satan with all power and false signs and wonders" (2 Thessalonians 2:9). "The dragon [Satan] gave his power and his throne and great authority" to the antichrist (Revelation 13:2). Such verses make it clear that Satan will empower and energize the antichrist. No wonder the antichrist's desires, motivations, and actions will be identical to those of Satan.

THE ANTICHRIST DECEIVES THE WAY SATAN DOES

We learn from Scripture that Satan is the "father of lies" (John 8:44). This means he originates and inspires lies and deception. In fact, Satan is a master deceiver and the greatest among all liars. His lies are often religious, distorting the biblical picture of God, Jesus, and the true gospel. Satan is "the deceiver of the whole world" (Revelation 12:9) and "the dragon, that ancient serpent" (Revelation 20:2). This title hearkens back to the Garden of Eden, where Satan through the serpent deceived Eve (Genesis 3; see also 2 Corinthians 11:3; 1 Timothy 2:14). Satan's deception began in the Garden of Eden, but it will continue right on through the tribulation period.

Because Satan is the father of lies and the deceiver of the whole world, it makes sense that the one whom he energizes—the antichrist—will also be characterized by lies and deception. The "false signs and wonders" the antichrist performs (2 Thessalonians 2:9) will cause all the more deception because they will seem to exalt the antichrist as God among us, just as Christ was God among us (Matthew 1:23).

The antichrist is full of poisonous, lethal deception, and Satan all the while blinds the minds of unbelievers so they cannot perceive the truth (2 Corinthians 4:4). I infer from this that during the future tribulation period, Satan will be busy blinding the minds of people so that they are all the more vulnerable to believing the self-exalting claims of the antichrist.

Tragically, unbelievers during the tribulation period will have turned their backs on God, so God will hand them over to a powerful delusion. Paul makes this point in a powerful way in 2 Thessalonians 2:9-11: "The coming of the lawless one is by the activity of Satan with all power and false signs and wonders, and with all wicked deception for those who are perishing, because they refused to love the truth and so be saved. Therefore God sends them a strong delusion, so that they may believe what is false." This indicates that even though God desires all to be saved (1 Timothy 2:4-6) and desires that none perish (2 Peter 3:9), throngs of people will utterly turn their backs on God's truth and offer of salvation and become hardened in their hearts. When that happens, God eventually allows them to experience the full brunt of the consequences of falsehood (see Romans 1:18-25).

THE ANTICHRIST PERSECUTES THE WAY SATAN DOES

In Revelation 12:12-17, we find a sobering description of Satan's ousting from heaven, after which he engages in heavy persecution of the Jews.

> "Therefore, rejoice, O heavens and you who dwell in them! But woe to you, O earth and sea, for the devil has come down to you in great wrath, because he knows that his time is short!"
>
> And when the dragon saw that he had been thrown down to the earth, he pursued the woman who had given birth to the male child. But the woman was given the two wings of the great eagle so that she might fly from the serpent into the wilderness, to the place where she is to be nourished for a time, and times, and half a time. The serpent poured water like a river out of his mouth after the

woman, to sweep her away with a flood. But the earth came to the help of the woman, and the earth opened its mouth and swallowed the river that the dragon had poured from his mouth. Then the dragon became furious with the woman and went off to make war on the rest of her offspring, on those who keep the commandments of God and hold to the testimony of Jesus. And he stood on the sand of the sea.

We are here told that Satan will be cast out of heaven and "thrown down to the earth." He is filled with fury because he knows that his time is short. More specifically, he knows that his time is limited to a mere 1260 days, which is the last three and a half years of the tribulation period.

Who is the woman who becomes the object of Satan's great persecution? For the answer to this, we go back to the beginning of Revelation 12.

A great sign appeared in heaven: a woman clothed with the sun, with the moon under her feet, and on her head a crown of twelve stars. She was pregnant and was crying out in birth pains and the agony of giving birth…The dragon stood before the woman who was about to give birth, so that when she bore her child he might devour it. She gave birth to a male child, one who is to rule all the nations with a rod of iron, but her child was caught up to God and to his throne, and the woman fled into the wilderness, where she has a place prepared by God, in which she is to be nourished for 1,260 days (verses 1-6).

In this passage, the woman represents Israel, building on Old Testament imagery in which Israel was viewed as the wife of God (Isaiah 54:5-6; Jeremiah 3:6-8; 31:32; Ezekiel 16:32; Hosea 2:16). The 12 stars represent the 12 tribes of Israel, and the moon may allude to God's covenant relationship with Israel (new moons are associated with covenant worship) (1 Chronicles 23:31; 2 Chronicles 2:4; 8:13).

The male child refers to Jesus Christ. The mention of the dragon seeking to devour the child likely alludes to the massacre of male children commanded by Herod and other threats on Jesus' life (Matthew 2:13-18; Luke 4:28-29). The child was caught up to God in the sense that He ascended into heaven following His resurrection (Acts 1:9; 2:33-34; Hebrews 1:1-3; 12:2). The child—the divine Messiah—is destined to rule the nations (see Psalm 2:6-9).

In Revelation 12:12 and following, we see that Satan—knowing that he has very little time left—seeks to persecute Israel with fury. But God provides supernatural aid, and the Jews manage to find shelter in a secret place. John F. Walvoord, in *The Bible Knowledge Commentary*, provides this comment:

> This hiding place was not clearly identified. Some suggest that it might be Petra, fortress capital of the Nabateans in Edom, south of the Dead Sea. This city has a narrow access which could easily be blocked but which opens up into a large canyon capable of caring for many thousands of people.[1]

The two wings probably refer to God's supernatural delivering power (see Exodus 19:4; Deuteronomy 32:11-12; see also Matthew 24:16; Mark 13:14; Luke 21:21).

God will preserve a remnant of Jews through this persecution, but this should not be taken to mean that all Jews will survive, for they will not. Many prophecy scholars relate this passage to Zechariah 13:8: "In the whole land, declares the LORD, two thirds shall be cut off and perish, and one third shall be left alive." Many will die, but a remnant will survive the onslaught.

God preserves the Jews for "a time, times, and half a time." This refers to the last three and a half years of the tribulation period. Keep in mind that "a time" equals one year, "times" equals two years, and "half a time" equals half a year (Daniel 7:25; 12:7). This period also coincides with the 42-month period referenced in Revelation 11:2 and 13:5. The last three and a half years of the tribulation period is often referred to as the great tribulation.

So Satan is a great persecutor of God's people. But we also find that the antichrist—who is empowered and energized by Satan—is likewise a great persecutor of God's people.

> The beast [the Antichrist] was allowed to make war on the saints and to conquer them. And authority was given it over every tribe and people and language and nation, and all who dwell on earth will worship it, everyone whose name has not been written before the foundation of the world in the book of life of the Lamb who was slain. If anyone has an ear, let him hear:
> > If anyone is to be taken captive,
> > > to captivity he goes;
> > if anyone is to be slain with the sword,
> > > with the sword must he be slain.
> Here is a call for the endurance and faith of the saints (Revelation 13:7-10).

A parallel passage, Daniel 7:21, tells us the antichrist "made war with the saints and prevailed over them." Many will die. The Revelation passage tells us that the antichrist will conquer them, and the Daniel passage tells us he will prevail over them. There will be many martyrs during the future tribulation period.

"[The antichrist] makes war with God's people and overcomes many of them. They die rather than submit to him. His rule extends over all the world—the last world empire before Christ's reign."[2] God's people are willing to die because they know they will live forever with the true Christ, Jesus the divine Messiah.

The antichrist is also a great persecutor of the Jewish people. Daniel 9:27 tells us that the tribulation period begins when the antichrist makes a covenant with the Jewish people. The antichrist will break this covenant at the midpoint of the tribulation, when he "takes his seat in the temple of God, proclaiming himself to be God" (2 Thessalonians 2:4). This desolates the Jewish temple (see Matthew 24:15). When that happens, Jesus says, the Jews in Jerusalem should try to escape.

> Let those who are in Judea flee to the mountains. Let the one who is on the housetop not go down to take what is in

his house, and let the one who is in the field not turn back to take his cloak. And alas for women who are pregnant and for those who are nursing infants in those days! Pray that your flight may not be in winter or on a Sabbath. For then there will be great tribulation, such as has not been from the beginning of the world until now, no, and never will be (Matthew 24:16-21).

The persecution of the Jews by the antichrist will be relentless. There will be countless casualties.

CONCLUSION

In a sense, the antichrist will be Satan's CEO on the earth. A CEO is a chief executive officer who carries the authority of leadership in an organization. He implements the vision of the organization. The antichrist will head up Satan's evil enterprise in a seven-year reign of terror, using perpetual lies, fraud, deceit, theft, abuse of power, duplicity, self-interest, self-aggrandizement, persecution, murder, and the like—all under Satan's power.

THE DEATH AND RESURRECTION OF THE ANTICHRIST

In Revelation 13:1-3 we read about a seemingly mortal head wound that the antichrist had suffered.

> And I saw a beast rising out of the sea, with ten horns and seven heads, with ten diadems on its horns and blasphemous names on its heads. And the beast that I saw was like a leopard; its feet were like a bear's, and its mouth was like a lion's mouth. And to it the dragon gave his power and his throne and great authority. One of its heads seemed to have a mortal wound, but its mortal wound was healed, and the whole earth marveled as they followed the beast.

There has been much debate and speculation through the centuries regarding what this passage may be referring to. Some believe it refers to the pagan Roman Empire, which died in the past but will be revived in the end times. Some say a historical character of the past (Nero, Judas Iscariot, Mussolini, Hitler, and Stalin are common suggestions) will come back to life and fulfill the role of the antichrist in the end times. Others say the antichrist will be killed and then be resurrected back to life. Others say that perhaps the antichrist will be merely wounded, and Satan will supernaturally heal this wound so that he is brought back to health. As John F. Walvoord explains it, "While the resurrection of a dead person seems to be beyond Satan's power, the healing of a wound would be possible for Satan, and this may be the explanation."[1] Still others say that the antichrist will only appear to be killed, though he really is not, and through satanic trickery will give the appearance of having been resurrected from the dead. What is really going on in this controversial passage?

A PERSON, NOT A KINGDOM

There is room for debate on this issue, but I believe Revelation 13:3 is referring not to a kingdom (the revived Roman Empire) but to a person—more specifically, the antichrist. I say this because Revelation 13:12 makes specific reference to "the first beast, whose mortal wound was healed." The first beast is clearly the person of the antichrist. He is mentioned alongside another beast, the false prophet. Then, verse 14 refers to "the beast that was wounded by the sword and yet lived." The most natural interpretation is that this verse refers to a person.

NOT A HISTORICAL PERSON

Does Revelation 13 refer to a historical person of the past coming back to life to fulfill the role of the antichrist in the end times? This hypothesis is a fascinating one, but I personally reject it. It seems to be based more on eisogesis (reading a meaning into the text) than exegesis (deriving the meaning out of the text). It is a highly speculative view, and I find virtually no biblical facts to support it. Passages such as Daniel 2, Daniel 7, 2 Thessalonians 2, and the book of Revelation point to the emergence of a unique person who is ultimately unlike any other person who has ever lived.

But questions still remain. Will Satan actually resurrect the antichrist? Or will this so-called resurrection be an example of satanic trickery? Let's focus brief attention on some scriptural teachings that can help guide our thinking on this matter.

SATAN IS POWERFUL AND INFLUENTIAL

In a previous chapter, I noted that Satan—though possessing creaturely limitations—is nevertheless pictured in Scripture as being extremely powerful and influential in the world. We have seen that he is "the ruler of this world" (John 12:31), "the god of this world" (2 Corinthians 4:4), and the "prince of the power of the air" (Ephesians 2:2). He deceives the whole world (Revelation 12:9; 20:3). He has power in the governmental realm (Matthew 4:8-9; 2 Corinthians 4:4), the physical realm (Luke 13:11,16; Acts 10:38), the angelic realm (Ephesians 6:11-12; Jude 9), and the ecclesiastical (church) realm (Revelation 2:9; 3:9). So at the outset, we must recognize that Satan certainly has supernatural abilities. But he is not powerful enough to actually resurrect people from the dead. (More on this shortly.)

SATAN HAS VAST EXPERIENCE

Scripture also reveals that Satan's vast experience observing and dealing with human beings is far greater than that of any human being. By his very longevity, Satan has acquired a breadth of experience that easily eclipses the limited knowledge of man. He has observed people firsthand in every conceivable situation, so he can predict with accuracy how they will respond to a variety of circumstances.[2] So even though Satan is not omniscient (only God is), his wide experience gives him knowledge that is far superior to anything any man could have.

Now, here is an important consideration. Because Satan has vast experience, he has learned many wiles and tricks regarding how to deceive human beings. He is the "father of lies" (John 8:44). Therefore, much of what he does is rooted in lies and trickery. We can infer that some of his deceitful tricks relate to the counterfeit miracles he inspires. This is one reason Christians are urged to beware (2 Corinthians 2:11; 1 Peter 5:8).

Perhaps Satan will pull off a master trick, creating an illusion that the antichrist has been resurrected from the dead. Perhaps he will heal a nonfatal wound or simply engage in supernatural trickery. In any event, if this scenario is correct, Satan's vast experience in tricking and influencing human beings will be his major asset in pulling this off.

If talented Las Vegas magicians can deceive large crowds of people by sleight of hand, how much more so will Satan—the master trickster who has thousands of years of experience—be able to deceive multitudes about the antichrist's apparent resurrection. These will be times of deception (John 8:44; 1 Thessalonians 2:3; see also 1 Timothy 4:1; 2 Timothy 4:3-4).

SATAN, THE APE OF GOD

Augustine called the devil *Simius Dei*—"the ape of God." Satan is the great counterfeiter.[3] He mimics God in many ways. A primary tactic Satan uses to attack God and His program in general is to offer a counterfeit kingdom and program.[4] This is hinted at in 2 Corinthians 11:14, which refers to Satan masquerading as an angel of light. In what ways does Satan act as the ape of God?

- Satan has his own church—the "synagogue of Satan" (Revelation 2:9).

- He has his own ministers—ministers of darkness who bring false sermons (2 Corinthians 11:4-5).

- He has formulated his own system of theology—"doctrines of demons" (1 Timothy 4:1; Revelation 2:24).

- His ministers proclaim a counterfeit gospel—a gospel contrary to the one Paul preached (Galatians 1:7-8).

- He has his own throne (Revelation 13:2) and his own worshippers (13:4).

- He inspires false christs and self-constituted messiahs (Matthew 24:4-5).

- He employs false teachers who bring in "destructive heresies" (2 Peter 2:1).

- He sends out false prophets (Matthew 24:11).

- He sponsors false apostles who imitate the true apostles (2 Corinthians 11:13).

"Satan's plan and purposes have been, are, and always will be to seek to establish a rival rule to God's kingdom. He is promoting a system of which he is the head and which stands in opposition to God and His rule in the universe."[5]

Scripture indicates that Satan performs counterfeit signs and wonders. Indeed, 2 Thessalonians 2:9 tells us, "The coming of the lawless one is by the activity of Satan with all power and false signs and wonders."

An apparent resurrection would be in perfect keeping with Satan's character as the ape of God. This counterfeit resurrection will mimic the genuine resurrection of Jesus Christ, the slain Lamb (Revelation 5:6). Many will marvel at it.

CAN SATAN PERFORM MIRACLES?

Satan does have supernatural power, but there is a gigantic difference between the devil and God. Satan does not possess attributes that belong to God alone—he is not omnipresent (everywhere-present), omnipotent (all-powerful), or omniscient (all-knowing). Satan is a creature, and as a creature he is lesser than (and is responsible to) the Creator. Satan can be in only one place at a time. His strength, though great, is limited. And his knowledge, though vast, has its bounds.

So God is infinite in power (omnipotent), but the devil (like demons) is finite and limited. Only God can create life (Genesis 1:1,21; Deuteronomy 32:39); the devil cannot (see Exodus 8:19). We infer from this that only God can truly raise the dead (John 10:18; Revelation 1:18).

Certainly the devil has great power to deceive people (Revelation 12:9), to oppress those who yield to him, and even to possess them (Acts 16:16). He is a master magician and a superscientist. And with his vast knowledge of God, man, and the universe, he is able to perform false signs and wonders (2 Thessalonians 2:9; see also Revelation 13:13-14). For example, Simon the sorcerer in the city of Samaria amazed people with his Satan-inspired magic (Acts 8:9-11), but the miracles accomplished through Philip were much, much greater (Acts 8:13). The devil's counterfeit miracles do not compete with God's mighty works.

Perhaps the best illustration of Satan's counterfeit wonders is found in the Exodus account. In Exodus 7:10, for example, we read that Moses's rod was turned into a snake by the power of God. Then, according to verse 11, Pharaoh "summoned the wise men and the sorcerers, and they, the magicians of Egypt, also did the same things by their secret arts." The purpose of these acts, of course, was to convince Pharaoh that his magicians possessed as much power as Moses and Aaron and that he did not need to yield to their request to let Israel go. It worked, at least for the first three encounters (Aaron's rod, the plague of blood, and the plague of frogs). However, when Moses and Aaron, by the power of God, brought forth living lice from the sand, the magicians were not able to counterfeit this miracle. They could only exclaim, "This is the finger of God" (Exodus 8:19). Satan cannot create life.

Biblical scholars differ as to whether Satan performs convincing tricks or genuine (albeit limited) miraculous works. Some scholars assert that the feats of Egypt's magicians, inspired by Satan, were done by sleight of hand. Perhaps the magicians had enchanted the snakes so that they became stiff and appeared to be rods. When thrown on the floor, they came out of their trance and began to move as snakes. Satan is the "father of lies" (John 8:44), so he very well may have pulled some kind of trick instead of performing a true miracle.

Other scholars say these were supernatural and miraculous acts of Satan, who actually turned the rods of the magicians into snakes. Dr. Henry Morris, for example, believes the devil and demons may be able to perform some "grade-B" miracles. They may be capable of "great juggling of the world's natural processes."[6]

Still others, such as theologian John Witmer, believe Satan sometimes does tricks and sometimes does supernatural (albeit limited) miraculous works.

> Some of these spectacles are mere trickery, spurious miracles. Others of them are truly supernatural events, but Satanic in origin and power, not divine. Remember that the devil showed the Lord Jesus "all the kingdoms of the world in a moment of time" (Luke 4:5) and is able to transform himself "into an angel of light" (2 Corinthians 11:14).[7]

Reformed theologian Charles Hodge, in his *Systematic Theology*, notes that whether Satan can perform a miracle hinges on how one defines *miracle*.

> The question is, Are they to be regarded as *true* miracles?
> The answer to this question depends on the meaning of
> the word. If by a miracle we mean any event transcend-
> ing the efficiency of physical causes and the power of man,
> then they are miracles. But if we adhere to the definition…
> which requires that the event be produced by the immedi-
> ate power of God, they of course are not miracles.[8]

Whether Satan has the ability to perform a few limited grade-B miracles or whether his works are just impressive tricks, the scriptural evidence is undeniably clear that only God can perform grade-A miracles.
Only God can fully control and supersede the natural laws He Himself created, though on one occasion He did grant Satan the power to
bring a whirlwind on Job's family (Job 1:19). As the account of Job illustrates, all the power the devil has is granted him by God and is carefully
limited and monitored (see verses 10-12). In other words, Satan is on
a leash. His finite power is under the control of God's infinite power.

In view of this scriptural evidence, it seems reasonable to conclude
that Satan will either engage in a limited grade-B miracle in healing the
wounded antichrist (that is, wounded but not dead) or he will engage
in some kind of masterful deception—or perhaps a combination of
both. In any event, the world will be amazed.

DISCERNING BETWEEN GOD'S MIRACLES AND SATAN'S LYING WONDERS

While we are on the topic, let's note that Scripture gives us the key
to discerning between the true miracles of God and the lying wonders
of Satan. We find this key summarized in Deuteronomy 13:1-3.

> If a prophet or a dreamer of dreams arises among you and
> gives you a sign or a wonder, and the sign or wonder that
> he tells you comes to pass, and if he says, "Let us go after
> other gods," which you have not known, "and let us serve
> them," you shall not listen to the words of that prophet or
> that dreamer of dreams. For the LORD your God is testing
> you, to know whether you love the LORD your God with
> all your heart and with all your soul.

This means that if a person claiming to perform a miracle of God is teaching false doctrine, we may assume without hesitation that this person's miracle is not done in the power of God but is a lying wonder from Satan. Christian apologist Norman Geisler notes that there are a variety of false teachings or activities that might be connected to a satanically inspired counterfeit miracle.

> Numerous evils are mentioned in the Bible, such as idolatry (1 Corinthians 10:19), immorality (Ephesians 2:2), divination (Deuteronomy 18:10), false prophecies (Deuteronomy 18:22), occult activity (Deuteronomy 18:14), worshipping other gods (Deuteronomy 13:1,2), deceptive activity (2 Thessalonians 2:9), contacting the dead (Deuteronomy 18:11,12), messages contrary to those revealed through true prophets (Galatians 1:8), and prophecies that do not center on Jesus Christ (Revelation 19:10).[9]

If the miracle confirms or supports any of the items listed above, it cannot be of the God of truth. God's miracles are never connected to the kingdom of darkness.[10]

This key truth will help anchor those who become believers in God during the tribulation period. They will witness what seems to be a mighty miracle—the supposed resurrection of the antichrist. But they will not ascribe deity to him or worship him, as so many others will do during the tribulation period. They will recognize that this sign or wonder is connected to one who disseminates falsehood.

SATAN BLINDS MINDS

Previously in the book I noted 2 Corinthians 4:4: "The god of this world [Satan] has blinded the minds of the unbelievers, to keep them from seeing the light of the gospel of the glory of Christ, who is the image of God." This passage indicates that Satan inhibits the unbeliever's ability to think or reason properly in regard to spiritual matters.[11] Might we infer from this that if Satan pulls off some kind of counterfeit resurrection (a grade-B healing of a wound or satanic trickery), he will be able to blind the minds of people on earth so that they accept this as an indication of the antichrist's power and deity and subsequently worship him? There is good reason to think so.

AN APPEARANCE OF DEATH

Some prophecy experts, such as Tim LaHaye and Jerry Jenkins, believe the antichrist will not just be wounded, but rather will actually die. "We believe that the Beast really is killed, for John twice says that he 'ascends out of the bottomless pit' (11:7; 17:8); we believe this means that the Beast is killed, descends to the pit, and ascends from there to the earth when he is resurrected."[12] However, with all due respect to these esteemed interpreters, this is not the only possible interpretation of these verses. Bible scholar Walter Price is representative of those who hold that the antichrist will appear to be dead but not actually be dead:

> The apostle Paul…was stoned in Lystra, and the citizens "dragged him out of the city, supposing that he was dead" (Acts 14:19). While in an unconscious state, Paul "was caught up into Paradise, and heard unspeakable words, which it is not lawful for a man to utter" (2 Cor. 12:4). Paul had received, as it were, what seemed like a death stroke. At the same time he was thought to be dead, his spirit was caught up into the third heaven and there received a profound revelation from God. This same thing, in reverse, will happen to the Antichrist. The Antichrist, sometime during his career as Caesar, will receive a death stroke. He will be no more dead than was the apostle Paul. But just as the citizens of Lystra thought Paul was dead, so the Antichrist will be thought dead.[13]

Price then raises the possibility that just as Paul's spirit departed from his body and was taken up to God's domain, where he received further revelations, so the antichrist's spirit may depart from his body (appearing to be dead) and be taken into the abyss by Satan, where Satan will offer the world's kingdoms to him.

> Just as Satan took Jesus up into a high mountain and showed him all the kingdoms of the world, and offered

them to him, if he would fall down and worship him; so Satan will take the Antichrist into the depths of the Abyss and show him all the kingdoms of the world...Jesus refused to bow down to Satan. The Antichrist will not refuse.[14]

Price suggests that the antichrist's spirit will then return from the abyss (Revelation 11:7), reenter what appears to be a dead body, thereby giving the appearance of a resurrection from the dead, and continue on his satanically inspired mission. Mark Hitchcock suggests that while in the abyss, the "Antichrist probably receives his orders and strategy from Satan, literally selling his soul to the devil, and then comes back to earth with hellish ferocity to establish his world domination over a completely awestruck earth."[15]

CONCLUSION

My assessment is that only God can do grade-A miracles, such as resurrecting people from the dead. However, I also believe that Satan has supernatural abilities, can perform what might be called grade-B miracles, is a superscientist and a master trickster, and has thousands of years of experience in duping human beings. I believe that all of this will come to play in the future tribulation period, when Satan pulls off one of the greatest hoaxes of all time—making it appear that the antichrist has actually risen from the dead, just as Jesus did.

THE ROLE OF THE FALSE PROPHET

Scripture reveals that in the end times, many false prophets will emerge on the religious landscape (Matthew 24:24). Such prophets are mouthpieces of Satan, spreading doctrines of demons (1 Timothy 4:1). However, Scripture also reveals that during the tribulation period, one supreme false prophet will emerge who will be the right-hand man of the antichrist. The antichrist will primarily be a military and political leader, but the false prophet will primarily be a religious leader. As Randall Price puts it, "Just as many 'antichrists' appeared during the Last Days to prepare for the Antichrist (1 Jn. 2:18, 22), so many 'false prophets and false Christs' will appear throughout the tribulation (cf. Matt. 24:10,24) to prepare for the greater deception of the second beast (Rev. 13:13-14) as the superlative 'false prophet' (Rev. 13:14 with Matt. 24:24; cf. Rev. 19:20)."[1]

The antichrist will not carry out his diabolical plans alone. He will be assisted by a first lieutenant. The Bible—particularly the book of Revelation—tells us a great deal about this devious and deceptive false prophet.

ANOTHER BEAST

The apostle John introduces us to the false prophet in Revelation 13:11: "I saw another beast rising out of the earth. It had two horns like a lamb and it spoke like a dragon." What does this strange imagery mean?

Just as the antichrist will be a beast, so will the false prophet be a beast. The Greek word for *another* is *allos*, meaning "another of the same kind." Together, this beastly duo will wreak havoc on the earth for seven years.

This second beast rises out of the earth. Some expositors argue that the antichrist is a Gentile who emerges out of the sea of nations (Revelation 13:1), but the false prophet will be a Jew. J. Dwight Pentecost writes, "This individual is evidently a Jew, since he arises out of the earth, or land, that is Palestine (13:11)."[2] David Reagan agrees.

> Just as the sea is used symbolically in prophecy to refer to the Gentile nations, the land (or earth) is used to refer to Israel. This does not mean the false prophet will be an Orthodox Jew. It only means that he will be of Jewish heritage. Religiously, he will be an apostate Jew who will head up the One World Religion of the Antichrist.[3]

Others, including John F. Walvoord, hold that the term *earth* gives no indication regarding the false prophet's ethnic identity.

> While the first beast was a Gentile, since he came from the entire human race as symbolized by "the sea" (v. 1), the second beast was a creature of the earth. Some have taken this as a specific reference to the Promised Land and have argued that he was therefore a Jew. There is no support for this in the context as the word for "earth" is the general word referring to the entire world (*ghv*). Actually his nationality and geographic origin are not indicated.[4]

Bible expositor John MacArthur suggests another meaning for the fact that the false prophet arises from the earth. "[This] suggests that he will be subtler, gentler, less overpowering and terrifying than the Antichrist. He will be winsome and persuasive, the epitome of the wolves in sheep's clothing Jesus warned of (Matt. 7:15)."[5] Clearly there is room for debate among Christians as to the meaning of "out of the earth."

In any event, the false prophet has "two horns like a lamb and it spoke like a dragon" (Revelation 13:11). Recall that the antichrist has ten horns (13:1). Horns indicate power and authority, so we can infer from the false prophet's two horns that he has less power and authority than the antichrist. Compared to the antichrist, the false prophet is like a lamb—more meek and more gentle in his dealings with others. He speaks like a dragon in the sense that he speaks words inspired by the dragon, or Satan. Just as true prophets are inspired by the Holy Spirit, so the false prophet is inspired by the unholy spirit— Satan. As Ed Hindson puts it, "He looks religious, but he talks like the devil."[6] MacArthur suggests, "He will speak winsome, deceiving words of praise about the Antichrist, luring the world to worship that vile, satanic dictator."[7]

We can infer from Scripture that the false prophet will be a gifted communicator who is particularly adept at inspiring commitment to the false world religion and to the antichrist. John Phillips offers this explanation:

> The role of the False Prophet will be to make the new religion appealing and palatable to men. No doubt it will combine all the features of the religious systems of men, will appeal to man's total personality, and will take full advantage of his carnal appetite. The dynamic appeal of the False Prophet will lie in his skill in combining political expediency with religious passion, self-interest with benevolent philanthropy, lofty sentiment with blatant sophistry, moral platitude with unbridled self-indulgence. His arguments will be subtle, convincing, and appealing. His oratory will be hypnotic, for he will be able to move the masses to tears or whip them into a frenzy. He will control the communication media of the world and will skillfully organize mass publicity to promote his ends. He will be the master of every promotional device and public relations gimmick. He will manage the truth with guile beyond words, bending it, twisting it, and distorting it. Public opinion will be his to command. He will mold world thought and

shape human opinion like so much potter's clay. His deadly appeal will lie in the fact that what he says will sound so right, so sensible, so exactly what unregenerate men have always wanted to hear.[8]

THE AUTHORITY OF THE FALSE PROPHET

Revelation 13:12 tells us that the false prophet "exercises all the authority of the first beast in its presence, and makes the earth and its inhabitants worship the first beast, whose mortal wound was healed." When the text says that he "exercises all the authority of the first beast in its presence," we should keep two primary ideas in mind. First, the source of the false prophet's authority is the same as the antichrist's authority—Satan. Both are empowered by this diabolical spirit. Second, the authority of the false prophet is a delegated authority—that is, he speaks on behalf of the antichrist.

The goal of the false prophet will be to make "the earth and its inhabitants worship the first beast, whose mortal wound was healed." In his efforts to move the entire world to worship the antichrist, he will be the epitome of a false prophet because he will point to a god other than the God in the Bible.

THE MIRACULOUS WORKS OF THE FALSE PROPHET

Revelation 13:13-15 describes some of the false prophet's activities.

> It performs great signs, even making fire come down from heaven to earth in front of people, and by the signs that it is allowed to work in the presence of the beast [the antichrist] it deceives those who dwell on earth, telling them to make an image for the beast [the antichrist] that was wounded by the sword and yet lived. And it was allowed to give breath to the image of the beast, so that the image of the beast might even speak and might cause those who would not worship the image of the beast to be slain.

As we have seen, Satan does not have the power to inspire the kind of grade-A miracles that God does. However, he can apparently do grade-B miracles, and he empowers the false prophet to perform these (see Exodus 7:11). He does this to induce people to worship Satan's substitute for Christ, the antichrist (see Daniel 9:27; 11:31; 12:11; Matthew 24:15).

Bible scholar J. Hampton Keathley notes that the word *performs* in Revelation 13:13 is a present tense in the original Greek, indicating that "he engages in a display of miraculous signs one after another."[9] In other words, the seemingly miraculous works of the false prophet will be ongoing and perpetual. People will be impressed.

Our text describes these miracles as "great"—from the Greek word *megas*, meaning "large" or "great." This Greek word is typically used of that which is outstanding, significant, important, or prominent. We can thus infer that the signs performed by the false prophet will not be "the run of the mill miracles that one hears about with pseudo healers or the paranormal events of today."[10] Some of the signs performed by the false prophet seem similar to those of Elijah (1 Kings 18:38) or God's two prophetic witnesses (Revelation 11:5; see also 2 Kings 1:9-11; Leviticus 10:1-2).

Our text also tells us that these miraculous signs are designed to deceive people (Revelation 13:14). The word *deceive* in the Greek (*planaw*) literally means "to lead astray, cause to wander, mislead, deceive." The word is often used in the Bible as related to false teachers who lead people into false forms of worship (see, for example, 2 Thessalonians 2:9-12).

In one of his more impressive miraculous and deceptive acts, the false prophet will animate an image of the beast in the Jewish temple. The apostle Paul earlier revealed that the antichrist himself will sit in God's temple (see 2 Thessalonians 2:4) and receive worship that properly belongs only to God. Some suggest that when the antichrist is not present in the temple, an image of him will provide an object of worship there in his absence (see Revelation 13:14-15; 14:9,11; 15:2; 16:2; 19:20; 20:4).

What is meant when Scripture affirms that the false prophet gives breath to the image of the beast, so that it can even speak? Bible expositors have different opinions on this matter. Some believe the beast's image is able to give an impression of breathing and speaking mechanically, as with animatronics today. Perhaps some kind of holographic deception may be employed. Recall that Satan has great intelligence—including scientific intelligence—and likely has the know-how to accomplish all this.

Other expositors, such as Hampton Keathley, see something more supernatural going on here, though not a miracle of actually making the image alive (giving life is something only God can do).

> We are told that the false prophet is able to give breath to the image. This gives it the appearance of life. However, it isn't real life but only breath. Since breath or breathing is one of the signs of life, men think the image lives, but John is careful *not* to say that he gives life to the image. Only God can do that. It is something miraculous, but also deceptive and false…Then we are told the image of the beast, through this imparted breath, speaks. This is to be a further confirmation of the miraculous nature of the beast's image. Some might see this as the result of some product of our modern electronic robot-type of technology. But such would hardly convince people of anything spectacular. Evidently it will go far beyond that.[11]

Christian scholars may have different opinions on the matter, but notice that the apparent animation that the false prophet gives the image sets it apart from typical idols in Old Testament times. "The idols of the nations are silver and gold, the work of human hands. They have mouths, but do not speak; they have eyes, but do not see" (Psalm 135:15-16). "Woe to him who says to a wooden thing, Awake; to a silent stone, Arise! Can this teach? Behold, it is overlaid with gold and silver, and there is no breath at all in it" (Habakkuk 2:19). Contrary to such inanimate idols, this idolatrous image of the antichrist seems to be alive. Perhaps the false prophet—using Satan's power—brings all this about to give the impression that unlike a dead idol, the antichrist really is God.

GOAL OF THE FALSE PROPHET

The ultimate goal of the false prophet's supernatural acts is to induce people around the world to worship the antichrist—a worship that rightfully should be rendered to God alone. Because the antichrist puts himself in the place of Christ, the antichrist seeks worship, just as Jesus was worshipped many times during His three-year ministry on earth (see, for example, Matthew 2:11; 8:2; 9:18; 15:25; 28:9,17; John 9:38; 20:28).* An important theological backdrop to all this is found in Exodus 34:14, which instructs us, "You shall worship no other god, for the LORD, whose name is Jealous, is a jealous God." Clearly, by demanding worship, the antichrist places himself in the position of deity.

Revelation 13:16-18 then tells us that the false prophet continues his controlling influence.

> [He] causes all, both small and great, both rich and poor, both free and slave, to be marked on the right hand or the forehead, so that no one can buy or sell unless he has the mark, that is, the name of the beast or the number of its name. This calls for wisdom: let the one who has understanding calculate the number of the beast, for it is the number of a man, and his number is 666.

I will deal with the mark of the beast in a separate chapter. For now, it is enough to note that the false prophet will bring about global economic bondage so that no one can buy or sell anywhere on the planet without receiving a mark that indicates allegiance and submission to the antichrist.

THE FALSE RELIGION OF THE END TIMES

Revelation 17 informs us about religious Babylon. Verses 1-7 describe it with symbolic language, and verses 8-18 interpret the description. The passage indicates that Babylon is a great prostitute whose religious unfaithfulness influences the people of many nations.** This "great prostitute" (blasphemous religion) sits on (or controls) a scarlet beast (the antichrist).

We also read of "seven mountains on which the woman [that is, the

---

* One of the meanings for the Greek word *anti* is "in the place of."

** Prostitution is a graphic metaphor symbolizing utter unfaithfulness to God. See Jeremiah 3:6-9; Ezekiel 20:30; Hosea 4:15; 5:3; 6:10; 9:1.

prostitute] is seated" (Revelation 17:9). Apparently, the seven mountains symbolize the seven kingdoms and their kings mentioned in verse 10. Mountains often symbolize kingdoms in Scripture (Psalm 30:7; Jeremiah 51:25; Daniel 2:44-45).

These seven kingdoms refer to the seven great world empires—Egypt, Assyria, Babylon, Medo-Persia, Greece, Rome, and that of the antichrist. The biblical text tells us that five of these kingdoms have fallen, one still exists, and one is yet to come (Revelation 17:10). More specifically, at the time of John's writing, the Egyptian, Assyrian, Babylonian, Medo-Persian, and Greek empires had already fallen. Rome, however, still existed, and the antichrist's kingdom was yet to come. The Bible thus indicates that false and paganized religion affected *all* these empires.

Based on clues in Revelation 17, we infer that this apostate religious system will be in force in the first half of the tribulation period and will have a worldwide impact (see verse 15). It will also be utterly unfaithful to the truth (a "harlot"—verses 1,5,15-16), will exercise powerful political clout (verses 12-13), will seem outwardly glorious while being inwardly corrupt (implied in verse 4), and will persecute new believers during the first half of the tribulation period (see verse 6).

It is instructive to compare Revelation 17 with other key verses that relate to this end-times false religious system. To begin, assuming the truth of pretribulationism, the rapture of the church occurs before the tribulation period (Romans 5:9; 1 Thessalonians 1:9-10; 5:9; Revelation 3:10), so all so-called Christians who are left behind will be apostates and may form the core of this end-times false religious system (see 2 Thessalonians 2:8-12). We should also keep in mind that the spirit of antichrist is already at work (1 John 4:3) promoting apostasy and unbelief among liberal Christians and others. The massive apostasy already evident in churches today may be setting the stage for this end-times false religious system.

The false prophet will force these apostates to accept and worship the antichrist (see 1 Timothy 4:1-4; 2 Timothy 3:1-5; 4:1-4; 2 Peter 2:1; 1 John 2:18-19; Jude 4; Revelation 17:1-6). He will force everyone to receive a mark on the right hand or the forehead, without which they cannot buy or sell (Revelation 13:17). This squeeze play will force human beings to make a choice: Worship the antichrist or starve!

THE DESTRUCTION OF THE FALSE RELIGIOUS SYSTEM

Revelation 17:16-18 reveals that the ten kings who are under the antichrist's authority will destroy the false world church.

> The ten horns that you saw, they and the beast will hate the prostitute. They will make her desolate and naked, and devour her flesh and burn her up with fire, for God has put it into their hearts to carry out his purpose by being of one mind and handing over their royal power to the beast, until the words of God are fulfilled.

This passage indicates that the beast—that is, the antichrist—and the ten kings who submit to his authority will bring ruination upon the prostitute, or false religious system. The text does not indicate when this event will take place. However, it seems most logical and coherent to place it halfway through the tribulation period, when the beast will assume the role of world dictator by proclamation (see Daniel 9:27; Matthew 24:15). This means that the antichrist will come into world domination politically and religiously at the same time, demanding even to be worshipped (Daniel 11:36-38; 2 Thessalonians 2:4; Revelation 13:8,15).

The false religious system that dominated during the first half of the tribulation will be obliterated when the antichrist takes the religious center stage. The final world religion will involve worship of the antichrist.

THE ANTICHRIST AND GOD'S TWO WITNESSES

During the tribulation period, God will raise up two mighty witnesses who will testify to the true God. Their astounding power reminds us of Elijah (1 Kings 17; Malachi 4:5) and Moses (Exodus 7–11). In the Old Testament, two witnesses were required to confirm testimony (see Deuteronomy 17:6; 19:15; see also Matthew 18:16; John 8:17; Hebrews 10:28). These two witnesses will confirm God's truth to those living in tribulation times. They will fearlessly proclaim God's judgment, wrath, and vengeance as well as the need for repentance.

> I will grant authority to my two witnesses, and they will prophesy for 1,260 days, clothed in sackcloth.
>
> These are the two olive trees and the two lampstands that stand before the Lord of the earth. And if anyone would harm them, fire pours from their mouth and consumes their foes. If anyone would harm them, this is how he is doomed to be killed. They have the power to shut the sky, that no rain may fall during the days of their prophesying, and they have power over the waters to turn them into blood and to strike the earth with every kind of plague, as often as they desire (Revelation 11:3-6).

These witnesses will wear clothing made of goat or camel hair, garments that symbolically express mourning and grief over the wretched condition and lack of repentance in the world. One Bible expositor suggests that these two witnesses "will serve as the conscience of the world and will be hated by most people."[1] The olive trees and lampstands symbolize the light of spiritual revival. Eventually, at the end of the tribulation, Israel will indeed experience national revival, but many other people will want no such revival.

The miracles will serve to authenticate these witnesses. In both the Old and New Testaments, God often used miracles to authenticate His messengers. As one expositor puts it, "In the Tribulation time when the world is overrun by supernatural demonic activity, false religion, murder, sexual perversion, and rampant wickedness, the supernatural signs performed by the two witnesses will mark them as true prophets of God."[2]

I mentioned earlier that many expositors believe the two witnesses will actually be Moses and Elijah. Here are some reasons why.

- In the tribulation, God deals with the Jews, just as He did in the first 69 weeks of Daniel. Moses and Elijah are unquestionably the two most influential figures in Jewish history. It would thus make good sense that they be on the scene during the tribulation period.

- Both Old Testament and Jewish tradition expected Moses (Deuteronomy 18:15,18) and Elijah (Malachi 4:5) to return in the future.

- Moses and Elijah appeared on the mount of transfiguration with Jesus. This shows their centrality. It would be appropriate for them to be on the scene during the future tribulation period as well.

- The miracles portrayed in Revelation 11 are very similar to those Moses and Elijah performed in Old Testament times (see Exodus 7–11; 1 Kings 17; Malachi 4:5).

- John MacArthur makes this note: "[Both Moses and Elijah] left the earth in unusual ways. Elijah never died, but was transported to heaven in a fiery chariot (2 Kings 2:11-12), and God supernaturally buried Moses' body in a secret location (Deut. 34:5-6; Jude 9)."[3]

Factors such as these have led Bible expositor Walter Price to make this suggestion:

> In those [tribulation] days God will send two of his great-est servants: Moses, the liberator, the spiritual legislator of Israel; and Elijah, one of the greatest of the prophets. Each of these Old Testament figures saved Israel from bondage and idolatry during their respective days upon earth in Old Testament times. They will appear again to warn Israel and to keep many in the nation from total capitulation to the cult of the beast.[4]

Other expositors suggest that perhaps the two witnesses will be Enoch and Elijah. David Reagan explains this view:

> [Both Enoch and Elijah] were men of righteousness who were raptured to Heaven. Neither experienced death. Both were prophets, and one was a Gentile (Enoch) and the other was a Jew (Elijah)…This was the unanimous opinion of the Church Fathers during the first three hundred years of the Church. All of them identified the two witnesses in their writings as Enoch and Elijah.[5]

It is suggested that perhaps God will ordain one of the witnesses to speak to the Jews and the other witness to speak to the Gentiles.

Still other expositors, such as John F. Walvoord, say that these two witnesses are not biblical personalities of the past. "While there is room for considerable discussion of these various views, the fact is that the passage does not identify the two witnesses, and they probably do not have historic identification."[6] Bible expositor Thomas Constable con-curs. "I agree with those who believe that they will be individuals liv-ing at this time rather than former prophets brought back to earth for this ministry (cf. Matt. 11:14)."[7]

Regardless of their actual identity, the time frame of these two witness—1260 days—measures out to precisely three and a half years. It is not clear from Revelation 11 whether this is the first or second half of the tribulation. It may be best to conclude that the two witnesses do their miraculous work during the first half, for the antichrist's execution of them seems to fit best with other events that will transpire in the middle of the tribulation, such as the antichrist's exaltation of himself to godhood. Moreover, the resurrection of the two witnesses—after being dead for three days—would make a bigger impact on the world in the middle of the tribulation than at the end, just prior to the glorious second coming of Christ.

Before the antichrist executes the two witnesses, God supernaturally sustains and protects them during the years of their ministry. This is similar to the way God providentially protected Jesus during the years of His ministry.

> The Antichrist will be powerless against them until the three-and-one-half years of their prophetic witness is finished. Finally he will be able to kill them—just as the antagonists of Jesus were powerless against his prophetic witness during the three-and-one-half years of his ministry on earth. When Jesus' ministry was finished, then his enemies could take Him. But not before. When the witness of [these two] is done, then they will be killed. However, just as with the Lord Jesus Christ, they too will rise again and ascend into heaven.[8]

Scripture describes in detail the martyrdom of the two witnesses.

> When they have finished their testimony, the beast that rises from the bottomless pit will make war on them and conquer them and kill them, and their dead bodies will lie in the street of the great city that symbolically is called Sodom and Egypt, where their Lord was crucified. For three and a half days some from the peoples and tribes and languages and nations will gaze at their dead bodies and refuse to let them be placed in a tomb, and those who

> dwell on the earth will rejoice over them and make merry
> and exchange presents, because these two prophets had
> been a torment to those who dwell on the earth. But after
> the three and a half days a breath of life from God entered
> them, and they stood up on their feet, and great fear fell on
> those who saw them. Then they heard a loud voice from
> heaven saying to them, "Come up here!" And they went
> up to heaven in a cloud, and their enemies watched them
> (Revelation 11:7-12).

Only when the two witnesses have finished their ministry will God
sovereignly permit the beast to kill them. They will not die prematurely.
All goes according to God's divine plan.

The bodies of the witnesses lie lifeless in Jerusalem. Jerusalem is fig-
uratively called "Sodom and Egypt" because of the people's apostasy
and rejection of God. "The description of Jerusalem as no better than
Sodom and Egypt was to show that the once holy city had become no
better than places which were known for their hatred of the true God
and His Word."[9]

How will "the peoples and tribes and languages and nations" gaze
at the dead witnesses for three days? Only modern technology—television and the Internet—can explain how the whole world will be able
to watch all of this, as Tim LaHaye and Jerry Jenkins explain.

> It is now possible for CNN (or its successor) to let the
> world view the dead bodies of the two prophets of God
> killed by the Antichrist in the middle of the Tribulation.
> We are the first generation ever to have that televising
> capability! The prophetic significance of this fact cannot
> be over-exaggerated. For the first time in history man has
> the technology to fulfill that Revelation prophecy. This, of
> course, did not take God by surprise—over nineteen hun-
> dred years ago He prophesied that such an event would be
> shared worldwide.[10]

In biblical times, the refusal to bury a corpse was a way of showing
contempt (see Acts 14:19; see also Deuteronomy 21:22-23). By leaving

the dead bodies in the street, the people of the world render the greatest possible insult to God's spokesmen. "This was the worst indignity that someone could perpetrate on a person in biblical times (cf. Ps. 79:2-3)."[11] It is equivalent to the people of the world collectively spitting upon the corpses.

Moreover, the people of the world have something like a Christmas celebration when the witnesses are put to death. They exchange presents, apparently in relief that the witnesses are no longer around. Based on biblical history, it seems that the only prophets people love are dead ones.

> This is the only instance of rejoicing during the Tribulation recorded in this book. It reflects the widespread wickedness of that day (cf. 1 Kings 18:17; 21:20). Earth-dwellers will celebrate because they do not have to listen to messages from God any longer. This will be the world's last great Mardi Gras type celebration.[12]

But then "a breath of life from God entered them, and they stood up on their feet, and great fear fell on those who saw them" (see Genesis 2:7). The Christmas celebration quickly gives way to fear as people witness this mighty act of God. The lifeless corpses suddenly stand up in full view of television and Internet feeds. Clips of this event will no doubt be replayed over and over again through various media. It will no doubt go viral on the Internet. This resurrection and ascension of the two witnesses serves as a huge exclamation point to their prophetic words throughout the three and a half years of their ministry.

Following this ascension, the city of Jerusalem—where the murder will take place and where the bodies will be displayed—will receive a sudden judgment (Revelation 11:13). Jerusalem will suffer an immense earthquake that will destroy one-tenth of the city and kill 7000 inhabitants. After witnessing this, many will give glory to God. This does not necessarily mean they will all become believers, but they will at least acknowledge God's hand in these events.

Some scholars suggest that the ministry, death, and resurrection of the two prophetic witnesses (seen around the world through television and the Internet) and the verbal witness of God's 144,000 Jewish evangelists will expose millions of souls to the truth about God. How wonderful that despite the horrific efforts of the antichrist and the false prophet to promote false religion, God will give a powerful testimony of Himself during the tribulation. Let's never forget that God has no pleasure in the death of the wicked (Ezekiel 18:32; 33:11) but rather desires that all people be saved (see 2 Peter 3:9). Despite the hardness of heart of many people during those days, many will nevertheless turn to the Lord and be saved. We know this to be true, for by the time the Lord comes again at the second coming, Christ will invite all believers who have survived the woes of the tribulation period into His millennial kingdom (see Matthew 25:31-46).

THE MARK OF
THE BEAST

In Revelation 13, we read that the diabolical duo—the antichrist and the false prophet—will subjugate the entire world so that no one who does not receive the mark of the beast will be able to buy or sell.

> [The false prophet] causes all, both small and great, both rich and poor, both free and slave, to be marked on the right hand or the forehead, so that no one can buy or sell unless he has the mark, that is, the name of the beast or the number of its name. This calls for wisdom: let the one who has understanding calculate the number of the beast, for it is the number of a man, and his number is 666 (Revelation 13:16-18).

The book of Revelation reveals that followers of both the antichrist *and* Jesus Christ will have identifying marks during the tribulation period. Revelation 14:1 tells us: "Then I looked, and behold, on Mount Zion stood the Lamb, and with him 144,000 who had his [the Lamb, Jesus Christ's] name and his Father's name written on their foreheads." It would seem that the antichrist's mark is a parody of God's sealing of the 144,000 witnesses of Revelation 7 and 14.

God's seal of His witnesses most likely is invisible and for the purpose of protection from the Antichrist. On the other hand, Antichrist offers protection from the wrath of God—a promise he cannot deliver—and his mark is visible and external…For the only time in history, an outward indication will identify those who reject Christ and His gospel of forgiveness of sins.[1]

Receiving the mark of the beast is a serious business. "If anyone worships the beast and its image and receives a mark on his forehead or on his hand, he also will drink the wine of God's wrath, poured full strength into the cup of his anger, and he will be tormented with fire and sulfur in the presence of the holy angels and in the presence of the Lamb" (Revelation 14:9-10). We are likewise told that "the first angel went and poured out his bowl on the earth, and harmful and painful sores came upon the people who bore the mark of the beast and worshiped its image" (Revelation 16:2).

Such words are sobering. Any who express loyalty to the antichrist and his cause will suffer the wrath of our holy and just God. How awful it will be for these to experience the full force of God's divine anger and unmitigated vengeance (see Psalm 75:8; Isaiah 51:17; Jeremiah 25:15-16).

In contrast, believers in the Lord Jesus Christ will refuse the mark of the beast and choose death instead. "I saw the souls of those who had been beheaded for the testimony of Jesus and for the word of God, and who had not worshiped the beast or its image and had not received its mark on their foreheads or their hands. They came to life and reigned with Christ for a thousand years" (Revelation 20:4).

WHAT IS THE MARK?

During the future seven-year tribulation period, human beings will somehow be branded, just as animals today are branded and as slaves were once branded by their slave owners. We cannot be certain, however, about how the number 666 relates specifically to the antichrist or his mark.

For centuries, Bible interpreters have offered many suggestions as to the meaning of 666. According to one popular theory, the number

7 is a number of perfection, and the number 777 reflects the perfect Trinity, so perhaps 666 points to a being who aspires to perfect deity but never attains it. (In reality, the antichrist is ultimately just a man, though influenced and possibly indwelt by Satan.)

Others have suggested that perhaps the number refers to a specific man—such as the Roman emperor Nero. It is suggested that if Nero's name is translated into the Hebrew language, the numerical value of its letters is 666. Some suggest that the antichrist will be a man like Nero of old. Of course, all this is highly speculative. The truth is, Scripture does not clearly define what is meant by 666. Interpreting this verse therefore involves some guesswork.

One thing is certain. In some way that is presently unknown to us, this number will be a crucial part of the antichrist's identification. It is sobering to realize that receiving the mark of the beast is apparently an unpardonable sin (Revelation 14:9-10). The decision to receive the mark is an irreversible decision. Once made, there is no turning back.

Receiving the mark signifies approval of the antichrist as a leader and agreement with his purpose. No one takes this mark accidentally. One must volitionally choose to do so, with all the facts on the table. It will be a deliberate choice with eternal consequences. Those who choose to receive the mark will do so with the full knowledge of what they have done.

The choice will cause a radical polarization. There is no possible middle ground. One chooses either for or against the antichrist, for or against God. People in our present day may think they can avoid God and His demands on their lives by feigning neutrality, but no such neutrality will be possible during the tribulation, for one's very survival will be determined by a decision for or against God. One must choose to either receive the mark and live (being able to buy and sell) or reject the mark and face suffering and death. One must choose to follow antichrist and eat well or reject the antichrist and starve.

A COMMERCE PASSPORT

The mark of the beast will be a commerce passport during the future tribulation period.

> [It] will be given to all who submit themselves to the
> authority of the Antichrist and accept him as god. The
> mark will serve as a passport for business…They will be
> able to neither buy nor sell anything unless they have the
> mark…Only those who have this number will be permit-
> ted to work, to buy, to sell, or simply to make a living.[2]

This mark will apparently be required during the second half of the tribulation period.

Prophecy scholar Mark Hitchcock suggests that there is ancient historical precedence for such a mark.[3] For example, he points to Ezekiel 9:4: "The LORD said to him, 'Pass through the city, through Jerusalem, and put a mark on the foreheads of the men who sigh and groan over all the abominations that are committed in it.'" In this context, the mark on the forehead was one of preservation, just as the blood on the doorposts spared the Israelites from death during the tenth plague that was inflicted on the Egyptians (see Exodus 12:21-29).

Such a mark was also used in connection with pagans and false deities in ancient times, as Bible scholar Robert Thomas explains.

> The mark must be some sort of branding similar to that
> given soldiers, slaves, and temple devotees in John's day.
> In Asia Minor, devotees of pagan religions delighted in
> the display of such a tattoo as an emblem of ownership
> by a certain god. In Egypt, Ptolemy Philopator I branded
> Jews, who submitted to registration, with an ivy leaf in
> recognition of their Dionysian worship (cf. 3 Mace. 2:29).
> This meaning resembles the long-time practice of carrying
> signs to advertise religious loyalties (cf. Isa. 44:5) and fol-
> lows the habit of branding slaves with the name or special
> mark of their owners (cf. Gal. 6:17). *Charagma* ("mark")
> was a [Greek] term for the images or names of emperors
> on Roman coins, so it fittingly could apply to the beast's
> emblem put on people.[4]

John MacArthur offers a similar note.

In the Roman Empire, this was a normal identifying symbol, or brand, that slaves and soldiers bore on their bodies. Some of the ancient mystical cults delighted in such tattoos, which identified members with a form of worship. Antichrist will have a similar requirement, one that will need to be visible on the hand or forehead.[5]

The mark of the beast will serve to indicate that one is religiously orthodox—that is, orthodox as defined by the antichrist and the false prophet, as David Jeremiah explains. "The mark will allow the Antichrist's followers to buy and sell because it identifies them as religiously orthodox—submissive followers of the Beast and worshipers of his image. Those without the mark are forbidden to buy because they are identified as traitors."[6] So, though receiving the mark is essentially a spiritual decision, it will have life-and-death economic consequences.

TECHNOLOGY AND THE MARK

Though I believe that modern technology will make it possible for the antichrist and false prophet to bring about a cashless society and then control all commerce on earth, we must differentiate between this technology and the mark of the beast, for the technology itself is not the mark. I make this point because some prophecy expositors in the past have claimed that the mark will be a high-tech chip inserted under the skin, a barcode on the hand or the forehead, some kind of universal product code, or some other such technology.

This is not the case. The mark itself will identify allegiance to the antichrist, but that is separate and distinct from the technology that enables him to enforce his economic system. My former prophecy mentor John F. Walvoord comments on how technology will enable such economical control, based on whether people have received the mark.

> There is no doubt that with today's technology, a world ruler, who is in total control, would have the ability to keep a continually updated census of all living persons and know day-by-day precisely which people had pledged their allegiance to him and received the mark and which had not.[7]

It is highly likely that "chip implants, scan technology, and biometrics will be used as tools to enforce his policy that one cannot buy or sell without the mark."[8]

Notice that this mark will be *on* people, not *in* them (like some kind of microchip). It will be on the right hand or forehead and will be visible to the eye (perhaps like a tattoo), not hidden beneath the skin. It will be universally rejected by believers in God but universally accepted by those who choose against God.

END-TIMES INFLATION AND FAMINE

I would be remiss to discuss the economics of the end times without noting that during the tribulation, there will be war, severe inflation, and famine. Because of widespread famine, people will be all the more motivated to receive the mark of the beast so they can buy or sell food. Let's consider the details by taking a brief look at the four horsemen of the apocalypse.

The First Horseman

The four horsemen of the apocalypse relate to the seal judgments that are poured out on humankind during the tribulation. We first read of a person riding a white horse (Revelation 6:2). Some have speculated that perhaps the rider is Jesus Christ because Jesus rides a white horse in Revelation 19:11. However, the contexts are entirely different. In Revelation 19 Christ returns to the earth as a conqueror on a horse at the end of the tribulation. By contrast, Revelation 6 refers to the beginning of the tribulation, and the rider on the white horse (along with his three fellow riders) is associated with the seal judgments. Most scholars believe the rider of the white horse in Revelation 6:2 is none other than the antichrist (Daniel 9:26). The crown suggests that this individual is a ruler. The bow without an arrow may symbolically reveal that the antichrist will initially establish his world government without warfare. His government seems to begin with a time of peace, but it is short-lived, for destruction will surely follow (see 1 Thessalonians 5:3).

The Second Horseman

A second horse is mentioned in Revelation 6:3-4 and it is red—a color that represents bloodshed, killing with the sword, and war (see also Matthew 24:6-7). The rider carries a large sword. These verses symbolize that man's efforts at bringing about peace will be utterly frustrated, for peace will be taken from the entire earth. As bad as this will be, however, it will only represent the initial "birth pangs" of what is yet to come upon the earth (see Matthew 24:8; Mark 13:7-8; Luke 21:9). Of course, history tells us that war always brings economic instability and food shortages.

The Third Horseman

A third horse mentioned in Revelation 6:5-6 is black. The rider is carrying a pair of scales in his hand. This apparently symbolizes famine and death, for the prices for wheat and barley are extravagantly high, requiring a full day's wages just to buy a few meals (see Lamentations 5:8-10). Such a famine would be expected following global war.

There will be runaway inflation during this time. The buying power of money will drop dramatically.

> To put it in ordinary language, the situation would be such that one would have to spend a day's wages for a loaf of bread with no money left to buy anything else. The symbolism therefore indicates a time of economic devastation and famine when life will be reduced to the barest necessities.[9]

Things will get so bad that people will be looking for someone to solve the dilemma, and that someone will be the antichrist.

Black is an appropriate color, for it points to the lamentation and sorrow that naturally accompanies extreme deprivation. Black represents hunger in Lamentations 4:8-9 as well: "Now their face is blacker than soot; they are not recognized in the streets; their skin has shriveled on their bones; it has become as dry as wood. Happier were the victims of the sword than the victims of hunger, who wasted away, pierced by lack of the fruits of the field."

Such famine is in keeping with Jesus' own words regarding the end times. He affirmed that the first three birth pangs of the end times will be false messiahs, war, and famine (Matthew 24:5-7). While some of this famine will be due to the outbreak of war (the second horse), some famine may also relate to the fact that those who refuse to take the mark of the beast (the believers in God) will not be permitted to buy or sell, which means they will have much less food than everyone else. As economic outcasts, believers during the tribulation will experience much hunger. By contrast, those who reject God will be motivated to receive the mark of the beast so they can eat. These will be black days indeed.

The Fourth Horseman

A fourth horse mentioned in Revelation 6:7-8 is pale—literally, yellowish green, the color of a corpse. The rider of this horse is appropriately named Death. The death symbolized here seems to be the natural consequence of the previous three judgments. The death toll will be catastrophic—a fourth of earth's population. Woe to those who dwell on the earth during this time!

THE JUDGMENT OF THE NATIONS

Another issue that relates to end-time economics is the judgment of the nations—an event that takes place after the tribulation. This judgment directly relates to the fact that one will not be able to buy or sell in the tribulation period without receiving the mark of the beast (Revelation 13:16-17). I am referring specifically to the "brothers" mentioned in connection with the judgment of the nations in Matthew 25:31-46.

> When the Son of Man comes in his glory, and all the angels with him, then he will sit on his glorious throne. Before him will be gathered all the nations, and he will separate people one from another as a shepherd separates the sheep from the goats. And he will place the sheep on his right, but the goats on the left. Then the King will say to those on his right, "Come, you who are blessed by my Father, inherit the kingdom prepared for you from the foundation

of the world. For I was hungry and you gave me food, I was thirsty and you gave me drink, I was a stranger and you welcomed me, I was naked and you clothed me, I was sick and you visited me, I was in prison and you came to me." Then the righteous will answer him, saying, "Lord, when did we see you hungry and feed you, or thirsty and give you drink? And when did we see you a stranger and welcome you, or naked and clothe you? And when did we see you sick or in prison and visit you?" And the King will answer them, "Truly, I say to you, as you did it to one of the least of these my brothers, you did it to me."

Then he will say to those on his left, "Depart from me, you cursed, into the eternal fire prepared for the devil and his angels. For I was hungry and you gave me no food, I was thirsty and you gave me no drink, I was a stranger and you did not welcome me, naked and you did not clothe me, sick and in prison and you did not visit me." Then they also will answer, saying, "Lord, when did we see you hungry or thirsty or a stranger or naked or sick or in prison, and did not minister to you?" Then he will answer them, saying, "Truly, I say to you, as you did not do it to one of the least of these, you did not do it to me." And these will go away into eternal punishment, but the righteous into eternal life.

Notice the basis of the judgment of these people. One's destiny—entering Christ's kingdom or entering into punishment—hinges on how one treated Christ's brothers.

Who are these brothers? A comparison of this passage with the details of the tribulation as recorded in Revelation 4–19 suggests the possibility that the term *brothers* may refer to the 144,000 (Revelation 7), Christ's Jewish brothers who bear witness of Him during the tribulation. Bible expositor Stan Toussaint, one of my former professors at Dallas Theological Seminary, notes, "It seems best to say that 'brothers of Mine' is a designation of the godly remnant of Israel that will proclaim the gospel of the kingdom unto every nation of the world."[10] Bible expositor Merrill F. Unger writes this concerning the brothers:

They are Jews saved by the preaching of "the gospel of the kingdom" after the rapture of the church (Mt. 24:14). During the tribulation period, God will sovereignly call and save 144,000 Jews...So glorious and wonderful will be the ministry of the 144,000 saved Jews and so faithful will be their powerful testimony, the King on His throne of glory will not be ashamed to call them "My brothers." More than that, He will consider Himself so intimately united to them that what was done or not done to them is the same as being actually done or not done to Himself...The fact that the Lord's brothers endured hunger, thirst, homelessness, nakedness, sickness, and imprisonment suggests their fidelity to their newfound Savior and Lord. They proved their willingness to suffer for Him amid the terrible persecutions and trials of the tribulation through which they passed. They proved their loyalty to their King. He attests His identity with them.[11]

Bible expositor J. Dwight Pentecost, another of my former professors at Dallas Theological Seminary, agrees.

That phrase ["My brothers"] may refer to...the 144,000 of Revelation 7, who will bear witness of Him during the Tribulation. Such ones will be under a death sentence by the beast. They will refuse to carry the beast's mark, and so they will not be able to buy and sell. Consequently, they will have to depend on those to whom they minister for hospitality, food, and support. Only those who receive the message will jeopardize their lives by extending hospitality to the messengers. Therefore what is done for them will be an evidence of their faith in Christ, that is, what is done for them will be done for Christ.[12]

Bible scholar Herman Hoyt also agrees, noting that "an unconverted person would not risk his life to befriend a Jew during the great tribulation; these acts of mercy are therefore evidence of salvation."[13] *The Bible Knowledge Commentary* provides this summary:

The expression "these brothers" must refer to a third group that is neither sheep nor goats. The only possible group would be Jews, physical brothers of the Lord. In view of the distress in the Tribulation period, it is clear that any believing Jew will have a difficult time surviving (cf. 24:15-21). The forces of the world dictator will be doing everything possible to exterminate all Jews (cf. Rev. 12:17). A Gentile going out of his way to assist a Jew in the Tribulation will mean that Gentile has become a believer in Jesus Christ during the Tribulation. By such a stand and action, a believing Gentile will put his life in jeopardy. His works will not save him; but his works will reveal that he is redeemed.[14]

So, then, here is the main point. Prophetic Scripture reveals that even though the antichrist and the false prophet will wield economical control over the world during the tribulation period, God will still be at work. Indeed, God's redeemed will come to the aid of Christ's Jewish brethren as they bear witness to Christ all around the world. Many will still suffer famine and many will die, but there will be a great harvest of souls during this time. Praise the Lord!

MODERN TECHNOLOGIES AND BIBLICAL PROPHECY

In studying Bible prophecy, an important factor to keep in mind is that while the prophecies are quite specific, very often people living during the time of the prophets had no awareness of the providential circumstances that would one day emerge to bring about their fulfillment. For example, Micah 5:2 prophesied that the Messiah would be born in Bethlehem. But Joseph and Mary lived in Nazareth. So why would Joseph and Mary be in Bethlehem?

Luke 2:1 gives us the answer: "In those days a decree went out from Caesar Augustus that all the world should be registered." Verse 3 then tells us that people had to register for this census in their original hometown. Bethlehem is Joseph's hometown. While they were in Bethlehem at the government's request, Mary gave birth to Jesus. In Micah's day, though, people had no idea that a government census would enable the prophecy to be fulfilled. Only God Himself knew that detail.

We might say the same thing about Zechariah 12:10, which speaks of the Messiah as "him whom they have pierced." Zechariah's original hearers may have wondered how the Messiah would be pierced. After all, this prophecy was written hundreds of years before crucifixion was Rome's chosen method of execution. So people in Zechariah's day were unaware of the providential circumstances that would one day emerge to bring about the fulfillment of that prophecy (execution by crucifixion).

Likewise, when the Bible prophesies about the one-world economy, a cashless society, and the antichrist's control of the economy in the tribulation period, it doesn't specifically mention computers or cyberspace or the Internet or biometrics (involving, for example, thumbprint scanners or retina scanners). But very clearly these new technologies, for the first time in human history, make it possible for these prophecies to be fulfilled. Now all becomes clear.

It now seems apparent that a cashless system will be the means by which the antichrist will control who can buy or sell. After all, if the world economy were still cash-based, people anywhere who possessed cash could still buy and sell. It would be impossible for the antichrist to enforce who can buy or sell in such a cash-based society. Only in a cashless world—with a centralized electronic transaction system, where all is controlled electronically—would such control be possible. Thomas Ice and Timothy Demy provide this explanation:

> It is becoming increasingly apparent that today's developing cashless system will become the instrument through which the Antichrist will seek to control all who buy or sell, based upon whether they are a follower of Jesus Christ or a follower of the European ruler, and thus, Satan. It is obvious that any leader wanting to control the world's economy would avail themselves of the power that an electronic cashless system holds as a tool for implementing total control.[15]

Someone once said that prophetic events cast their shadows before them. David Jeremiah draws this conclusion:

> We are on the cutting edge of having all the technology that the Antichrist and False Prophet would need to wire this

world together for their evil purposes. Right now it is well within the range of possibility for a centralized power to gain worldwide control of all banking and purchasing...As we see things that are prophesied for the tribulation period beginning to take shape right now, we are made aware of the fact that surely the Lord's return is not far off.[16]

To learn more about the specific kinds of technologies that relate to our coming cashless society and the mark of the beast, see my book *Cyber Meltdown: Bible Prophecy and the Imminent Threat of Cyberterrorism* (Harvest House, 2011).

THE DEFEAT AND DOOM OF THE ANTICHRIST

The word *Armageddon* literally means "Mount of Megiddo" and refers to a location about 60 miles north of Jerusalem. This is the location of Barak's battle with the Canaanites (Judges 4) and Gideon's battle with the Midianites (Judges 7). This will be the site for the final horrific battles of humankind just prior to the second coming of Jesus Christ (Revelation 16:16).

Napoleon is reported to have once commented that this site is perhaps the greatest battlefield he had ever witnessed. Of course, the battles Napoleon fought will dim in comparison to Armageddon. So horrible will Armageddon be that no one would survive if it were not for Christ coming again (Matthew 24:22). Armageddon will constitute the worst human suffering in the great tribulation.

The campaign of Armageddon includes a number of stages. I will document eight specific stages in this unfolding campaign. In view of all that occurs during Armageddon, it would be wrong to refer to it as the battle of Armageddon, as if it were a single event. Armageddon will involve an extended escalating conflict, and it will be catastrophic. We will see that the antichrist is intimately involved in this escalating conflict.

PHASE 1: THE ANTICHRIST'S ALLIES ASSEMBLE FOR WAR

Scripture reveals that at the end of the tribulation period, the allied armies of the antichrist will gather for the final destruction of the Jews.

> The sixth angel poured out his bowl on the great river Euphrates, and its water was dried up, to prepare the way for the kings from the east. And I saw, coming out of the mouth of the dragon and out of the mouth of the beast and out of the mouth of the false prophet, three unclean spirits like frogs. For they are demonic spirits, performing signs, who go abroad to the kings of the whole world, to assemble them for battle on the great day of God the Almighty. ("Behold, I am coming like a thief! Blessed is the one who stays awake, keeping his garments on, that he may not go about naked and be seen exposed!") And they assembled them at the place that in Hebrew is called Armageddon (Revelation 16:12-16).

Scripture indicates that the assembling of these armies takes place at the unleashing of the sixth bowl judgment. The Euphrates River will be dried up, thereby making it easier for the armies of the east to assemble. The Euphrates River—the longest river of western Asia (almost 1800 miles)—begins in modern-day Turkey, heads toward the Mediterranean Sea, then turns south, flows more than 1000 miles to eventually converge with the Tigris River, and then flows into the Persian Gulf. Many ancient cities, including Ur and Babylon, are located at various points along the river.

Who are the kings of the east? Bible scholars have varying opinions. In fact, a survey of 100 prophecy books reveals more than 50 different interpretations as to who they are. For example, some suggest that it may refer to the seven kings of Daniel 7 that have submitted to the authority of the antichrist. However, prophecy scholar John F. Walvoord provides a different perspective.

> The simplest and best explanation…is that this refers to kings or rulers from the Orient or East who will participate in the final world war. In the light of the context of this

passage indicating the near approach of the second coming
of Christ and the contemporary world situation in which
the Orient today contains a large portion of the world's
population with tremendous military potential, any interpretation other than a literal one does not make sense.[1]

This is what makes the Euphrates River so significant. Indeed, this
river is the primary water boundary between the Holy Land and Asia
to the east. For this reason, theologian Charles Ryrie observes that "the
armies of the nations of the Orient will be aided in their march toward
Armageddon by the supernatural drying up of the Euphrates River."[2]
Interestingly, the drying up of the Euphrates River is predicted in Isaiah 11:15.

The goal of the invading coalition will be to once and for all destroy
the Jewish people. Christian prophecy scholar Arnold Fruchtenbaum
suggests that the satanic trinity will be behind it all.

> The gathering for this final campaign against the Jews is
> clearly the work of the counterfeit trinity. All three mem-
> bers of the counterfeit trinity are involved: the dragon, or
> Satan who is the counterfeit father, the beast [antichrist]
> who is the counterfeit son; and the False Prophet who
> is the counterfeit holy spirit. The summons will be rein-
> forced by demonic activity to make sure that the nations
> will indeed cooperate in assembling their armies together.
> These demonic messengers will be empowered to perform
> signs in order to assure compliance and defeat any reluc-
> tance to fall into line on the part of the other kings.[3]

PHASE 2: BABYLON IS UTTERLY DESTROYED

The second phase of Armageddon will be the destruction of Babylon. Recall that Babylon lay in the land of Shinar (Genesis 10:10). This
influential civilization, ruled by kings and priests, was situated on the
banks of the Euphrates River, a little more than 50 miles south of modern Baghdad. Because of its ideal location, Babylon was an important commercial and trade center in the ancient world. It became a

powerful kingdom under the leadership of Hammurabi (1792–1750 BC).

False religious beliefs have long been a characteristic of Babylon. Like other pagan nations of the Ancient Near East, the Babylonians believed in many false gods and goddesses. These gods were thought to control the entire world of nature, so people who wanted to be successful in life placated the gods. In Babylonian religion, the behavior of the gods was considered unpredictable at best.

Each city in Babylon had a patron god with an accompanying temple. There were also a number of small shrines scattered about each city where people often met to worship various other deities. The chief of the Babylonian gods was Anu, considered the king of heaven, and the patron god of Babylon was Marduk.

The Babylonians were well known for their practice of divination. Astrology can trace its roots back to Babylon around 3000 BC. The ancient Babylonians observed how orderly and rhythmically the planets moved across the sky, and they concluded that the planets were gods of the night. The planets were assigned godlike powers and character and were worshipped. These gods were believed to control the fate of human beings on earth in a broad sense—that is, they controlled the destiny of nations (see Daniel 1:20; 2:2,10,27; 4:7; 5:7,11,15). The priests of Babylon sought to understand and predict the movements of these planets so that perhaps they could use this knowledge beneficially on their nation's behalf. To study and worship these deities, the Babylonians built towers called ziggurats. Apparently, the Tower of Babel was such a ziggurat.

In view of this dire history, it is not surprising that Babylon is often represented in Scripture as being arrayed against God and His people (2 Kings 24:10). In 597 BC, for example, King Nebuchadnezzar took some 3000 Jews into exile in Babylon. Jerusalem and the temple were obliterated (Lamentations 1:1-7). God sovereignly used Babylon as His powerful whipping rod in chastening Israel, but Babylon was to be utterly destroyed by God's hand of judgment for its continual standing against His people (Isaiah 13).

A literal approach to Scripture leads to the conclusion that Babylon will be revived in the end times, rebuilt by the forces of the antichrist (see Revelation 17–18). It may become a worldwide economic and religious center. It is noteworthy that when the late Saddam Hussein was in power, he spent more than a billion dollars in oil money to enhance the city—essentially as a monument to himself.

Fast-forward to the future tribulation period, when we witness an interesting irony. While phase 1 of Armageddon is underway, with the antichrist preparing with his armies to attack Israel, God judges and destroys the antichrist's headquarters of Babylon (see Jeremiah 50:11-27).

Isaiah 13:19 informs us that Babylon's destruction "will be like Sodom and Gomorrah when God overthrew them." Jeremiah 50:40 likewise portrays Babylon's destruction: "As when God overthrew Sodom and Gomorrah and their neighboring cities, declares the LORD, so no man shall dwell there, and no son of man shall sojourn in her." The book of Revelation graphically describes Babylon's destruction.

> Then a mighty angel took up a stone like a great millstone and threw it into the sea, saying, "So will Babylon the great city be thrown down with violence, and will be found no more; and the sound of harpists and musicians, of flute players and trumpeters, will be heard in you no more, and a craftsman of any craft will be found in you no more, and the sound of the mill will be heard in you no more, and the light of a lamp will shine in you no more, and the voice of bridegroom and bride will be heard in you no more, for your merchants were the great ones of the earth, and all nations were deceived by your sorcery. And in her was found the blood of prophets and of saints, and of all who have been slain on earth" (Revelation 18:21-24).

This destruction will come upon Babylon as a direct, decisive judgment from the hand of God. God will settle the score for Babylon's long history of standing against His people of Israel. And just as Babylon showed no mercy to its oppression against Israel in the past, so God will now show no mercy to Babylon during the tribulation.

Thomas Ice and Timothy Demy provide these helpful words regarding how Jews are able to escape from Babylon before judgment falls on the city.

> When Babylon is destroyed, the Antichrist will not be present in the city. He will be told of its destruction by messengers (Jeremiah 50:43; 51:31,32)…The attack will be swift, but there will be some warning or opportunity for Jews who are living in Babylon to flee from the city (Jeremiah 50:6-8,28; 51:5,6). Even in these last days, God will preserve a remnant of His people. These refugees are to go to Jerusalem and tell them of the city's destruction and their escape (Jeremiah 51:10,45,50; Revelation 18:4,5).[4]

This will occur at the very end of the tribulation period.

PHASE 3: JERUSALEM FALLS AND IS RAVAGED

As we have seen, God will destroy the antichrist's capital, Babylon, in phase 2 of Armageddon. However, even the destruction of his capital is not enough to deter him from his goal of destroying the Jewish people. The antichrist and his forces promptly move south to attack Jerusalem. We read about it in Zechariah 12:1-3.

> The burden of the word of the LORD concerning Israel: Thus declares the LORD, who stretched out the heavens and founded the earth and formed the spirit of man within him: "Behold, I am about to make Jerusalem a cup of staggering to all the surrounding peoples. The siege of Jerusalem will also be against Judah. On that day I will make Jerusalem a heavy stone for all the peoples. All who lift it will surely hurt themselves. And all the nations of the earth will gather against it."

Zechariah 14:1-2 adds this:

> Behold, a day is coming for the LORD, when the spoil taken from you will be divided in your midst. For I will gather all

the nations against Jerusalem to battle, and the city shall be taken and the houses plundered and the women raped. Half of the city shall go out into exile, but the rest of the people shall not be cut off from the city.

With heavy losses, Jerusalem will fall and be ravaged. The antichrist's forces gain initial victory. However, as we will see, Israel will soon attain victory through the direct intervention of their Messiah.

PHASE 4: THE ANTICHRIST MOVES SOUTH AGAINST THE REMNANT

Not all of the Jews will be in Jerusalem. Remember that in the middle of the tribulation period, the antichrist will break his covenant with Israel and exalt himself as deity, even putting an image of himself in the Jewish temple. Christ, in His Olivet Discourse, warned of how quickly the Jews must flee for their lives (Matthew 24:16-31). Many of the Jews apparently flee to the deserts and mountains, perhaps in the area of Bozrah (Petra), about 80 miles south of Jerusalem.

This escape from Jerusalem is described in Revelation 12:6: "The woman [a metaphor referring to Israel] fled into the wilderness, where she has a place prepared by God, in which she is to be nourished for 1,260 days." Verse 14 adds, "The woman was given the two wings of the great eagle so that she might fly from the serpent into the wilderness, to the place where she is to be nourished for a time, and times, and half a time" (or three and a half years).

Despite the antichrist's concerted efforts to move against and destroy the remnant, God Himself will be their protector. God Himself promised in Micah 5:12, "I will surely assemble all of you, O Jacob; I will gather the remnant of Israel; I will set them together like sheep in a fold, like a flock in its pasture, a noisy multitude of men." And yet, prior to God's deliverance of His people, the Jews sense impending doom about to come upon them as the forces of the antichrist gather in the rugged wilderness, poised to attack and annihilate them. From an earthly perspective, they are helpless and utterly defenseless. This sets the stage for phase 5 of Armageddon.

PHASE 5: ISRAEL IS THREATENED, DELIVERED, AND REGENERATED

The Jews are endangered, acutely aware of the forces of antichrist that have gathered to destroy them. Their spiritual blindness is removed, and they call out to their Messiah, Jesus Christ. At this point, the remnant experiences national regeneration.

To understand the significance of this, recall that in Romans 11:25 the apostle Paul, himself a Jew who turned to the Messiah, writes, "I want you to understand this mystery, brothers: a partial hardening has come upon Israel, until the fullness of the Gentiles has come in"—that is, until the full number of Gentiles who will be saved have, in fact, become saved. "Israel...pursued a law [literally, 'kept on pursuing a law'—the Mosaic law] that would lead to righteousness [but] did not succeed in reaching that law. Why? Because they did not pursue it by faith, but as if it were based on works. They have stumbled over the stumbling stone" (Romans 9:31-33). The stumbling stone is Jesus Christ.

Put another way, Israel had sought a relationship with God by means of a righteousness earned by keeping the law. Instead of seeking a faith-based relationship with God, they sought to do everything the law prescribed so they could earn a relationship with Him (see Galatians 2:16; 3:2,5,10).

Failure was unavoidable, for attaining a righteousness by observing the law requires perfect obedience (James 2:10), which no man is capable of. To make matters worse, the Jews refused to admit their inability to perfectly keep the law and turn by faith to God for His forgiveness. They rejected Jesus Christ as the Messiah, refusing to turn to Him in faith because He did not fit their preconceived ideas about the Messiah (see, for example, Matthew 12:14,24). They stumbled over Him.

Therefore, a partial judicial blindness or hardness of heart came upon Israel. Israel thus lost her favored position before God, and the gospel was then preached to the Gentiles so the Jews would become jealous and be saved (Romans 11:11). Israel's hardening and casting off is only temporary.

Now fast-forward to the campaign of Armageddon. The armies of the antichrist are gathered in the desert wilderness, poised to attack the Jewish remnant. Desperate, the Jewish leaders call for the people of the nation to repent and turn to God. Their collective repentance takes two days.

> Come, let us return to the LORD; for he has torn us, that he may heal us; he has struck us down, and he will bind us up. After two days he will revive us; on the third day he will raise us up, that we may live before him. Let us know; let us press on to know the LORD; his going out is sure as the dawn; he will come to us as the showers, as the spring rains that water the earth (Hosea 6:1-3).

Prophecy scholar Arnold Fruchtenbaum suggests that just as the Jewish leaders once led the Jewish people to reject Jesus as their Messiah, so now the Jewish leaders will urge repentance and instruct all to turn to Jesus as their Messiah.[5] This the remnant will do, and they will be saved.

This is in keeping with Joel 2:28-29, which informs us that there will be a spiritual awakening of the Jewish remnant. Armageddon seems to be the context in which Israel finally becomes converted (Zechariah 12:2–13:1). In terms of chronology, the restoration of Israel will include the confession of Israel's national sin (Leviticus 26:40-42; Jeremiah 3:11-18; Hosea 5:15), and then Israel will be saved, thereby fulfilling Paul's prophecy in Romans 11:25-27. In dire threat at Armageddon, Israel will plead for their newly found Messiah to return and deliver them (they will "mourn for Him, as one mourns for an only child"—Zechariah 12:10; see also Isaiah 53:1-9; Matthew 23:37-39), at which point their deliverance will surely come (see Romans 10:13-14). Israel's leaders will have finally realized why the tribulation has fallen on them—perhaps due to the Holy Spirit's enlightenment of their understanding of Scripture, or the testimony of the 144,000 Jewish evangelists, or the testimony of the two prophetic witnesses.

Sadly, according to Zechariah 13:7-9, some two-thirds of the Jewish people will lose their lives during the tribulation period. However, one-third—the remnant—will survive, turn to the Lord, and be saved (see Isaiah 64:1-12).

Later, in the millennial kingdom, Israel will experience a full possession of the promised land and the reestablishment of the Davidic throne. It will be a time of physical and spiritual blessing based on the new covenant (Jeremiah 31:31-34).

PHASE 6: THE SECOND COMING OF CHRIST

The prayers of the Jewish remnant are answered! The divine Messiah returns personally and rescues His people from danger. The very same Jesus who ascended into heaven will come again at the second coming (Acts 1:9-11).

The second coming will involve a visible, physical, bodily coming of the glorified Jesus (see 1 Peter 4:13). It will involve "the appearing of the glory of our great God and Savior Jesus Christ" (Titus 2:13; see also 1 Timothy 6:14).

At the time of the second coming, there will be magnificent signs in the heavens (Matthew 24:29-30). Christ will come as the King of kings and Lord of lords, wearing many crowns (representing absolute sovereignty). His eyes will be like blazing fire (Revelation 19:11-16).

Old Testament prophetic Scripture reveals that Jesus returns first to the mountain wilderness of Bozrah, where the Jewish remnant is endangered (Isaiah 34:1-7; 63:1-6; Habakkuk 3:3; Micah 2:12-13). Jesus will confront the antichrist and his forces and slay them with the word of His mouth. The description of the second coming in the book of Revelation makes it clear that the enemies of Christ suffer instant defeat.

> Then I saw heaven opened, and behold, a white horse! The one sitting on it is called Faithful and True, and in righteousness he judges and makes war. His eyes are like a flame of fire, and on his head are many diadems, and he has a name written that no one knows but himself. He is clothed in a robe dipped in blood, and the name by which he is called is The Word of God. And the armies of heaven, arrayed in fine linen, white and pure, were following him on white horses. From his mouth comes a sharp sword with which to strike down the nations, and he will rule them with a rod of iron. He will tread the winepress of the fury of the wrath

of God the Almighty. On his robe and on his thigh he has a name written, King of kings and Lord of lords (Revelation 19:11-16).

It will be a glorious event, and every eye will see Him. "Then will appear in heaven the sign of the Son of Man, and then all the tribes of the earth will mourn, and they will see the Son of Man coming on the clouds of heaven with power and great glory" (Matthew 24:30). "Behold, he is coming with the clouds, and every eye will see him, even those who pierced him, and all tribes of the earth will wail on account of him. Even so. Amen" (Revelation 1:7).

PHASE 7: CHRIST DEFEATS THE ANTICHRIST

Deliverance now comes to the Jewish remnant. As we have seen, the antichrist and his forces are poised for attack against the remnant in the wilderness. The remnant has no chance of survival. The Jewish leaders urge the remnant to repent and turn to Jesus the Messiah. The second coming of Jesus Christ then occurs.

Here, at phase 7 of Armageddon, Christ will defeat those who stand against Israel. The antichrist will be slain. Habakkuk 3:13 prophesies of Christ's victory over the antichrist: "You went out for the salvation of your people, for the salvation of your anointed. You crushed the head of the house of the wicked, laying him bare from thigh to neck." In 2 Thessalonians 2:8 we read of the antichrist, "whom the Lord Jesus will kill with the breath of his mouth and bring to nothing by the appearance of his coming."

The antichrist will be shown to be impotent and powerless in the face of the true Christ. All the forces of the antichrist will also be destroyed from Bozrah all the way back to Jerusalem (Joel 3:12-13; Zechariah 14:12-15; Revelation 14:19-20).

PHASE 8: CHRIST ASCENDS TO THE MOUNT OF OLIVES

In the eighth and final phase of the campaign of Armageddon, Jesus Christ victoriously ascends to the Mount of Olives.

Then the LORD will go out and fight against those nations

as when he fights on a day of battle. On that day his feet shall stand on the Mount of Olives that lies before Jerusalem on the east, and the Mount of Olives shall be split in two from east to west by a very wide valley, so that one half of the Mount shall move northward, and the other half southward (Zechariah 14:3-4).

The seventh angel poured out his bowl into the air, and a loud voice came out of the temple, from the throne, saying, "It is done!" And there were flashes of lightning, rumblings, peals of thunder, and a great earthquake such as there had never been since man was on the earth, so great was that earthquake. The great city was split into three parts, and the cities of the nations fell, and God remembered Babylon the great, to make her drain the cup of the wine of the fury of his wrath. And every island fled away, and no mountains were to be found. And great hailstones, about one hundred pounds each, fell from heaven on people; and they cursed God for the plague of the hail, because the plague was so severe (Revelation 16:17-21).

Clearly, when Christ ascends to the Mount of Olives, some cataclysmic events will bring an end to the tribulation period.

- An earthquake of globally staggering proportions (compare with Revelation 8:5 and 11:19) will be felt around the world. Mountains will be leveled. Islands will vanish. The topography of the earth will be drastically changed.
- Jerusalem will be split into three areas.
- The Mount of Olives will split into two parts, creating a valley.
- There will be a horrific hail storm, and the sun and moon will be darkened (see Joel 3:14-16; Matthew 24:29).

As these horrific events subside, the tribulation period finally comes to a close. But judgments now remain on the horizon prior to the beginning of Christ's millennial kingdom—the judgment of the nations (Matthew 25), the judgment of Israel (Ezekiel 20), and the judgment of the antichrist and the false prophet. (Satan's final judgment will take place at the end of the millennial kingdom.)

THE DESTINY OF THE ANTICHRIST: THE LAKE OF FIRE

In Revelation 19:20 we read that the antichrist and the false prophet—two malevolent foes who come into power during the future tribulation period—will be "thrown alive into the lake of fire that burns with sulfur." This takes place before the beginning of Christ's millennial kingdom—that 1000-year period following the second coming of Christ in which Christ will physically rule on earth from the throne of David.

At the end of the millennial kingdom—1000 years after the antichrist and the false prophet were thrown into the lake of burning sulfur—the devil himself will also be "thrown into the lake of fire and sulfur where the beast and the false prophet were, and they will be tormented day and night for ever and ever" (Revelation 20:10).

Notice that the antichrist and false prophet are not burned up or annihilated at the time the devil is thrown into the lake of burning sulfur. They are still burning after 1000 years. These sinister beings, along with unbelievers of all ages, will be tormented day and night forever (Revelation 20:14-15).

> It is appropriate…that the members of this satanic trinity share the same destiny. At the conclusion of the Battle of Armageddon the False Prophet and the Antichrist are plucked alive from the battlefield and tossed bodily into the lake of fire, where they are joined a thousand years later by Satan. There they will (together, but very much alone) be tormented day and night forever and ever—not ruling over the damned, as some think, but "punished with everlasting destruction from the presence of the Lord and from the glory of His power" (2 Thessalonians 1:9).[6]

IS THE ANTICHRIST ALIVE TODAY?

Many of the prophetic signs of the times seem to be coming to pass in our own day, or at least the stage is being set for the fulfillment of some of these signs. Consequently, many believe the antichrist may be alive in our world today. Let's give brief consideration to some of these signs.

In our study, a sign of the times is an event of prophetic significance that points to the end times. In a way, signs might be considered God's intel in advance. Today, powerful nations have their own intelligence agencies that provide intel to their respective governments. For example, the United States has the Central Intelligence Agency (CIA). We might say that the signs of the times found in the pages of prophetic Scripture constitute God's intel regarding what the world will look like as we enter into the end times.

Many of the prophetic signs recorded in the pages of Scripture relate directly to the future seven-year tribulation period. Recall that in Matthew 24:3, the disciples asked Jesus, "What will be the sign of your coming and of the close of the age?" Jesus proceeded to reveal a number of signs of the times that will predominate in the years prior to the second coming—that is, during the tribulation period.

Jesus wanted His followers to be aware of these signs and to become thoughtful observers of the times. To the Sadducees and Pharisees, who rejected Him as the divine Messiah, He said, "When it is evening, you say, 'It will be fair weather, for the sky is red.' And in the morning, 'It will be stormy today, for the sky is red and threatening.' You know how to interpret the appearance of the sky, but you cannot interpret the signs of the times" (Matthew 16:1-3).

These Jewish leaders were supposed to be experts in interpreting the Old Testament Scriptures. In messianic passages like Isaiah 11 and 35, we are told that when the Messiah would come, the lame would walk, the deaf would hear, and the blind would see. When Jesus came on the scene, this is precisely what happened. Therefore, these Jewish leaders should have been able to read the signs of the times and recognize that Jesus indeed was the promised Messiah. But they were blind to this reality. The lesson we learn from this is that Jesus calls you and me to be thoughtful observers of the times. We are to be aware of the biblical signs and keep a close eye on unfolding events in the world so we notice the correlations.

We are never to set dates because we do not know the specific day or hour of Jesus' coming (Matthew 24:36; Acts 1:7). But we can know the general season of the Lord's return by virtue of the signs of the times. Jesus instructed His followers to pay attention: "From the fig tree learn its lesson: as soon as its branch becomes tender and puts out its leaves, you know that summer is near. So also, when you see all these things, you know that he is near, at the very gates" (Matthew 24:32-33).

Jesus indicates in this passage that God has revealed certain things in prophecy that ought to cause people who know the Bible to understand that a fulfillment of prophecy is taking place—or perhaps, in our present day, that the stage is being set for a prophecy to eventually be fulfilled. Jesus is thus informing His followers to become accurate observers of the times so that when biblical prophecies are fulfilled, or the stage is being set, they will recognize what is happening (see also Luke 21:25-28).

GEOLOGICAL AND METEOROLOGICAL SIGNS OF THE END TIMES

Scripture reveals that the future tribulation period will include a great increase in frequency and intensity of earthquakes, famine, pestilence, and signs in the heavens (Matthew 24:7). Consider Luke 21:11, for example: "There will be great earthquakes, and in various places famines and pestilences. And there will be terrors and great signs from heaven." Such things are the beginning of birth pangs (Matthew 24:8). Just as birth pangs increase in frequency and intensity, so will these signs.

Most scholars believe these signs refer to the future seven-year tribulation period. However, just as tremors (or foreshocks) often occur before major earthquakes, so preliminary manifestations of some of these signs may emerge prior to the tribulation period. Someone said that prophecies cast their shadows before them. I think this is true. Prophecies that relate specifically to the tribulation are presently casting their shadows before them in our day. That's why it's important to be thoughtful observers!

Luke 21:11 mentions terrors but does not tell us specifically what these events are. But we can't help but notice that global terrorism has never been more prominent and is likely to get even worse.

What about the signs in the heavens? Scholars have debated what this may refer to, but they likely include strange weather patterns, falling stars, a darkening of the moon and other celestial bodies (during the tribulation period), and large bodies striking the earth. The reference to "wormwood" in Revelation 8:10-12 is likely an example.

> The third angel blew his trumpet, and a great star fell from heaven, blazing like a torch, and it fell on a third of the rivers and on the springs of water. The name of the star is Wormwood. A third of the waters became wormwood, and many people died from the water, because it had been made bitter.
>
> The fourth angel blew his trumpet, and a third of the sun was struck, and a third of the moon, and a third of the stars, so that a third of their light might be darkened, and a third of the day might be kept from shining, and likewise a third of the night.

It would appear that the fall of this "star" will in fact be a near-extinction-level "deep impact" of a large meteor or an asteroid that strikes the earth with catastrophic force. It will look like a star because it will burst into flames as it plummets through earth's atmosphere. It results in turning a third of the waters bitter so that people who drink it die. It may contaminate this large volume of water by the residue that results from the meteor disintegrating as it blasts through earth's atmosphere. Or it may be that the meteor plummets into the head-waters from which some of the world's major rivers and underground water sources flow, thereby spreading the poisonous water to many people on earth.

This deep impact may well be what ultimately causes a reduction in light from the sun and other celestial bodies. Following the impact, a catastrophic level of dust will be released into the atmosphere, thereby blocking light.

MORAL SIGNS OF THE END TIMES

The world will take on a particularly dark moral climate in the end times.

> But understand this, that in the last days there will come times of difficulty. For people will be lovers of self, lovers of money, proud, arrogant, abusive, disobedient to their parents, ungrateful, unholy, heartless, unappeasable, slanderous, without self-control, brutal, not loving good, treacherous, reckless, swollen with conceit, lovers of pleasure rather than lovers of God, having the appearance of godliness, but denying its power. Avoid such people (2 Timothy 3:1-5).

Notice that in the last days, people will increase their love of self (we might call this *humanism*), love of money (we might call this *materialism*), and love of pleasure (we might call this *hedonism*). Humanism, materialism, and hedonism are three of the most prominent philosophies in our world today and often go hand in hand.

Jesus describes the end times in similar fashion.

> Because lawlessness will be increased, the love of many will grow cold...As were the days of Noah, so will be the coming of the Son of Man. For as in those days before the flood they were eating and drinking, marrying and giving

in marriage, until the day when Noah entered the ark, and they were unaware until the flood came and swept them all away, so will be the coming of the Son of Man (Matthew 24:12,37-39).

This passage specifically refers to the future tribulation period, but I cannot help but notice that we see the attitude Jesus described even in our own day. People are merrily going about their way, seemingly with no concern for the things of God.

As a thoughtful observer of the times, I believe America is presently engulfed in a moral crisis. The moral fiber of this country is eroding before our very eyes, and if the trend continues, it is only a matter of time before the country capitulates. Today there is widespread acceptance of homosexuality. Abortion—especially the barbaric practice of partial-birth abortion—continues to be widely practiced, with some 50 million unborn babies murdered since the enactment of *Roe v. Wade* in 1973.

Pornography is freely available on the Internet, enslaving millions of sex addicts. Drug abuse and alcoholism are pervasive as well among both teenagers and adults. Promiscuity, fornication, and adultery continue to escalate, bringing about the carnage of sexually transmitted diseases.

A number of prophecy experts have also noted that the family unit seems to be disintegrating before our eyes. The divorce rate is around 50 percent, and many today are living together outside of marriage. Out-of-wedlock births have escalated to new highs, with 40 percent of women not being married when they give birth. As well, gay couples are adopting children, raising them in a homosexual atmosphere. The moral atmosphere is darkening by the day.

RELIGIOUS SIGNS OF THE END TIMES

There are also many religious signs that point to the imminent end times.

The emergence of false christs. Jesus warned of the rise of religious peril in the end times in Matthew 24:24: "For false christs and false prophets will arise and perform great signs and wonders, so as to lead astray, if possible, even the elect" (see also Mark 13:22). The apostle Paul also warned of a different Jesus (2 Corinthians 11:4). The danger, of course, is that a counterfeit Jesus who preaches a counterfeit gospel yields a counterfeit salvation (compare with Galatians 1:8). There are no exceptions to this maxim. Even in our day, we witness an unprecedented rise in false christs and self-constituted messiahs affiliated with the kingdom of the cults and the occult. This will no doubt continue as we move further into the end times.

The emergence of false prophets and teachers. Scripture often warns believers against false prophets and false teachers. Why so? Because it is entirely possible that God's own people will be deceived. Ezekiel 34:1-7, for example, indicates that God's sheep can be abused and led astray by wicked shepherds. Jesus Himself warned His followers, "Beware of false prophets, who come to you in sheep's clothing but inwardly are ferocious wolves" (Matthew 7:15). Why would Jesus warn His followers to beware if they could not be deceived? Luke and the apostle Paul likewise warned their readers that Christians can be deceived (Acts 20:28-30; 2 Corinthians 11:2-3). The apostle John exhorts believers to test those who claim to be prophets (1 John 4:1-3).

Scripture explains how to recognize false prophets.

- They give prophecies that do not come true (Deuteronomy 18:21-22).

- They sometimes entice people to follow false gods or idols (Deuteronomy 13:1-3).

- They often deny the deity of Jesus Christ (Colossians 2:8-9).

- They sometimes deny the humanity of Jesus Christ (1 John 4:1-2).

- They sometimes advocate abstaining from certain foods for spiritual reasons (1 Timothy 4:3-4).

- They sometimes deprecate or deny the need for marriage (1 Timothy 4:3).

- They often promote immorality (Jude 4-7).

- They often encourage legalistic self-denial (Colossians 2:16-23).

If a so-called prophet says anything that clearly contradicts any part of God's Word, his teachings should be rejected (Acts 17:11; 1 Thessalonians 5:21). All of this is particularly relevant to the rise of the false prophet in the end times.

The emergence of false apostles. Scripture warns of false apostles who are "deceitful workmen, disguising themselves as apostles of Christ" (2 Corinthians 11:13). The two key characteristics we see here are that these individuals deceive people doctrinally and that they pretend to be true apostles of Jesus Christ. In Revelation 2:2, we read Christ's commendation to the church of Ephesus for taking a stand against false apostles: "I know your works, your toil and your patient endurance, and how you cannot bear with those who are evil, but have tested those who call themselves apostles and are not, and found them false."

How can we test the claims of apostles? The Word of God is our sole doctrinal litmus test. Like the ancient Bereans, all Christians should make a regular habit of testing all things against Scripture (Acts 17:11), for Scripture is our only infallible barometer of truth. No true apostle will ever say anything that contradicts the Word of God (see Galatians 1:8).

The escalation of apostasy. Apostasy is a theological term that derives from the Greek word *apostasia.* It literally means "falling away." The word refers to a determined, willful defection from the faith or an abandonment of the faith. In the New Testament, Judas Iscariot's betrayal of Jesus for 30 pieces of silver is a classic example of apostasy and its effects (see Matthew 26:14-25,47-56; 27:3-10). Other examples include Hymenaeus and Alexander, who made "shipwreck" of their faith (1 Timothy 1:19-20), and Demas, who turned away from the apostle Paul because of his love for the present world (2 Timothy 4:10).

False teachers often encourage apostasy (Matthew 24:11; Galatians 2:4). Apostasy typically escalates during times of trial (Matthew 24:9-10; Luke 8:13). Apostasy certainly occurred in Old Testament times among the Israelites (Joshua 22:22; 2 Chronicles 33:19; Jeremiah 2:19; 5:6).

Prophetic Scripture points to a great end-times apostasy involving a massive defection from the truth (2 Thessalonians 2:3; see also Matthew 24:10-12). The apostle Paul offers these warnings:

- "The Spirit expressly says that in later times some will depart from the faith by devoting themselves to deceitful spirits and teachings of demons, through the insincerity of liars whose consciences are seared" (1 Timothy 4:1-2).

- "The time is coming when people will not endure sound teaching, but having itching ears they will accumulate for themselves teachers to suit their own passions, and will turn away from listening to the truth and wander off into myths" (2 Timothy 4:3-4).

Can there be any doubt that we are witnessing such things in our own day?

People can apostatize by denying various things, including...

> God (2 Timothy 3:4-5)
>
> Christ (1 John 2:18)
>
> Christ's return (2 Peter 3:3-4)
>
> the faith (1 Timothy 4:1-2)
>
> sound doctrine (2 Timothy 4:3-4)
>
> morals (2 Timothy 3:1-8)
>
> authority (2 Timothy 3:4)

We are living in days of deception!

TECHNOLOGICAL SIGNS OF THE END TIMES

Certain prophesies about the tribulation period require specific technological advances in order to be fulfilled. We might call these technological signs. Many prophecy scholars believe that the technology is now in place for these things to occur.

Global evangelism. Prophetic Scripture tells us that prior to the second coming of Christ, the gospel must be preached to every nation (Matthew 24:14). With today's technology—satellites, the Internet, global media, translation technologies, publishing technologies, rapid transportation, and the like—this has never been more possible.

Economic control. We do not know specifically what form the mark of the beast will take, but we do know that the false prophet will control who will be able to buy and sell, depending on whether they submit to worshipping the antichrist (Revelation 13:16-17). With today's satellites, the Internet, supercomputers, biometric identification procedures (such as hand scanners, retina scanners, and facial recognition scanners), RFID chips, and smart cards, the technology now exists to facilitate the fulfillment of this prophecy.

Nuclear detonations. It might surprise you to learn of evidence in prophetic Scripture that there may be nuclear detonations in the end times. For example, Revelation 8:7 tells us that "a third of the earth was burned up, and a third of the trees were burned up, and all the green grass was burned up." Moreover, Revelation 16:2 tells us that people around the world will break out with harmful and painful sores. Could this be a result of radiation poisoning following the detonation of nuclear weapons? Some believe Jesus may have alluded to nuclear weaponry: "And there will be…people fainting with fear and with foreboding of what is coming on the world. For the powers of the heavens will be shaken" (Luke 21:25-26). Regardless of whether this is so, technology clearly now exists to burn a third of the earth and cause mass casualties.

SIGNIFICANCE OF THE SIGNS

Prophetic signs are now casting their shadows before them. We are even now experiencing the foreshocks of some of these prophetic signs. The stage is now being set for the future seven-year tribulation period! Consequently, we can logically infer that the antichrist *may* be alive somewhere in the world today, waiting in the wings to step onto center stage to rule the world. Has he actually been born? Is he a youngster, a teenager, a twenty- or thirtysomething? We do not know—indeed, we cannot know—but it is entirely possible that he may be alive in our day.

Perhaps it would be good to repeat something I said earlier in the book. Satan has had a man ready to play the role of the antichrist in every generation. He does not know God's sovereign and providential timing of the end times with divine precision, so he must always have a man ready, waiting in the wings. As one prophecy expert put it, "Satan has always had a Nimrod, a Pharaoh, a Nebuchadnezzar, an Alexander the Great, an Antiochus, a Caesar, a Napoleon, a Hitler, a Stalin, and a someone alive today to set up a rival kingdom and to usurp the rightful place of the King of kings."[1]

When you think about it, if Jesus really is coming back in the next 40 or 50 years, the antichrist is likely to be alive right now.

> While the Bible never tells us how old Antichrist will be when he comes on the world scene, we would assume he would be in his forties or fifties. Moreover, while I am certainly not saying that Jesus is coming in the next forty to fifty years, because no one can set a time for His coming, I do think is it highly probable. If this is true, then the Antichrist is alive somewhere on the earth today. He may even be on the world political scene waiting in the wings for his moment.[2]

Might Christians be able to know the precise identity of the antichrist before the rapture? My answer to this is no. The tribulation period will begin when the antichrist signs a covenant with Israel (see Daniel 9:27). As we have seen, the rapture of the church precedes the signing of this covenant, so Christians could not possibly know the precise identity of this individual. Speaking tongue-in-cheek, if you have clearly identified the antichrist based on the criteria in Daniel 9:27, you have been left behind.

To be fair, some Christians have argued that they believe the antichrist is alive in our day because of the belief that the generation that sees the reestablishment of Israel (which took place in 1948) will live to see all the end-time prophecies fulfilled.[3] This is based on Matthew 24:34: "Truly, I say to you, this generation will not pass away until all these things take place."

Other Christians suggest that Christ is simply saying that those people who witness the signs stated just earlier in Matthew 24—the abomination of desolation (verse 15), the great tribulation such as has never been seen before (verse 21), and the sign of the Son of Man in heaven (verse 30)—will see the coming of Jesus Christ within *that* very generation. It was common knowledge among the Jews that the future tribulation period would last only seven years (Daniel 9:24-27), so it is obvious that those living at the beginning of this time would likely live to see the second coming seven years later (except for those who lose their lives during this tumultuous time).

So Christians differ in their interpretation of this verse and its significance for the manifestation of the antichrist. Most prophecy experts continue to affirm that Christians will not know the identity of the antichrist before the rapture. This is my personal position.

FREQUENTLY ASKED QUESTIONS ABOUT THE ANTICHRIST

I have been asked many questions about the antichrist, the false prophet, and Satan through my many years of ministry. I have addressed most of these questions in this book. Other questions, however, have not fit neatly into the previous chapters. I have therefore compiled them in this chapter to tie up any loose ends on this fascinating prophetic topic.

1. Will the antichrist experience a supernatural birth?

Some people have wondered whether the antichrist will experience some kind of supernatural birth, perhaps mimicking the supernatural birth of Jesus Christ. The antichrist is a counterfeit of Christ in many other ways, so just as the Holy Spirit overshadowed Mary to bring about the virgin birth (Luke 1:35), might the *un*holy spirit (Satan) overshadow a human mother so that the product will be a supernatural antichrist?

You might be surprised to learn that this was essentially the viewpoint of Jerome in the fourth century AD. Jerome was a Catholic priest and was best known for his translation of the Bible into Latin (the Vulgate). He was respected by many people, and the fact that such a weighty voice from ancient times held to such a view is significant. If true, this would make the antichrist the actual son of Satan, as portrayed in movies like *The Omen*.

Genesis 3:15 is sometimes cited as biblical support for this view. In this verse, God speaks judgment against the serpent: "I will put enmity between you and the woman, and between your offspring and her offspring; he shall bruise your head, and you shall bruise his heel." The woman's offspring is clearly the Messiah. The offspring of the serpent would become the archenemy of the Messiah. So as one prophecy scholar put it, "For those who hold to a supernatural origin for the Antichrist, Genesis 3:15 is seen as the first prophecy of the coming Messiah as well as the first prophecy of the Antichrist."[1]

Such a view is not impossible, but Scripture seems to consistently indicate that the antichrist is just a human being who will be heavily influenced and perhaps even indwelt by Satan. He is called "the man of lawlessness" in 2 Thessalonians 2:3. We are told that "the coming of the lawless one is by the activity of Satan with all power and false signs and wonders" (verse 9). So even though the antichrist is a man, Satan will empower him to do seemingly supernatural things.

We likewise read in Revelation 13:4 that the dragon (Satan) "had given his authority to the beast" (the antichrist). The beast is portrayed as a man who is born from the people who destroyed Jerusalem—a Roman (Daniel 9:26)—but he will be given the power and authority of the *un*holy spirit, Satan.

A tenth-century writer named Adso suggested that the antichrist will be born of a human father and a human mother. "[But the devil will] enter the womb of his mother at the very instant of conception. He will be fostered by the power of the devil and protected in his mother's womb."[2] This view has been held by an impressive number of people throughout church history.

However, the idea of the devil entering the antichrist's mother's womb is speculative and has no explicit biblical support. Some believe the idea may conflict with Revelation 12:7-9, which refers to Satan being thrown out of the domain of heaven, apparently in the middle of the tribulation period. Some interpreters suggest that Satan will indwell the antichrist at this point—in the middle of the tribulation— and not before.

Others suggest that the idea of the devil entering the antichrist's mother's womb may conflict with the idea that Satan may have an adult man ready in every age to step out of the wings in order to fulfill the role of the antichrist. This view seems reasonable, for Satan is not omniscient and therefore does not know God's sovereign timing of end-time events with pinpoint precision. He has to engage in eschatological guesswork.

In any event, the important thing to remember is that the antichrist will be a human being who will be energized by Satan. He will be endowed with seemingly supernatural abilities. Of that we can be certain.

2. Will the antichrist know that he is the antichrist as he is growing up?

I do not know of a single verse in Scripture that even remotely addresses this issue. Based on my general knowledge of biblical prophecy, however, my answer to this question is no.

The point I made above is relevant to this issue. Satan is not omniscient, so he does not know God's sovereign timing of end-time events with pinpoint precision. He has to guess about the timing of end-time events—including the timing of the initial emergence of a full-grown adult antichrist.

Satan's inability to pinpoint prophetic events even a few decades down the road would seem to make impossible the idea of a child growing up who knows he is the antichrist. It is difficult to fathom how a child could know he is the antichrist and then three or four decades later emerge as an adult political leader in perfect synchronization with God's overall prophetic plan—a plan requiring the rapture first (1 Thessalonians 4:13-17), followed by the emergence of a revived Roman Empire (Daniel 2; 7), with its leader (the antichrist) signing a covenant with Israel (Daniel 9:26-27).

3. How old will the antichrist be when he comes into power?

This is another question the Scriptures shed no light on. Jesus was apparently about 30 when He began His public ministry. Evidence for this includes the fact that he sought "to fulfill all righteousness" in obedience to Jewish law (Matthew 3:15). This would have included meeting the Jewish legal requirements for His role as a priest (after the order of Melchizedek—Hebrews 7). One priestly requirement is a minimum age of 30 (Numbers 4:3).

Some might argue that if the antichrist is a true counterfeit who is parallel to Jesus Christ, perhaps he too will be at least 30 when he rises to power. But this is purely speculative. The truth is, Scripture reveals nothing on this issue. We might note, however, that most political leaders of the world are a bit older—from the early forties and up. It seems reasonable to assume that the antichrist will emerge on the world scene around this general age.

4. Could the antichrist emerge from the United States?

I do not think so. Keep in mind the explicit statement in Daniel 9:26: "The people of the prince who is to come shall destroy the city and the sanctuary." The people who destroyed Jerusalem and its temple in AD 70 were the Romans. This means that the "prince who is to come" (the antichrist) will emerge from the Roman Empire, not the United States.

5. What are the clearest markers for identifying the antichrist?

Scripture reveals many markers. Here are some of the most notable:

- He will rise to power in the last days (Daniel 8:19,23).
- He will make a peace treaty with Israel (Daniel 9:27).
- He will rule the whole world (Revelation 13:7).
- His headquarters will be in Rome (Revelation 17:8-9).
- He will control the world economy (Revelation 13:16-17).
- He will seemingly die and be resurrected (Revelation 13:3,12).
- He will claim to be God (2 Thessalonians 2:4).

6. Does the current trend of globalism fit in with the imminent appearance of the antichrist?

I am convinced that this is indeed the case. The present U.S. administration seems to be moving us away from American national sovereignty and is open to handling more and more problems globally. More specifically, the current trend is to submit to multinational treaties, organizations, and courts of law.[3] Former presidential advisor Dick Morris gave this report after a 2009 meeting of the G-20 in London: "Now we may no longer look to presidential appointees, confirmed by the Senate, to make policy for our economy. These decisions will be made internationally."[4] He also commented: "It's a whole new world of financial regulation in which, essentially, all of the U.S. regulatory bodies and all U.S. companies are put under international regulation, international supervision. It really amounts to a global economic government."[5]

We can also surmise that the Ezekiel invasion—that is, the invasion into Israel by Russia, Iran, Sudan, Turkey, Libya, and other Muslim nations that is prophesied in Ezekiel 38–39—will help facilitate and solidify globalism. After all, if this invasion takes place either before the tribulation period or in the early part of the tribulation period, with God's subsequent destruction of all these foreign invaders, the revived Roman Empire could quickly rise to dominance in the world. This would also facilitate the rapid ascension of the antichrist as a world leader, setting the stage for his eventual global dominion (see Revelation 13:12-17).

7. Will the antichrist be able to read other peoples' minds?

I do not think so. Scripture indicates that only God has the ability to "know the hearts of all the children of mankind" (1 Kings 8:39). God is omniscient, and He certainly knows our thoughts. "Even before a word is on my tongue, behold, O Lord, you know it altogether" (Psalm 139:4).

The antichrist, by contrast, is just a man. He will be energized by Satan, but no Scripture indicates that Satan has the ability to read people's minds. Satan is a creature with creaturely limitations. Nevertheless, Satan is a highly intelligent being (Ezekiel 28:12) who has had thousands of years of experience dealing with human beings and thus may give the appearance of knowing people's thoughts. Satan is also the head of a vast network of demonic spirits who answer to him (Revelation 12:7), and this too may give the appearance of Satan being omniscient. But again, he is just a creature with creaturely limitations. There is certainly no indication anywhere in Scripture that he has the capability of actually reading people's minds. And he cannot energize the antichrist to do what he himself cannot do.

8. Why do Satan and the antichrist hate the Jewish people?

The antichrist, like Satan, who energizes him, hates the Jews primarily because they represent the genealogical line of the Messiah. Revelation 12:1-17 clearly reveals that Satan has sought to persecute the nation that gave birth to the Messiah (Israel). The text even indicates that Satan was behind the massacre of male children commanded by Herod, who tried to kill the King of the Jews as a babe (Matthew 2:13-18; see also Luke 4:28-29). The antichrist, too, is portrayed as persecuting the Jewish people (Daniel 9:27; Matthew 24:15; 2 Thessalonians 2:4).

Another point bears mentioning. Scripture reveals that Jesus will come again at the second coming only when the Jewish people are endangered at Armageddon and the Jewish leaders of the nation cry out for deliverance from Him, their divine Messiah (see Zechariah 12:10).

> This explains Satan's war against the Jews throughout history in general and during the tribulation in particular. Satan knows that once Messiah returns, his freedom ends. Satan also knows that Jesus will not come back until the Jewish leaders ask Him to come back. So if Satan can succeed in destroying the Jews once and for all before they come to national repentance, then Jesus will not come back and Satan's career is eternally safe...He [therefore] expends all of his satanic energies to try to destroy the Jews once and for all. Anti-Semitism in any form, active or passive, whether it is racial, ethnic, national, economic, political, religious, or theological, is all part of the satanic strategy to avoid the second coming.[6]

9. What is "the day of the Lord" referenced in 2 Thessalonians 2 in connection with the antichrist?

The term *day of the Lord* is used in several senses in Scripture. The Old Testament prophets sometimes used the term of an event to be fulfilled in the near future. At other times, they used the term of an event in the distant eschatological future (the future tribulation period). The immediate context of the term generally indicates which sense is intended. In both cases, the day of the Lord is characterized by God actively intervening supernaturally in order to judge sin in the world. The day of the Lord is a time in which God actively controls and dominates history in a direct way instead of working through secondary causes.

Among the New Testament writers, the term is generally used of the judgment that will climax in the future seven-year tribulation period (2 Thessalonians 2:2; Revelation 16–18) as well as the judgment that will usher in the new earth in the end times (2 Peter 3:10-13; Revelation 20:7–21:1; see also Isaiah 65:17-19; 66:22; Revelation 21:1). This theme of judgment against sin runs like a thread through the many references to the day of the Lord.

In 2 Thessalonians, Paul informed the Thessalonian believers that any concern that some might have about the coming day of the Lord (that is, the tribulation period) having already arrived is ill-conceived, for that day will not come until the antichrist is first revealed.

> We ask you, brothers, not to be quickly shaken in mind or alarmed, either by a spirit or a spoken word, or a letter seeming to be from us, to the effect that the day of the Lord has come. Let no one deceive you in any way. For that day will not come, unless the rebellion comes first, and the man of lawlessness is revealed (2 Thessalonians 2:1-3).

10. Will raptured believers be able to observe the antichrist and the events of the tribulation period from heaven?

Some Christians think so, based on Hebrews 12:1: "Since we are surrounded by so great a cloud of witnesses, let us also lay aside every weight, and sin which clings so closely, and let us run with endurance the race that is set before us."

Christians have two interpretations of this verse. The first view holds that people in heaven are able to watch us on earth, looking over heaven's balcony as a cloud of witnesses, or spectators in a vast arena.

In support of this view, it is suggested that people in the afterlife do seem to be aware of things transpiring on earth. For example, when Samuel the prophet, following his death, appeared to King Saul, he seemed to be aware of the events in Saul's life (1 Samuel 28:16-18). Likewise, Luke 9:31 tells us that Moses and Elijah "appeared in glory [to Jesus] and spoke of his departure, which he was about to accomplish at Jerusalem." Moses and Elijah seemed to be aware of events transpiring on earth relating to Christ's upcoming resurrection and ascension. Moreover, the angels in heaven seem to know what is going on in the earthly realm (see 1 Corinthians 4:9), and if angels know, why not redeemed humans? We are also told, "There will be more joy in heaven over one sinner who repents than over ninety-nine righteous persons who need no repentance" (Luke 15:7). It is suggested that this rejoicing could include not only angels but also Christians who have already gone to heaven. Further, the Christian martyrs mentioned in Revelation 6:9-10 are aware of the circumstances of their persecutors on earth. Finally, those in heaven who are mentioned in Revelation 19:1-6 are aware that Babylon has been destroyed on earth. This being the case, it is suggested that perhaps Christians in heaven can watch the antichrist and unfolding events on earth during the tribulation period.

This may seem a compelling case, but other Christians suggest that it may be reading too much into Hebrews 12:1 to conclude that there are saints looking over heaven's balcony, observing tribulation events. First, there are other possible explanations for the verses cited above. For example, Samuel was a prophet of God, and it is quite possible (even likely) that God personally informed him of Saul's circumstances before He caused Samuel to appear to Saul. The rejoicing in heaven over those who convert on earth could result not from saints looking over heaven's balcony, but from regular evangelism reports being issued in heaven—like a celestial newscast from the throne room. The same could be true regarding the martyrs in Revelation 6 and those in Revelation 19 who become aware that Babylon has been destroyed. Moreover, a case could be made that if Christians in heaven were looking over the balcony at earth, how could there be no more mourning or tears in heaven, since horrific things occur on a minute-by-minute basis on earth, especially during the tribulation period?

Many thus believe that the main idea of Hebrews 12:1 is that we have been preceded by superheroes of the faith (the "cloud" of great witnesses, or testifiers, who are specifically mentioned in Hebrews 11), so we should seek to mimic their behavior, following their lead in righteous, godly behavior.

If this latter view is correct, Christians in heaven are not looking over heaven's balcony at the earth. This is my personal view.

11. Will babies and young children be raptured before the tribulation along with all Christians, or will they be left behind to encounter the antichrist and the judgments of the tribulation?

Scholars may have different views on this issue, but I believe the scriptural evidence supports the idea that infants and young children will be raptured along with all Christians. I say this because of my firm belief that babies and young children who die before the age of accountability are saved.

At some time, each child becomes morally responsible before God. Christians have often debated what age constitutes the age of accountability. Actually, it is not the same for everyone. Some children mature faster than others. Some come into an awareness of personal evil and righteousness before others do.

We read in James 4:17, "Whoever knows the right thing to do and fails to do it, for him it is sin." It would seem that when children truly come into a full awareness and moral understanding of "oughts" and "shoulds," they have reached the age of accountability.

I believe that at the moment infants die—and not before—the benefits of Jesus' atoning death on the cross are applied to them. At that moment, infants become saved and are immediately issued into the presence of God in heaven. Consider these thoughts:

- In all the descriptions of hell in the Bible, we never read of infants or little children there. Not once. Only adults capable of making moral decisions are seen there.

- Nor do we read of infants and little children standing before the great white throne judgment, which is the judgment of the wicked dead and the precursor to the lake of fire (Revelation 20:11-15). The complete silence of Scripture regarding the presence of infants in eternal torment militates against their being there.

- The basis of the judgment of the lost involves deeds done while on earth (Revelation 20:11-13). Infants and young children cannot possibly be the objects of this judgment because they are not responsible for their deeds. Such a judgment against infants would be a travesty.

- Jesus indicated that children have a special place in His kingdom (Matthew 18:1-14). In fact, He said that adults must become like little children to enter into His kingdom.

- King David in the Old Testament certainly believed he would again be with his son who died. "While the child was still alive, I fasted and wept, for I said, 'Who knows whether the LORD will be gracious to me, that the child may live?' But now he is dead. Why should I fast? Can I bring him back again? I shall go to him, but he will not return to me" (2 Samuel 12:22-23). David displayed complete confidence that his little one was with God in heaven and that he would one day join his son there.

For these and other reasons, I am convinced that infants and young children who die before the age of accountability are saved. We can thus infer that God will apply this same kind of saving grace to infants and young children at the rapture, sparing them of any encounter with the antichrist or the horrific judgments of the tribulation period. For a full discussion of heaven for those who don't have an opportunity to believe, see my book *The Wonder of Heaven* (Harvest House, 2009).

12. If the antichrist's revived Roman Empire is to be a dominant world power in the tribulation period, will the United States be in a weakened state?

Many prophecy scholars believe that the United States will be weakened in the end times. Consider these possibilities:

Moral implosion. The United States may eventually implode from ever-escalating moral and spiritual degeneration. God Himself may choose to judge America for its immorality as He has done to other sinful nations of the past.

Nuclear bombs. The United States could also be weakened by nuclear weapons. Top government advisors are presently saying that a nuclear attack on U.S. soil within the next ten years is more likely than not. Of course, it may be a stretch to say that the entire United States could be destroyed, but the destruction of one major city would have a devastating effect on the U.S. economy.

EMP attack. Perhaps the United States will become incapacitated due to an electromagnetic pulse (EMP) attack. A single nuclear weapon, delivered by a missile to an altitude of a few hundred miles over the United States, would yield catastrophic damage to the nation. The electromagnetic pulse produced by such a weapon would have a high likelihood of severely damaging electrical power systems, electronics, and information systems—all of which Americans depend on. Electronic control, the infrastructures for handling electric power, sensors and protective systems of all kinds, computers, cell phones, telecommunications, cars, boats, airplanes, trains, transportation, fuel and energy, banking and finance, emergency services, and even food and water would be at high risk. Repairing such damage could take years.

The rapture. The rapture will likely have a catastrophic effect on the United States because of its high concentration of Christians. Following the rapture, many companies will be without some of their leaders and workers; many bills, mortgages, and other loans will go unpaid; many police, fire, and medical personnel will be gone; and the ensuing panic will likely lead to a stock-market crash. This and much more will result from the rapture.

The United States could become weakened in the end times because of any of these factors, let alone several of them working in concert with each other. Once this happens, the revived Roman Empire will more easily ascend to supremacy in the world.

13. Could the United States be in league with the antichrist in the end times?

I hate to say it, but yes. Following the rapture of the church, the United States could be in general cooperation with Europe—the revived Roman Empire headed by the antichrist. Many U.S. citizens have come from Europe, so the U.S. could naturally become an ally of this Roman power in the end times.

When Armageddon breaks out at the end of the tribulation period, troops from the United States may be there. I hate to say that, but Zechariah 12:3 seems rather clear about it: "On that day I will make Jerusalem a heavy stone for all the peoples. All who lift it will surely hurt themselves. And all the nations of the earth will gather against it." The phrase "all the nations of the earth" would certainly seem to include the United States. Zechariah 14:2 repeats the theme: "For I will gather all the nations against Jerusalem to battle, and the city shall be taken and the houses plundered and the women raped. Half of the city shall go out into exile, but the rest of the people shall not be cut off from the city." Again, "all the nations" would appear to include the United States. Likewise, we read in Revelation 16:14 that "the kings of the whole world" will be gathered together "for battle on the great day of God the Almighty." This would certainly include the president of the United States.

Following the rapture of the church, no Christians will be left on the earth—including in the United States. This means that many of the people in the United States who have long supported Israel have vanished and gone to be with the Lord in heaven. It is easy to see how a Christian-less United States could ally with the revived Roman Empire and then find itself in league with the antichrist.

14. Will the antichrist and false prophet be punished with much greater severity in the lake of fire than other unredeemed sinners?

Yes, I believe this will be the case. Scripture indicates that there will be degrees of punishment in hell (Matthew 10:15; 16:27; Luke 12:47-48; Revelation 20:12-13; 22:12). Christ's justice is perfect, and this requires that extremely evil persons will experience much greater punishment than, for example, a non-Christian moralist. This punishment will last forever.

15. How do we know that the antichrist and false prophet will suffer for all eternity in the lake of fire?

Scripture is clear that the punishment in hell is eternal. Annihilationism—the obliteration of existence—is a false doctrine. People in hell do not get annihilated and thereby lose consciousness. Annihilation avoids punishment rather than encountering it.

Matthew 25:46 explicitly refers to "eternal punishment" in hell, and many other passages uses similar phrases. Annihilationism or an extinction of consciousness cannot possibly be forced into this passage. The adjective *aionion* in this verse literally means "everlasting, without end." This same adjective is predicated of God—the "eternal" or "everlasting" God (see Romans 16:26; 1 Timothy 1:17; Hebrews 9:14; 13:8; Revelation 4:9). The ongoing punishment of the wicked—including the antichrist, the false prophet, and Satan—will be just as eternal as our eternal God.

In keeping with this, the fire of hell is called an "unquenchable fire" (Mark 9:43), the worm of the wicked "does not die" (Mark 9:48), and the "smoke of their torment rises for ever and ever" (Revelation 14:11).

Revelation 20:10 specifically refers to Satan, the antichrist, and the false prophet being tormented in the lake of fire "day and night forever and ever." This is significant because the Greek word translated "for ever and ever" is used elsewhere in Revelation in reference to the endless worship of God (Revelation 1:6; 4:9; 5:13). The word is also used of the endless life of God (4:10; 10:6). The suffering of the antichrist, the false prophet, and Satan will be endless.

16. Could preterism be correct—the idea that the prophecies about the tribulation and the antichrist in Revelation and Matthew 24–25 have already been fulfilled?

I am fully convinced that this theological model is brimming with error. The word *preterism* derives from the Latin *preter*, meaning "past." In this view, the biblical prophecies in the book of Revelation (especially chapters 6–18) and Matthew 24–25 (Christ's Olivet Discourse) have already been fulfilled.

There are two forms of preterism: moderate (partial) preterism and extreme (full) preterism. Moderate preterism is represented by modern writers such as R.C. Sproul, Hank Hanegraaff, and Gary DeMar. They believe the literal resurrection and second coming are yet future, but the other prophecies in Revelation and Matthew 24–25 (including prophecies about the antichrist) were fulfilled when Jerusalem fell to Titus and his Roman army in AD 70. (Some relate the antichrist to General Titus.) Extreme or full preterism goes so far as to say that *all* New Testament predictions were fulfilled in the past, including those of the resurrection and second coming.

Preterists often point to Matthew 24:34, where Jesus asserted, "This generation will not pass away until all these things take place." This verse allegedly proves the prophecies would soon be fulfilled. Contrary to this view, many evangelicals believe Christ was simply saying that the generation that witnessed the signs stated earlier in Matthew 24—the abomination of desolation (verse 15), the great tribulation such as has never been seen before (verse 21), and the sign of the Son of Man in heaven (verse 30)—will see the coming of Jesus Christ. As we noted earlier, it was common knowledge among the Jews that the future tribulation period would last only seven years (Daniel 9:24-27), so those living at the beginning of this time would be likely live to see the second coming seven years later (except for those who lose their lives during this tumultuous time).

Other evangelicals hold that the word *generation* is to be take in its basic usage of "race, kindred, family, stock, or breed." If this is what is meant, then Jesus is here promising that the nation of Israel will be preserved—despite terrible persecution during the tribulation—until the consummation of God's program for Israel at the second coming. Many divine promises have been made to Israel—including land promises (Genesis 12; 14–15; 17) and a future Davidic kingdom (2 Samuel 7). Jesus could thus be referring to God's preservation of Israel in order to fulfill the divine promises to them (see Romans 11:11-27). Whichever view is correct, the verse does not support preterism.

Preterists also argue from Matthew 16:28 that Jesus said some of His followers standing there would not taste death until they saw Him return, or "coming in His kingdom." Contrary to the preterist view, many evangelicals believe that when Jesus said this, He had in mind the transfiguration, which happened precisely one week later (Matthew 17:1-13). In this view, the transfiguration served as a preview of the kingdom in which the divine Messiah would appear in glory. Moreover, some of the disciples standing there were no longer alive by AD 70—all but John had been martyred by then. Still further, no astronomical events occurred in AD 70, such as the stars falling from heaven and the heavens being shaken (Matthew 24:29). And Jesus did not return "coming on the clouds of heaven with power and great glory" (verse 30).

Preterists also point to verses that indicate that Jesus would come soon (Revelation 22:12,20) and that the events in the book of Revelation would soon take place (1:1; 22:6). Futurists point out, however, that the Greek word for *soon* often carries the meaning "swiftly, speedily, at a rapid rate." The term could simply indicate that when the predicted events first start to occur, they will progress swiftly, in rapid succession. The word can also mean "suddenly" as opposed to "soon."

A favorite argument among preterists is that the book of Revelation was written prior to AD 70, so the book must have been fulfilled in AD 70 when Rome overran Jerusalem. Futurists point out, however, that some of the earliest church fathers confirmed a late date (AD 90 or later), including Irenaeus (who knew Polycarp, John's disciple), who claimed the book was written at the close of the reign of Domitian (which took place from AD 81 to AD 96). Victorinus confirmed this date in the third century, as did Eusebius (263–340). The book was written well after AD 70, so it could hardly have been referring to events that would be fulfilled in AD 70.

Against preterism, futurists note that key events described in the book of Revelation simply did not occur in AD 70. For example, a third of mankind was not killed, as predicted in Revelation 9:18. Two hundred million soldiers from the East have never invaded Israel, as predicted in Revelation 9:13-15. Nor has every living thing died that was in the sea, as predicted in Revelation 16:3. In order to explain these texts, preterists must resort to an allegorical interpretation because they did not happen literally.

In view of such facts, I do not trust what preterism teaches about the antichrist in particular, or the tribulation period in general.

Postscript:

FEARLESS LIVING

A book on the antichrist, the false prophet, and the role of Satan in the horrific future tribulation period is not exactly what I call inspirational reading. We ought to keep all this in perspective, however. God has used prophecy to inform us what the future holds in order to encourage us and stimulate our faith. As my friend Walter Martin used to put it, "I read the last chapter in the book, and we win!" If we learn one thing from biblical prophecy, it is that God is in control of human history, and He is guiding history toward its culmination. One day, all who believe in Jesus Christ will live in a new heavens and a new earth, face-to-face with our Lord, never again having to give consideration to Satan or anything negative. We ought therefore to live fearlessly and follow a few guiding principles.

Maintain an eternal perspective. One of the best pieces of advice I can give you is to live your life as if the rapture could happen today but plan your life as if you will be here your entire lifetime expectancy. That way you will be prepared for time and eternity.

Your natural inclination might be to have a little fear regarding the things I have addressed in this book. Let me exhort you, however, not to be troubled at all, but rather to trust entirely in God. Jesus speaks words of great comfort to His disciples in John 14:1-3:

> Do not let your hearts be troubled. Believe in God; believe also in me. In my Father's house are many rooms. If it were not so, would I have told you that I go to prepare a place for you? And if I go and prepare a place for you, I will come again and will take you to myself, that where I am you may be also.

My former professor John F. Walvoord has a great insight on this passage:

> These verses are the Bible's first revelation of the rapture, in which Christ will come back to take His own to heaven. He exhorted the disciples not to be troubled. Since they trusted the Father, they also should trust Christ, whose power was demonstrated in His many miracles. Having referred to Himself as the Source of peace, Jesus spoke of His coming to take them to heaven. They need not be anxious about His leaving because later He would return for them.[1]

Regardless of what happens in this world, we need not be troubled. Why? Because we know the Prince of Peace, Jesus Christ. He is the source of peace, and the peace He gives does not depend on circumstances (John 14:27). Therefore, we need not worry. We need not fear. Besides, as Jesus said, He is now preparing our eternal homes (14:1-3). And one day—maybe even today—He will come for us at the rapture, before the antichrist manifests himself in the world.

Be sound minded. As we live day to day in the end times, we should aim to keep a sound mind, maintain a strong prayer life, and always be loving toward others. We find much wisdom on all this in 1 Peter 4:7-10.

> The end of all things is at hand; therefore be self-controlled and sober-minded for the sake of your prayers. Above all, keep loving one another earnestly, since love covers a multitude of sins. Show hospitality to one another without grumbling. As each has received a gift, use it to serve one another, as good stewards of God's varied grace.

It is unfortunate that many people tend to become sensationalistic and alarmist about end-time prophecies. God tells us to be sober minded. He instructs us to maintain sound judgment. The best way to be sober minded and maintain sound judgment is to regularly feed our minds with the Word of God. Keeping our minds stayed on the Scriptures will keep us on track in our thinking and in our life choices in the light of biblical prophecy.

Live righteously. When God reveals the future to us, He does not do so to show off. God does not give us prophecy to teach us mere intellectual facts about eschatology. Many verses in the Bible that deal with prophecy lead to exhortations to personal purity. This means that as we study Bible prophecy, it ought to change the way we live. It ought to have an effect on our behavior. Consider the apostle Paul's exhortation in Romans 13:11-14.

> Besides this you know the time, that the hour has come for you to wake from sleep. For salvation is nearer to us now than when we first believed. The night is far gone; the day is at hand. So then let us cast off the works of darkness and put on the armor of light. Let us walk properly as in the daytime, not in orgies and drunkenness, not in sexual immorality and sensuality, not in quarreling and jealousy. But put on the Lord Jesus Christ, and make no provision for the flesh, to gratify its desires.

We also see the connection between biblical prophecy and purity in 2 Peter 3:10-14.

> The day of the Lord will come like a thief, and then the heavens will pass away with a roar, and the heavenly bodies will be burned up and dissolved, and the earth and the works that are done on it will be exposed.
>
> Since all these things are thus to be dissolved, what sort of people ought you to be in lives of holiness and godliness, waiting for and hastening the coming of the day of God, because of which the heavens will be set on fire and dissolved, and the heavenly bodies will melt as they burn! But

according to his promise we are waiting for new heavens
and a new earth in which righteousness dwells.

Therefore, beloved, since you are waiting for these, be
diligent to be found by him without spot or blemish, and
at peace.

First John 3:2-3 provides a similar instruction.

Beloved, we are God's children now, and what we will be
has not appeared. But we know that when he appears, we
shall be like him, because we shall see him as he is. And
everyone who thus hopes in him purifies himself as he is
pure.

We find a helpful analogy in ancient Jewish marriage customs. In
biblical times, following the marriage betrothal, the groom would go
to his father's house to prepare a place for the couple to stay. Meanwhile,
the betrothed woman would eagerly await the coming of her groom to
take her away to his father's house in marriage celebration. During this
time of anticipation, the bride's loyalty to her groom was tested. Likewise, as the bride of Christ (the church) awaits the coming of the messianic Groom, the church is motivated to live in purity and godliness
until He arrives at the rapture (John 14:1-3). Let us daily choose purity.

Never set dates. God Himself controls the timing of end-time events,
and He has not provided us the specific details. In Acts 1:7 we read
Jesus' words to the disciples before He ascended into heaven: "It is not
for you to know times or seasons that the Father has fixed by His own
authority." This means that although we can be accurate observers of
the times, as Jesus instructed (Matthew 24:32-33; Luke 21:25-28), we
do not have pinpoint details on the precise timing. So we must simply
resolve to trust God with those details.

Bible prophecy points to the awesome greatness of God. I never tire of
reminding Bible students that biblical prophecy constantly and relent-
lessly points to the awesome greatness of God. Consider Isaiah 44:6-8.

Thus says the LORD, the King of Israel and his Redeemer,
the LORD of hosts: "I am the first and I am the last; besides

me there is no god. Who is like me? Let him proclaim it. Let him declare and set it before me, since I appointed an ancient people. Let them declare what is to come, and what will happen. Fear not, nor be afraid; have I not told you from of old and declared it? And you are my witnesses! Is there a God besides me? There is no Rock; I know not any."

In Daniel 2:20-22, we read this doxology:

Blessed be the name of God forever and ever, to whom belong wisdom and might. He changes times and seasons; he removes kings and sets up kings; he gives wisdom to the wise and knowledge to those who have understanding; he reveals deep and hidden things; he knows what is in the darkness, and the light dwells with him.

Can there be any doubt that our God is an awesome God?

In view of this, let me again exhort you not to worry about Satan, or the antichrist, or the false prophet. God is in control, and as we keep our minds focused on Him, we have peace. "You keep him in perfect peace whose mind is stayed on you" (Isaiah 26:3). Especially as we ponder living forever with the Lord in heaven, we have perfect peace.

I once had the opportunity to sit in a classroom with half a dozen students and well-known Christian author J.I. Packer. Packer says that "the lack of long, strong thinking about our promised hope of glory is a major cause of our plodding, lackluster lifestyle." He points to the Puritans as a much-needed example for us, for they believed that "it is the heavenly Christian that is the lively Christian." The Puritans understood that we "run so slowly, and strive so lazily, because we so little mind the prize...So let Christians animate themselves daily to run the race set before them by practicing heavenly meditation."[2]

Puritan Richard Baxter's daily habit was to "dwell on the glory of the heavenly life to which [he] was going." Baxter daily practiced "holding heaven at the forefront of his thoughts and desires." The hope of heaven brought him joy, and joy brought him strength. Baxter once said, "A heavenly mind is a joyful mind; this is the nearest and truest way to live a life of comfort…A heart in heaven will be a most excellent preservative against temptations, a powerful means to kill thy corruptions."[3]

Such comments reflect the exhortation of the apostle Paul in Colossians 3:1-2: "If then you have been raised with Christ, seek the things that are above, where Christ is, seated at the right hand of God. Set your minds on things that are above, not on things that are on earth." The original Greek of this verse is intense, communicating the idea, "Diligently, actively, single-mindedly pursue the things above." Moreover, the present tense in the original Greek communicates the idea, "Perpetually keep on seeking the things above…Make it an ongoing process."

This ought to be our attitude every single day.

Do not worry about the antichrist. Live fearlessly!

Appendix:

IF YOU ARE NOT
A CHRISTIAN

My friend, thank you for reading my book. I hope it has helped you learn a lot about what the Bible says about the antichrist and end-times prophecy.

Before I end the book, I need to let you know that choosing to have a personal relationship with Jesus is the most important decision you could ever make in your life. A relationship with Him is unlike any other. If you go into eternity without this relationship, you will spend eternity apart from Him.

If you will allow me, I would like to tell you how you can come into a personal relationship with Jesus.

First, you need to understand that God desires a personal relationship with you. He created you (Genesis 1:27). And He did not create you to exist all alone and apart from Him. He created you to have a personal relationship with Him.

God had face-to-face encounters and fellowship with Adam and Eve, the first couple (Genesis 3:8-19). Just as God fellowshipped with them, so He desires to enjoy fellowship with you—spiritual fellowship (1 John 1:5-7). God loves you (John 3:16). Never forget that fact.

The problem is, however, that human beings have a sin problem that blocks a relationship with God. Here is how it happened: When Adam and Eve chose to sin against God in the Garden of Eden, they catapulted the entire human race—to which they gave birth—into sin. Since that time, every human being has been born into the world with a propensity to sin. We call this a *sin nature*. "Sin came into the world through one man, and death through sin...By the one man's disobedience the many were made sinners" (Romans 5:12,19). This means that "by a man came death...in Adam all die" (1 Corinthians 15:21-22).

Jesus often spoke of sin in metaphors that illustrate the havoc sin can wreak in one's life. He described sin as blindness (Matthew 23:16-26), sickness (Matthew 9:12), being enslaved in bondage (John 8:34), and living in darkness (John 8:12; 12:35-36,44-46). Moreover, He taught that this is a universal condition and that all people are guilty before God (Luke 7:37-48).

Jesus also taught that both inner thoughts and external acts render a person guilty (Matthew 5:28). He taught that from within the human heart come evil thoughts, sexual immorality, theft, murder, adultery, greed, malice, deceit, envy, slander, arrogance, and folly (Mark 7:21-23). Moreover, He affirmed that God is fully aware of every person's sins, both external acts and inner thoughts; nothing escapes His notice (Matthew 22:18; Luke 6:8; John 4:17-19).

Of course, some people are more morally upright than others. However, we *all* fall short of God's infinitely holy standards (Romans 3:23). To illustrate, in a contest to see who can throw a rock to the moon, a muscular athlete would be able to throw the rock much farther than I could. But all human beings ultimately fall short of the task. No one can throw a rock to the moon. Similarly, though some people are more morally upright than others, all of us fall short of God's standards of perfect holiness.

Though the sin problem is a serious one, God has graciously provided a solution. The solution is that Jesus died for our sins and made salvation possible.

According to the Bible, God's absolute holiness demands that sin be punished. The good news of the gospel, however, is that Jesus has taken this punishment on Himself. God loves us so much that He sent Jesus to bear the penalty for our sins!

Jesus affirmed that it was for the very purpose of dying that He came into the world (John 12:27). Moreover, He perceived His death as being a sacrificial offering for the sins of humanity (Matthew 26:26-28). Jesus took His sacrificial mission with utmost seriousness, for He knew that without Him, humanity would certainly perish (Matthew 16:25; John 3:16) and spend eternity apart from God in a place of great suffering (Matthew 10:28; 11:23; 23:33; 25:41; Luke 16:22-28).

Jesus therefore described His mission this way: "The Son of Man came not to be served but to serve, and to give his life as a ransom for many" (Matthew 20:28). "The Son of Man came to seek and to save the lost" (Luke 19:10). "For God did not send his Son into the world to condemn the world, but in order that the world might be saved through him" (John 3:17).

I need to tell you in no uncertain terms, however, that the benefits of Christ's death on the cross are not automatically applied to your life. To receive the gift of salvation, you must believe in Jesus Christ, the Savior.

By His sacrificial death on the cross, Jesus took the sins of the entire world on Himself and made salvation available for everyone (1 John 2:2). But this salvation is not automatic. Only those who personally choose to believe in Christ are saved. This is Jesus' consistent testimony in the Bible.

- "God so loved the world, that he gave his only Son, that whoever believes in him should not perish but have eternal life" (John 3:16).

- "This is the will of my Father, that everyone who looks on the Son and believes in him should have eternal life, and I will raise him up on the last day" (John 6:40).

- "I am the resurrection and the life. Whoever believes in me, though he die, yet shall he live" (John 11:25).

Choosing *not* to believe in Jesus, by contrast, leads to eternal condemnation. "Whoever believes in him is not condemned, but whoever does not believe is condemned already, because he has not believed in the name of the only Son of God" (John 3:18).

The good news is that when you believe in Christ the Savior, God forgives you of your sins. All of them! He puts them completely out of His sight. Ponder for a few minutes the following verses, which speak of the forgiveness of those who have believed in Christ:

- "In him we have redemption through his blood, the forgive-ness of our trespasses, according to the riches of his grace" (Ephesians 1:7).

- "I will remember their sins and their lawless deeds no more" (Hebrews 10:17).

- "Blessed is the one whose transgression is forgiven, whose sin is covered. Blessed is the man against whom the LORD counts no iniquity" (Psalm 32:1-2).

- "For as high as the heavens are above the earth, so great is his steadfast love toward those who fear him; as far as the east is from the west, so far does he remove our transgressions from us" (Psalm 103:11-12).

Such forgiveness is wonderful indeed, for none of us can possibly work our way into heaven or be good enough to warrant God's good favor. Because of what Jesus has done for us, we can freely receive the gift of salvation. It is provided solely through the grace of God (Ephesians 2:8-9). It becomes ours when we place our faith in Jesus.

I feel a sense of urgency in communicating all this to you. Remember, it is highly dangerous to put off turning to Christ for salvation, for you do not know the day of your death. What if it happens this evening? "Death is the destiny of everyone; the living should take this to heart" (Ecclesiastes 7:2 NIV).

If God is speaking to your heart now, this is your door of opportunity to believe. "Seek the LORD while he may be found; call upon him while he is near" (Isaiah 55:6). "Now is the day of salvation" (2 Corinthians 6:2).

Would you like to place your faith in Jesus for the forgiveness of sins and guarantee your eternal place in heaven along His side? If so, pray the following prayer with me. Keep in mind that the prayer itself does not save you. The faith in your heart saves you. So let the following prayer be a simple expression of the faith that is in your heart.

> *Dear Jesus,*
>
> *I want to have a relationship with You.*
> *I know I cannot save myself, because I know I am a sinner.*
> *Thank You for dying on the cross on my behalf.*
> *I believe in You, my Savior and Redeemer. I believe You died for me, taking the punishment for sin that I deserved. I accept Your free gift of salvation.*
> *Thank You, Jesus.*
> *Amen.*

On the authority of the Word of God, I can now assure you that you are a part of God's forever family. If you prayed the above prayer with a heart of faith, you will spend all eternity by the side of Jesus in heaven. Welcome to God's family! Once we are all in heaven together, please introduce yourself to me!

Here is what you need to do next:

- Purchase a Bible and read from it daily. Because you are a new Christian, I recommend the New Living Translation. It is an easy-to-understand Bible. Read at least one chapter a day, followed by a time of prayer. I recommend starting with the Gospel of John.

- Join a Bible-believing church immediately. Get involved in it. Join a Bible study group at the church so you will have regular fellowship with other Christians.

- Please send me an e-mail at ronrhodes@earthlink.net. I want to e-mail you a free e-book that will help you get firmly established in your Christian faith. It will teach you all the basics of Christianity.

- Please visit my website, where you'll find many materials that can help you in your walk with God: www.ronrhodes.org.

BIBLIOGRAPHY

Ankerberg, John, and Dillon Burroughs. *Middle East Meltdown*. Eugene: Harvest House, 2007.

Ansari, Ali. *Confronting Iran: The Failure of American Foreign Policy and the Next Great Conflict in the Middle East*. New York: Basic Books, 2006.

Berman, Ilan. *Tehran Rising: Iran's Challenge to the United States*. New York: Rowman & Littlefield, 2005.

Block, Daniel. *The Book of Ezekiel: Chapters 25–48*. Grand Rapids: Eerdmans, 1998.

Corsi, Jerome. *Atomic Iran: How the Terrorist Regime Bought the Bomb and American Politicians*. Nashville: WND Books, 2005.

Dyer, Charles. *The Rise of Babylon: Sign of the End Times*. Chicago: Moody, 2003.

Feinberg, Charles. *The Prophecy of Ezekiel*. Eugene: Wipf and Stock, 2003.

Fruchtenbaum, Arnold. *The Footsteps of the Messiah*. San Antonio: Ariel, 2004.

Gaffney, Frank. *War Footing: Ten Steps America Must Take to Prevail in the War for the Free World*. Annapolis: Naval Institute Press, 2006.

Gold, Dore. *The Fight for Jerusalem: Radical Islam, the West, and the Future of the Holy City*. Washington: Regnery, 2007.

Hitchcock, Mark. *The Complete Book of Bible Prophecy*. Wheaton: Tyndale House, 1999.

———. *Iran: The Coming Crisis*. Sisters, OR: Multnomah, 2006.

———. *Is America in Bible Prophecy?* Sisters, OR: Multnomah, 2002.

———. *Is the Antichrist Alive Today?* Sisters, OR: Multnomah, 2003.

———. *The Coming Islamic Invasion of Israel*. Sisters, OR: Multnomah, 2002.

————. *The Second Coming of Babylon*. Sisters, OR: Multnomah, 2003.

Hoyt, Herman. *The End Times*. Chicago: Moody Press, 1969.

Ice, Thomas, and Randall Price. *Ready to Rebuild: The Imminent Plan to Rebuild the Last Days Temple*. Eugene: Harvest House, 1992.

Ice, Thomas, and Timothy Demy. *Prophecy Watch*. Eugene: Harvest House, 1998.

————. *When the Trumpet Sounds*. Eugene: Harvest House, 1995.

LaHaye, Tim. *The Beginning of the End*. Wheaton: Tyndale, 1991.

————. *The Coming Peace in the Middle East*. Grand Rapids: Zondervan, 1984.

LaHaye, Tim, ed. *Prophecy Study Bible*. Chattanooga: AMG, 2001.

LaHaye, Tim, and Ed Hindson. *Global Warning: Are We on the Brink of World War III?* Eugene: Harvest House, 2007.

LaHaye, Tim, and Ed Hindson, eds. *The Popular Bible Prophecy Commentary*. Eugene: Harvest House, 2006.

————. *The Popular Encyclopedia of Bible Prophecy*. Eugene: Harvest House, 2004.

LaHaye, Tim, and Thomas Ice. *Charting the End Times*. Eugene: Harvest House, 2001.

LaHaye, Tim, and Jerry Jenkins. *Are We Living in the End Times?* Wheaton: Tyndale, 1999.

Leeb, Stephen. *The Coming Economic Collapse*. New York: Warner Business Books, 2006.

Pentecost, J. Dwight. *Prophecy for Today*. Grand Rapids: Discovery House, 1989.

————. *Things to Come*. Grand Rapids: Zondervan, 1964.

Phares, Walid. *Future Jihad: Terrorist Strategies Against the West*. New York: Palgrave MacMillan, 2005.

Pink, Arthur W. *The Antichrist: A Study of Satan's Christ*. Blacksburg, VA: Wilder, 2008.

Pollack, Kenneth. *The Persian Puzzle: The Conflict Between Iran and America*. New York: Random House, 2005.

Price, Randall. *Fast Facts on the Middle East Conflict*. Eugene: Harvest House, 2003.

————. *Jerusalem in Prophecy*. Eugene: Harvest House, 1998.

————. *Unholy War*. Eugene: Harvest House, 2001.

Price, Walter K. *The Coming Antichrist*. Neptune, NJ: Loizeaux Brothers, 1985.

Reid, T.R. *The United States of Europe: The New Superpower and the End of American Supremacy*. New York: Penguin Books, 2004.

Rhodes, Ron. *The Coming Oil Storm: The Imminent End of Oil…and Its Strategic Global Role in End-Times Prophecy*. Eugene: Harvest House, 2010.

————. *Five Views on the Rapture: What You Need to Know*. Eugene: Harvest House, 2011.

————. *Is America in Bible Prophecy? What You Need to Know*. Eugene: Harvest House, 2011.

———. *The Middle East Conflict: What You Need to Know*. Eugene: Harvest House, 2009.

———. *Northern Storm Rising: Russia, Iran, and the Emerging End-Times Military Coalition Against Israel*. Eugene: Harvest House, 2008.

———. *The Popular Dictionary of Bible Prophecy*. Eugene: Harvest House, 2010.

———. *The Topical Handbook of Bible Prophecy*. Eugene: Harvest House, 2010.

Richardson, Joel. *The Islamic Antichrist*. Los Angeles: WND Books, 2009.

Rosenberg, Joel. *Epicenter: Why Current Rumblings in the Middle East Will Change Your Future*. Carol Stream: Tyndale House, 2006.

Ruthven, Jon Mark. *The Prophecy That Is Shaping History: New Research on Ezekiel's Vision of the End*. Fairfax: Xulon Press, 2003.

Ryrie, Charles. *Ryrie Study Bible*. Chicago: Moody, 2011.

Timmerman, Kenneth. *Countdown to Crisis: The Coming Nuclear Showdown with Iran*. New York: Three Rivers Press, 2006.

Unger, Merrill. *Beyond the Crystal Ball: What Occult Practices Cannot Tell You About Future Events*. Chicago: Moody, 1973.

Venter, Al. *Iran's Nuclear Option: Tehran's Quest for the Atomic Bomb*. Philadelphia: Casemate, 2005.

Walvoord, John F. *End Times*. Nashville: Word, 1998.

———. *The Millennial Kingdom*. Grand Rapids: Zondervan, 1975.

———. *The Prophecy Knowledge Handbook*. Wheaton: Victor Books, 1990.

———. *The Return of the Lord*. Grand Rapids: Zondervan, 1979.

Walvoord, John F., and John E. Walvoord. *Armageddon, Oil, and the Middle East Crisis*. Grand Rapids: Zondervan, 1975.

Yamauchi, Edwin. *Foes from the Northern Frontier: Invading Hordes from the Russian Steppes*. Eugene: Wipf and Stock, 1982.

NOTES

INTRODUCTION: RISING INTEREST IN THE EMERGENCE OF THE ANTICHRIST

1. Mark Hitchcock, *Is the Antichrist Alive Today?* (Sisters, OR: Multnomah, 2002), p. 7.
2. Herman Hoyt, *The End Times* (Chicago: Moody, 1969), pp. 115-16.
3. Cited in Walter K. Price, *The Coming Antichrist* (Neptune, NJ: Loizeaux Brothers, 1985), p. 12.

CHAPTER 2: DIFFERING CONCEPTS OF THE ANTICHRIST

1. Bernard McGinn, "Antichrist," in *Encyclopedia of Religion*, ed. Lindsay Jones (New York: Macmillan Reference USA, 2004).
2. Norman Geisler and Ron Brooks, *When Skeptics Ask* (Wheaton: Victor Books, 1990), p. 115.
3. Walter K. Price, *The Coming Antichrist* (Neptune, NJ: Loizeaux Brothers, 1985), p. 15.
4. Charles F. Pfieffer, John Rhea, and Howard F. Vos, "Antichrist," in *Wycliffe Bible Encyclopedia* (Chicago: Moody Press, 1975).
5. Pfieffer, Rhea, and Vos, "Antichrist."
6. Pfieffer, Rhea, and Vos, "Antichrist."
7. This view has been held by postmillennialists (for example, A.H. Strong, *Systematic Theology*, p. 1008), amillennialists (for example, C.F. Keil, *Commentary on Daniel*, at 9:26-27), and premillennialists (for example, Alva J. McClain, *The Greatness of the Kingdom*, pp. 452-53).
8. Price, *The Coming Antichrist*, p. 16.
9. Price, *The Coming Antichrist*, p. 17.
10. Price, *The Coming Antichrist*, p. 17.

CHAPTER 3: HISTORICAL IDENTIFICATIONS OF THE ANTICHRIST

1. Randall Price, "An Overview of the Antichrist." Available online at www.worldofthebible. com/Bible%20Studies/antichrist.pdf.

2. Cited in Price, "An Overview of the Antichrist."

3. Arthur W. Pink, *The Antichrist: A Study of Satan's Christ* (Blacksburg, VA: Wilder, 2008), p. 10.

4. Wayne Grudem, *Systematic Theology: An Introduction to Biblical Doctrine* (Grand Rapids: Zondervan, 1994), n.p.

5. Price, "An Overview of the Antichrist."

6. Augustine, *The City of God*, 20:19.

7. Pink, *The Antichrist*, p. 10.

8. Walter K. Price, *The Coming Antichrist* (Neptune, NJ: Loizeaux Brothers, 1985), pp. 20-21.

9. Price, *The Coming Antichrist*, p. 28.

10. Pope Urban, cited in Robert Eisner, "The Terminators: Eugen Weber traces the history of apocalyptic thinking and finds some eminent adherents," *New York Times*, August 8, 1999.

11. Cited in Price, *The Coming Antichrist*, p. 33.

12. Bernard McGinn, "Antichrist," in *Encyclopedia of Religion*, ed. Lindsay Jones (New York: Macmillan Reference USA, 2004).

13. Pink, *The Antichrist*, pp. 35-37.

14. See Mark Hitchcock, *The Complete Book of Bible Prophecy* (Wheaton: Tyndale House, 1999), p. 198.

15. David Gardner, "Obama is Antichrist, say one in four Republicans," *Daily Mail*, March 25, 2011.

16. Daniel Wallace, "Is Obama the Antichrist?" *Parchment and Pen* (blog), August 14, 2009, www.reclaimingthemind.org/blog/2009/08/2823/.

17. Wallace, "Is Obama the Antichrist?"

18. Wallace, "Is Obama the Antichrist?"

19. Thomas Ice and Timothy Demy, *Prophecy Watch* (Eugene: Harvest House, 1998), p. 146.

CHAPTER 4: UNDERSTANDING OUR TERMS

1. Irenaeus, *Against Heresies*, book 1, chapter 26.

2. Ed Hindson, "Antichrist," in *The Popular Encyclopedia of Bible Prophecy*, ed. Tim LaHaye and Ed Hindson (Eugene: Harvest House, 2004), p. 23.

3. Hindson, "Antichrist," p. 23.

4. Tim LaHaye and Ed Hindson, *Global Warning* (Eugene: Harvest House, 2007), p. 192.

5. Mark Hitchcock, *Is the Antichrist Alive Today?* (Sisters, OR: Multnomah, 2002), p. 15. See also Herman Hoyt, *The End Times* (Chicago: Moody Press, 1969), p. 116.

6. J. Dwight Pentecost, *Things to Come* (Grand Rapids: Zondervan, 1989), p. 338.

7. Cited in Pentecost, *Things to Come*, p. 338.

8. Hitchcock, *Is the Antichrist Alive Today?* pp. 18-20.

9. Arthur W. Pink, *The Antichrist: A Study of Satan's Christ* (Blacksburg, VA: Wilder, 2008), pp. 54-56.

10. Adapted from Pink, *The Antichrist*, pp. 56-57.

CHAPTER 5: IS THE ANTICHRIST A MUSLIM?

1. This brief summary is based in part on David R. Reagan, "The Muslim Antichrist Theory: An Evaluation," a paper presented at the annual conference of the Pre-Trib Research Center, Dallas, December 2010. Available online at www.lamblion.com/articles/articles_islam6.php.

2. For example, Joel Richardson, *The Islamic Antichrist* (Los Angeles: WND Books, 2009).

3. Richardson, *The Islamic Antichrist*, pp. 171-75.

4. Richardson, *The Islamic Antichrist*, p. 50.

5. Reagan, "The Muslim Antichrist Theory: An Evaluation."

6. Reagan, "The Muslim Antichrist Theory: An Evaluation."

7. Reagan, "The Muslim Antichrist Theory: An Evaluation." See also Ron Rhodes, *Reasoning from the Scriptures with Muslims* (Eugene: Harvest House, 2002), pp. 36-37.

8. Cited in Reagan, "The Muslim Antichrist Theory: An Evaluation." See also Ron Rhodes, *The 10 Things You Need to Know About Islam* (Eugene: Harvest House, 2007), pp. 43, 106.

9. Mahmoud Ahmadinejad, Iran's Muslim president, cited in Ewen MacAskill and Chris McGreal, "Israel should be wiped off map, says Iran's president." Available online at www.guardian.co.uk/world/2005/oct/27/israel.iran.

10. Richardson, *The Islamic Antichrist*, pp. 182-83.

11. Richardson, *The Islamic Antichrist*, p. 184.

12. Richardson, *The Islamic Antichrist*, pp. 182-83.

13. "Look Who Muslims Promote as 'Antichrist,'" *WorldNetDaily*, August 31, 2009. www.wnd.com/index.php?fa=PAGE.printable&pageId=108559.

14. Richardson, *The Islamic Antichrist*, p. 96.

15. Richardson, *The Islamic Antichrist*, pp. 86-87.

16. Richardson, *The Islamic Antichrist*, p. 92.

CHAPTER 6: IS THE ANTICHRIST A JEW?

1. Cited in Larry Witham, "Falwell Angers Jews with Antichrist Talk," *The Washington Times*, January 20, 1999.

2. Cited in Witham, "Falwell Angers Jews with Antichrist Talk."

3. Cited in Chana Shavelson, "Jews, Christians speak out after Falwell's assertion that Antichrist is Jewish man," *The Jewish Advocate*, March 25, 2011.

4. Cited in Shavelson, "Jews, Christians speak out."

5. Associated Press, "Falwell says Christ will return soon, Antichrist is Jewish, may be alive now," *The Virginian-Pilot*, January 16, 1999.

6. Cited in Shavelson, "Jews, Christians speak out."

7. Cited in Shavelson, "Jews, Christians speak out."

8. Arnold Fruchtenbaum, *The Nationality of the Anti-Christ* (Englewood Cliffs, NJ: American Board of Missions to the Jews, n.d.), p. 8.

9. Cited in Thomas Ice, "The Ethnicity of the Antichrist," a paper delivered at the annual conference of the Pre-Trib Research Center, Dallas, December 5–7, 2010. Available online at www.pre-trib.org/articles/view/ethnicity-of-antichrist.

10. Arthur W. Pink, *The Antichrist: A Study of Satan's Christ* (Blacksburg, VA: Wilder, 2008), p. 28.

11. Grant R. Jeffrey, *Prince of Darkness: Antichrist and the New World Order* (Toronto: Frontier Research, 1994), p. 39.

12. Pink, *The Antichrist*, p. 29.

13. David Parsons, "The Antichrist," *The Jerusalem Post*, January 24, 1999.

14. Fruchtenbaum, *The Nationality of the Anti-Christ*, p. 8.

15. David Reagan, "The Rise and Fall of the Antichrist." Available online at www.raptureready.com/featured/reagan/dr33.html.

16. "Revelation," in *Expositor's Bible Commentary*, ed. Frank E. Gaebelein (Grand Rapids: Zondervan, 1978), p. 482.

17. Robert H. Mounce, *The Book of Revelation*, pp. 169-70, in *The New International Commentary on the New Testament*, ed. Gordon Fee (Grand Rapids: Eerdmans, 1977).

18. Fruchtenbaum, *The Nationality of the Anti-Christ*, pp. 24, 26.

CHAPTER 7: IS THE ANTICHRIST "GOG"?

1. Thomas Ice, "Ezekiel 38 and 39, Part 2." Available online at www.pre-trib.org/data/pdf/Ice-(Part2)Ezekiel38&39.pdf. See also Tim LaHaye and Ed Hindson, eds., *The Popular Encyclopedia of Bible Prophecy* (Eugene: Harvest House, 2004), p. 119.

2. Mark Hitchcock, *Bible Prophecy* (Wheaton: Tyndale House, 1999), p. 128.

3. Joel Richardson, *The Islamic Antichrist* (Los Angeles: WND Books, 2009), p. 83.

4. Richardson, *The Islamic Antichrist*, p. 82.

5. Richardson, *The Islamic Antichrist*, p. 84.

CHAPTER 8: FORESHADOWING THE ANTICHRIST

1. *Webster's New International Dictionary of the English Language*, second ed., cited in John F. Walvoord, *Jesus Christ Our Lord* (Chicago: Moody Press, 1980), p. 62.

2. Donald K. Campbell, "The Interpretation of Types," *Bibliotheca Sacra*, July, 1955, p. 250.

3. Walvoord, *Jesus Christ Our Lord*, p. 62; see also Lewis Sperry Chafer, *Systematic Theology*, vol. 1 (Dallas: Dallas Theological Seminary, 1948), p. 30.

4. Paul Lee Tan, *The Interpretation of Prophecy* (Rockville, MD: Assurance, 1974), p. 168.

5. See, for example, Bernard Ramm, *Protestant Biblical Interpretation* (Grand Rapids: Baker Book House, 1978), pp. 215-40; A. Berkeley Mickelsen, *Interpreting the Bible* (Grand Rapids: Eerdmans, 1977), pp. 236-64. I discuss the types of Christ extensively in my book *Christ Before the Manger: The Life and Times of the Preincarnate Christ* (Eugene: Wipf and Stock, 2010).

6. Mickelsen, *Interpreting the Bible*, p. 237.

7. Some of this typological information on Antiochus Epiphanes is from Mark Hitchcock, *The Complete Book of Bible Prophecy* (Wheaton: Tyndale House, 1999), p. 133.

8. Walter K. Price, *The Coming Antichrist* (Neptune, NJ: Loizeaux Brothers, 1985), p. 114.

9. Price, *The Coming Antichrist*, p. 124.

10. Price, *The Coming Antichrist*, p. 127.

CHAPTER 9: THE RESTRAINER OF THE ANTICHRIST

1. "2 Thessalonians," in *The Bible Knowledge Commentary*, ed. John F. Walvoord and Roy B. Zuck (Colorado Springs: Cook, 1983).

2. Paul Feinberg, "2 Thessalonians 2 and the Rapture," in *When the Trumpet Sounds*, ed. Thomas Ice and Timothy Demy (Eugene: Harvest House, 1995), p. 307.

3. Arnold G. Fruchtenbaum, *Footsteps of the Messiah* (San Antonio: Ariel Ministries, 2004), n.p.

4. Fruchtenbaum, *Footsteps of the Messiah*.

5. Feinberg, "2 Thessalonians 2 and the Rapture," p. 307.

6. Feinberg, "2 Thessalonians 2 and the Rapture," p. 307.

7. Thomas Constable, "2 Thessalonians," in *The Popular Bible Prophecy Commentary*, ed. Tim LaHaye and Ed Hindson (Eugene: Harvest House, 2006), p. 455.

8. Constable, "2 Thessalonians," p. 455.

9. Mal Couch, "Restrainer," in *The Popular Encyclopedia of Bible Prophecy*, ed. Tim LaHaye and Ed Hindson (Eugene: Harvest House, 2004), p. 325.

10. Mark Hitchcock, *Is the Antichrist Alive Today?* (Sisters, OR: Multnomah, 2002), p. 83.

11. Couch, "Restrainer," p. 325.

12. Cited in David Jeremiah, *The Coming Economic Armageddon* (New York: Faith Words, 2010), p. 114.

13. Feinberg, "2 Thessalonians 2 and the Rapture," p. 308.

CHAPTER 10: THE 70 WEEKS OF DANIEL

1. John F. Walvoord, "Revelation," in *The Bible Knowledge Commentary*, ed. John F. Walvoord and Roy B. Zuck (Colorado Springs: Cook, 1983).

2. See Mark Hitchcock, *Is the Antichrist Alive Today?* (Sisters, OR: Multnomah, 2002), pp. 53-54.

3. Randall Price, "Abomination of Desolation," in *The Popular Encyclopedia of Bible Prophecy*, ed. Tim LaHaye and Ed Hindson (Eugene: Harvest House, 2004), p. 3.

CHAPTER 11: THE CHARACTER OF THE ANTICHRIST

1. Herman Hoyt, *The End Times* (Chicago: Moody Press, 1969), p. 120.

2. Ed Hindson, "Antichrist," in *The Popular Encyclopedia of Bible Prophecy*, ed. Tim LaHaye and Ed Hindson (Eugene: Harvest House, 2004), p. 25.

3. Hoyt, *The End Times*, p. 122.

4. Arthur W. Pink, *The Antichrist: A Study of Satan's Christ* (Blacksburg, VA: Wilder, 2008), p. 51.

5. David Levy, cited in J. Hampton Keathley III, "The Beast and the False Prophet (Rev 13:1-18)." Available online at bible.org/seriespage/beast-and-false-prophet-rev-131-18.

6. Hoyt, *The End Times*, p. 124.

7. Pink, *The Antichrist*, p. 51.

8. David Jeremiah, *The Coming Economic Armageddon: What Bible Prophecy Warns about the New Global Economy* (Brentwood, TN: FaithWords, 2010), p. 115.

9. Hoyt, *The End Times*, pp. 121-22.

10. Pink, *The Antichrist*, p. 52.

11. Thomas Constable, "Daniel." Available online at www.scribd.com/doc/56614880/Daniel.

CHAPTER 12: NAMES AND TITLES OF THE ANTICHRIST

1. J. Hampton Keathley III, "The Beast and the False Prophet (Rev. 13:1-18)." Available online at bible.org/seriespage/beast-and-false-prophet-rev-131-18.

2. Arthur W. Pink, *The Antichrist: A Study of Satan's Christ* (Blacksburg, VA: Wilder, 2008), pp. 41-42.

3. W.H. Marty, "Lawless One," in *The Popular Encyclopedia of Bible Prophecy*, ed. Tim LaHaye and Ed Hindson (Eugene: Harvest House, 2004), p. 199.

4. Herman Hoyt, *The End Times* (Chicago: Moody Press, 1969), p. 124.

5. Pink, *The Antichrist*, p. 41.

6. Tim LaHaye and Jerry Jenkins, *Are We Living in the End Times?* (Wheaton: Tyndale House, 1999), p. 273.

7. Walter K. Price, *The Coming Antichrist* (Neptune, NJ: Loizeaux Brothers, 1985), p. 147.

8. Price, *The Coming Antichrist*, p. 147.

9. Pink, *The Antichrist*, pp. 40-41.

10. LaHaye and Jenkins, *Are We Living in the End Times?* p. 273.

11. David Jeremiah, *The Coming Economic Armageddon* (New York: FaithWords, 2010), p. 105.

CHAPTER 13: THE ROLE OF SATAN

1. John F. Walvoord, "Revelation," in *The Bible Knowledge Commentary*, ed. John F. Walvoord and Roy B. Zuck (Colorado Springs: Cook, 1983).

2. William MacDonald, *Believer's Bible Commentary*, ed. Arthur L. Farsted (Nashville: Thomas Nelson, 1995), n.p.

CHAPTER 14: THE DEATH AND RESURRECTION OF THE ANTICHRIST

1. John F. Walvoord, "Revelation," in *The Bible Knowledge Commentary*, ed. John F. Walvoord and Roy B. Zuck (Colorado Springs: Cook, 1983).

2. Charles C. Ryrie, *Balancing the Christian Life* (Chicago: Moody Press, 1978), p. 124.

3. Charles C. Ryrie, *A Survey of Bible Doctrine* (Chicago: Moody Press, 1980), p. 94.

4. Charles C. Ryrie, *Basic Theology* (Wheaton: Victor Books, 1986), p. 147.

5. Ryrie, *Balancing the Christian Life*, p. 124.

6. Henry Morris, "Biblical Naturalism and Modern Science," in *Vital Apologetic Issues:*

Examining Reason and Revelation in Biblical Perspective, ed. Roy B. Zuck (Dallas: Dallas Theological Seminary, 1995), p. 58.

7. John A. Witmer, "The Doctrine of Miracles," *Bibliotheca Sacra*, vol. 120, no. 518 (1973), pp. 126-34.

8. Charles Hodge, *Systematic Theology*, n.p.

9. Norman L. Geisler, cited in *Miracles Are Heaven Sent* (Tulsa: Honor Books, 1995), p. 10.

10. Hodge, *Systematic Theology*, n.p.

11. Paul Enns, *The Moody Handbook of Theology* (Chicago: Moody Press, 1989), p. 297.

12. Tim LaHaye and Jerry Jenkins, *Are We Living in the End Times?* (Wheaton: Tyndale House, 1999), p. 281.

13. Walter K. Price, *The Coming Antichrist* (Neptune, NJ: Loizeaux Brothers, 1985), p. 145.

14. Price, *The Coming Antichrist*, pp. 146-47.

15. Mark Hitchcock, *The Complete Book of Bible Prophecy* (Wheaton: Tyndale House, 1999), pp. 199-200.

CHAPTER 15: THE ROLE OF THE FALSE PROPHET

1. Randall Price, "An Overview of the Antichrist." Available online at www.raptureready.com/featured/price/12rp.pdf.

2. J. Dwight Pentecost, *Things to Come* (Grand Rapids: Zondervan, 1964), pp. 336-37.

3. David Reagan, "The Rise and Fall of the Antichrist." Available online at www.raptureready.com/featured/reagan/dr33.html.

4. John F. Walvoord, "Revelation," in *The Bible Knowledge Commentary*, ed. John F. Walvoord and Roy B. Zuck (Colorado Springs: Cook, 1983).

5. John MacArthur, "Revelation," in *The MacArthur New Testament Commentary* (Nashville: Thomas Nelson, 2007).

6. Ed Hindson, "False Prophet," in *The Popular Encyclopedia of Bible Prophecy*, ed. Tim LaHaye and Ed Hindson (Eugene: Harvest House, 2004), p. 103.

7. MacArthur, "Revelation."

8. Cited in Mark Hitchcock, *The Complete Book of Bible Prophecy* (Wheaton: Tyndale House, 1999), p. 135.

9. J. Hampton Keathley III, "The Beast and the False Prophet (Rev. 13:1-18)." Available online at bible.org/seriespage/beast-and-false-prophet-rev-131-18.

10. Keathley, "The Beast and the False Prophet."

11. Keathley, "The Beast and the False Prophet."

CHAPTER 16: THE ANTICHRIST AND GOD'S TWO WITNESSES

1. David R. Reagan, "Who Are the Two Witnesses Who Will Preach in Jerusalem?" Available online at www.lamblion.com/articles/articles_revelation11.php.

2. John MacArthur, "Revelation," in *The MacArthur New Testament Commentary* (Nashville: Thomas Nelson, 2007).

3. MacArthur, "Revelation."

4. Walter K. Price, *The Coming Antichrist* (Neptune, NJ: Loizeaux Brothers, 1985), pp. 193-94.

5. Reagan, "Who Are the Two Witnesses?"

6. John F. Walvoord, "Revelation," in *The Bible Knowledge Commentary*, ed. John F. Walvoord and Roy B. Zuck (Colorado Springs: Cook, 1983).

7. Thomas L. Constable, "Notes on Revelation, 2001 edition." Available online at www.sonic light.com/constable/notes/pdf/revelation.pdf.

8. Price, *The Coming Antichrist*, p. 194.

9. MacArthur, "Revelation."

10. Tim LaHaye and Jerry Jenkins, *Are We Living in the End Times?* (Wheaton: Tyndale House, 1999), pp. 297-98.

11. Constable, "Notes on Revelation."

12. Constable, "Notes on Revelation."

CHAPTER 17: THE MARK OF THE BEAST

1. Thomas Ice and Timothy Demy, *The Coming Cashless Society* (Eugene: Harvest House Publishers, 1996), pp. 125-26.

2. Arnold Fruchtenbaum, *Footsteps of the Messiah* (San Antonio: Ariel Ministries, 2004), n.p. See also Mark Hitchcock, *Cashless: Bible Prophecy, Economic Chaos, and the Future Financial Order* (Eugene: Harvest House, 2010), pp. 163-64.

3. Mark Hitchcock, *The Complete Book of Bible Prophecy* (Wheaton: Tyndale House, 1999), pp. 163-64.

4. Cited in Thomas Ice and Timothy Demy, *Fast Facts on Bible Prophecy from A to Z* (Eugene: Harvest House, 2004), p. 129.

5. John MacArthur, *The MacArthur Study Bible* (Nashville: Thomas Nelson, 2003), n.p.

6. David Jeremiah, *The Coming Economic Armageddon: What Bible Prophecy Warns About the New Global Economy* (Brentwood, TN: FaithWords, 2010), p. 146.

7. John F. Walvoord, *The Prophecy Knowledge Handbook* (Wheaton: Victor, 1990), n.p.

8. John F. Walvoord, cited in Ice and Demy, *The Coming Cashless Society*, p. 132.

9. John F. Walvoord, "The Beginning of the Great Day of God's Wrath." Available online at bible.org/seriespage/6-beginning-great-day-god%E2%80%99s-wrath.

10. Stanley Toussaint, *Behold the King: A Study of Matthew* (Grand Rapids: Kregel, 2005), p. 291.

11. Merrill Unger, *Beyond the Crystal Ball* (Chicago: Moody, 1973), pp. 134-35.

12. J. Dwight Pentecost, *The Words and Works of Jesus Christ* (Grand Rapids: Zondervan, 1978), p. 410. See also J. Dwight Pentecost, *Things to Come* (Grand Rapids: Zondervan, 1973), p. 418.

13. Herman Hoyt, *The End Times* (Chicago: Moody, 1980), p. 220.

14. "Matthew," in *The Bible Knowledge Commentary*, ed. John F. Walvoord and Roy B. Zuck (Colorado Springs: Cook, 1983).

15. Ice and Demy, *The Coming Cashless Society*, pp. 85-86.

16. Jeremiah, *The Coming Economic Armageddon*, pp. 163-64.

CHAPTER 18: THE DEFEAT AND DOOM OF THE ANTICHRIST

1. John F. Walvoord, "Revelation," in *The Bible Knowledge Commentary*, ed. John F. Walvoord and Roy B. Zuck (Colorado Springs: Cook, 1983).

2. Charles Ryrie, *The Ryrie Study Bible* (Chicago: Moody Press, 2011), n.p.

3. Arnold Fruchtenbaum, *The Footsteps of the Messiah: A Study of the Sequence of Prophetic Events* (San Antonio: Ariel Ministries, 2004), n.p.

4. Thomas Ice and Timothy Demy, *Prophecy Watch* (Eugene: Harvest House, 1998), p. 191.

5. Fruchtenbaum, *The Footsteps of the Messiah*.

6. Tim LaHaye and Jerry Jenkins, *Are We Living in the End Times?* (Wheaton: Tyndale House, 1999), pp. 288-89.

CHAPTER 19: IS THE ANTICHRIST ALIVE TODAY?

1. Mark Hitchcock, *The Complete Book of Bible Prophecy* (Wheaton: Tyndale House, 1999), p. 205.

2. Mark Hitchcock, *Is the Antichrist Alive Today?* (Sisters, OR: Multnomah, 2003), p. 93.

3. David Reagan, "The Rise and Fall of the Antichrist." Available online at www.raptureready.com/featured/reagan/dr33.html.

CHAPTER 20: FREQUENTLY ASKED QUESTIONS ABOUT THE ANTICHRIST

1. Mark Hitchcock, *The Complete Book of Bible Prophecy* (Wheaton: Tyndale House, 1999), p. 194.

2. Cited in Hitchcock, *The Complete Book of Bible Prophecy*, p. 194.

3. Mark Hitchcock, *The Late Great United States* (Colorado Springs: Multnomah, 2009), p. 122.

4. "The Declaration of Independence Has Been Repealed." Available online at www.dickmorris.com/blog/the-declaration-of-independence-has-been-repealed/.

5. Greta Van Susteren, "Obama a 'Disaster' at the G20 Summit," *FoxNews.com*, April 3, 2009. Available online at www.foxnews.com/story/0,2933,512347,00.html. Cited in Thomas Ice, "The Late Great U.S.A." Available online at www.pre-trib.org/data/pdf/Ice-TheLate GreatUSA1.pdf.

6. Arnold Fruchtenbaum, "Conversion of Israel," in *The Popular Encyclopedia of Bible Prophecy*, ed. Tim LaHaye and Ed Hindson (Eugene: Harvest House, 2004), p. 59.

POSTSCRIPT: FEARLESS LIVING

1. John F. Walvoord, *End Times* (Nashville: Word, 1998), p. 218.

2. J.I. Packer, ed., *Alive to God* (Downers Grove: InterVarsity, 1992), p. 171.

3. Cited in Packer, *Alive to God*, p. 167.

Other Great Harvest House Books by Ron Rhodes

THE 10 MOST IMPORTANT THINGS SERIES
The 10 Most Important Things You Can Say to a Catholic
The 10 Most Important Things You Can Say to a Jehovah's Witness
The 10 Most Important Things You Can Say to a Mason
The 10 Most Important Things You Can Say to a Mormon
The 10 Things You Need to Know About Islam
The 10 Things You Should Know About the Creation vs. Evolution Debate

THE REASONING FROM THE SCRIPTURES SERIES
Reasoning from the Scriptures with Catholics
Reasoning from the Scriptures with the Jehovah's Witnesses
Reasoning from the Scriptures with Masons
Reasoning from the Scriptures with the Mormons
Reasoning from the Scriptures with Muslims

QUICK REFERENCE GUIDES
Christian Views of War: What You Need to Know
Five Views on the Rapture: What You Need to Know
Halloween: What You Need to Know
Is America in Bible Prophecy?: What You Need to Know
Islam: What You Need to Know
Jehovah's Witnesses: What You Need to Know
The Middle East Conflict: What You Need to Know